Ways of Being in the World

Ways of Being in the World

AN INTRODUCTION TO INDIGENOUS PHILOSOPHIES OF TURTLE ISLAND

edited by Andrea Sullivan-Clarke

broadview press

BROADVIEW PRESS – www.broadviewpress.com
Peterborough, Ontario, Canada

Founded in 1985, Broadview Press remains a wholly independent publishing house. Broadview's focus is on academic publishing; our titles are accessible to university and college students as well as scholars and general readers. With over 800 titles in print, Broadview has become a leading international publisher in the humanities, with world-wide distribution. Broadview is committed to environmentally responsible publishing and fair business practices.

Library and Archives Canada Cataloguing in Publication

Title: Ways of being in the world : an introduction to Indigenous philosophies of Turtle Island / edited by Andrea Sullivan-Clarke.
Other titles: Ways of being in the world (2023)
Names: Sullivan-Clarke, Andrea, editor.
Description: Includes bibliographical references.
Identifiers: Canadiana (print) 20230504582 | Canadiana (ebook) 2023050468X | ISBN 9781554815715 (softcover) | ISBN 9781770489158 (PDF) | ISBN 9781460408476 (EPUB)
Subjects: LCSH: Philosophy—North America—Textbooks. | CSH: Indigenous philosophy—Canada—Textbooks. | LCGFT: Textbooks.
Classification: LCC E98.P5 W39 2023 | DDC 191.089/97—dc23

Broadview Press handles its own distribution in North America:
PO Box 1243, Peterborough, Ontario K9J 7H5, Canada
555 Riverwalk Parkway, Tonawanda, NY 14150, USA
Tel: (705) 743-8990; Fax: (705) 743-8353
email: customerservice@broadviewpress.com

For all territories outside of North America, distribution is handled by Eurospan Group.

Canada Broadview Press acknowledges the financial support of the Government of Canada for our publishing activities.

Edited by Lisa Frenette
Book design by Em Dash Design

PRINTED IN CANADA

Contributing Editors and Writers

Editor
Andrea Sullivan-Clarke (Muscogee)

Editorial Coordinator
Stephen Latta (Canadian)

Copy Editor
Lisa Frenette (Mi'kmaw)

Proofreaders
Michel Pharand (Canadian)
Joe Davies (Canadian)

Production Editor
Tara Lowes (Canadian)

Permissions Coordinator
Jacqueline Kwan (Canadian)

Contributors
Joel Alvarez (Puerto Rican, Ecuadorian)
Kurtis Boyer (Métis)
Joseph Len Miller (Muscogee)
Paul Simard Smith (Métis)

Artwork
Portia "Po" Chapman (Anishinaabe–Haudenosaunee)
https://loveartbypo.wordpress.com

Cover Design and Layout
Elizabeth Broes (Canadian)
Matthew Jubb (Canadian)

Student Assistants
Krishali Kumar (Canadian)
Evelyn Clarke (Muscogee)

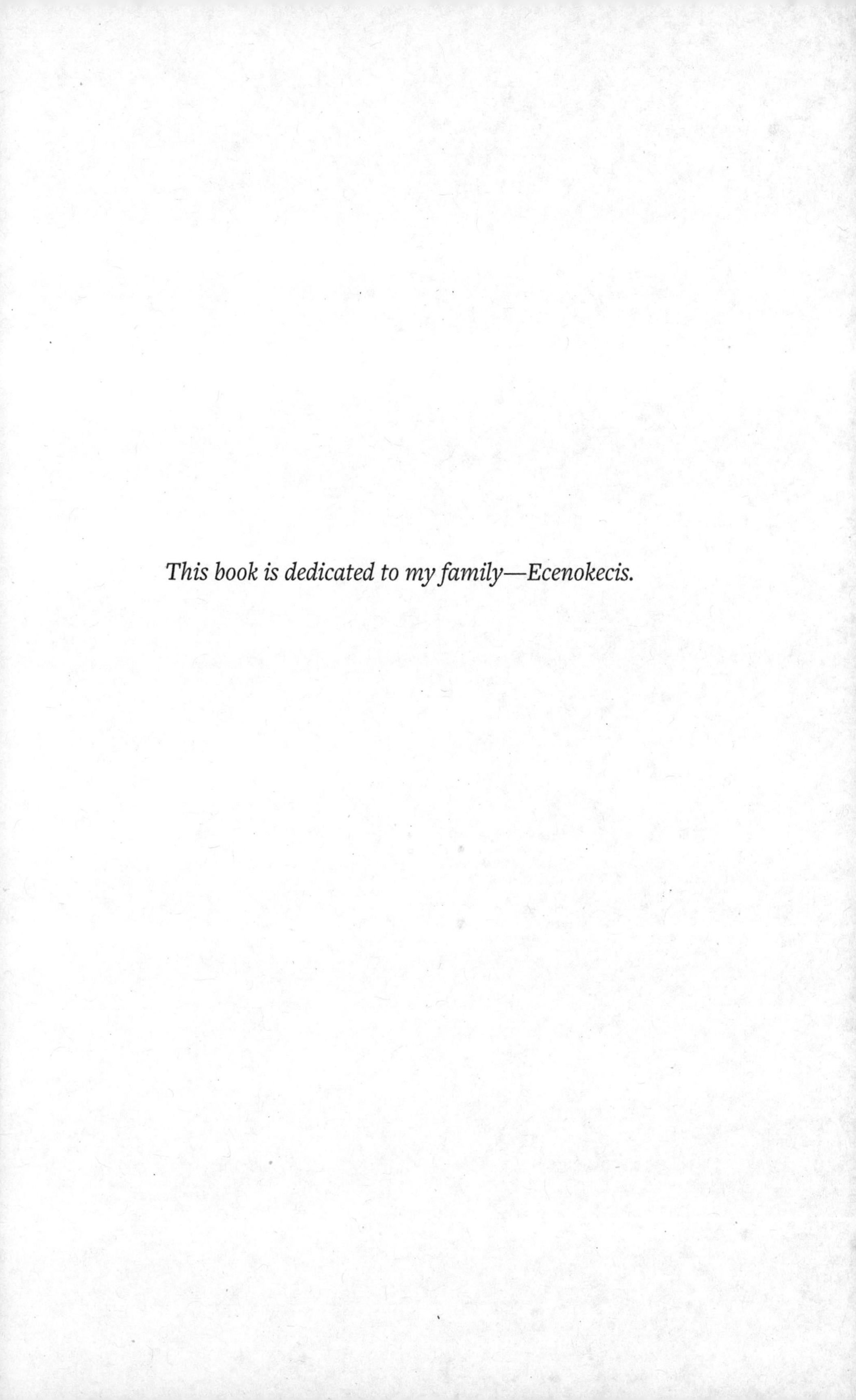

This book is dedicated to my family—Ecenokecis.

CONTENTS

ACKNOWLEDGEMENTS

This project could not have been undertaken without the valuable input and assistance from very generous scholars, including (but not limited to):

Claudia Mills, University of Colorado
Paul Franco, University of Washington
Colin Marshall, University of Washington
The anonymous reviewers, Broadview Press

I am humbled by the support and encouragement while working on this project. I would like to acknowledge Tina DeCastro, Teacher Consultant, as well as the Indigenous Education Team at the Windsor-Essex School District for their support of my Indigenous Philosophy Workshops. (A big shout-out to all the students who asked amazing questions when engaging with Indigenous philosophy!)

I am especially indebted to the Humanities Research Group at the University of Windsor who selected me (and this project) as their Fellow for 2021–22. Their support provided me with the much-needed time to develop the outline and manuscript for the book.

I wish to thank Portia Chapman, who was willing to work with me to develop the art that graces the cover and each chapter. It was a stroke of good fortune to find her and to think carefully about what would be appropriate for each section. I appreciate her guidance and her support as well. I am also grateful for the assistance provided by Krishali Kumar (University of Windsor) and Evelyn Clarke (University of Colorado) for assisting in the research and development of the accompanying materials. (Thank you also for helping me to make my deadline!)

To my family—especially my dear husband and parents—your encouragement and reminders of the importance of my project meant more than you will ever know.

Lastly, I thank my colleagues in the Philosophy Department at the University of Windsor for their support and encouragement.

Mvto! (Thank you!)

PREFACE

Hensci! (Greetings in the language of my people, the Muscogee Nation of Oklahoma.) I have thought about this book in its various iterations for quite a long time, and so I am pleased to be able to share a completed version with you. I developed this textbook to serve a few different purposes. First, I wanted to assist the non-Indigenous professor of philosophy, one who might be looking to introduce some diverse content into their course. Second, I wanted to provide a resource for the student interested in taking their learning beyond the traditional philosophical canon. Lastly, I put this together for the Indigenous people of Turtle Island, those who due to colonialism might not be familiar with the philosophical thought of Indigenous people. I wanted to provide a starting point for their journey; hopefully, one that is encouraging and supportive. Regardless of whether you are an instructor, student, or someone who is finding their way back—I am very glad that you are here and I want to offer resources that will contribute to cultural understanding.

I am a President's Indigenous People Scholar at the University of Windsor and an assistant professor in the Department of Philosophy. I received my PhD in Philosophy from the University of Washington in 2015 and have developed several courses on Indigenous philosophy. It has been my experience that many of my fellow academics would like to include Indigenous materials on their course syllabi, but they may not be familiar with the area. Some might even be apprehensive because they are worried about causing offense. (There is a wrong way to go about teaching Indigenous philosophy, so their concern is legitimate.) Even so, the number of Indigenous people who conduct research in philosophy as well as those able to teach such courses is quite small. So small, in fact, that it doesn't seem reasonable to expect only Indigenous people to teach this material even if that would be ideal. Arguably, Western institutions should devote space for Indigenous philosophy, especially that of the local communities. However, as it stands, I worry that if we wait until there are enough Indigenous professors to teach philosophy, it may never be offered at all.

When I teach Indigenous philosophy or give a talk to a public audience, I consider myself to be an ambassador of sorts. I not only represent my tribe, but I serve as a guide through philosophical thought. It is with this metaphor in mind that I created this book. Even though the face of the discipline is changing, philosophy still lacks diversity. I envision continuing the work of the early Indigenous philosophers who carved out a place for Indigenous philosophy by providing guidance for those students interested in taking their learning beyond the traditional canon. The end destination is to provide them with a broader understanding of my discipline. With that goal in mind, I created a roadmap contained within these pages. These sections, rightly or wrongly, are separated into those areas familiar to Western philosophers. The readings contained within offer a starting point for promoting inclusion in a discipline that would benefit from the diversity of Indigenous philosophy. Perhaps in the future, Indigenous philosophical thought will be as commonplace as reading the works of Hume, Descartes, or Kant.

I drew from personal experience while drafting the contents of this book. My hope was to inspire those who grew up like me—away from the teachings and community of my people. Colonialism is responsible for so many struggling to find their way home and be accepted as a member, and feeling lost through no fault of their own. Working in Indigenous philosophy provided an academic home base from which to branch out and make connections. I think of it as a journey, and who would not want help from their fellow traveller? These readings provide a trail for those who seek understanding but are unsure of where to begin. They are provided with good intentions and suggestions for continued study.

I started writing this book just as the COVID-19 pandemic began. I personally sought out contributors with the hopes that each article would be written solely for this book. As time went by, however, it became evident that many scholars were dealing with teaching online and battling unforeseen challenges. In an ideal world, this book would have an even broader representation of communities and include even more diverse perspectives. For example, it might include a section on contemporary topics such as resistance, Two-Spirit people, environmental issues, etc. Perhaps, in the future, what is missing will be added and the text will be improved. A wise Indigenous woman, however, once told me that I have created exactly what was intended. With those words written on my heart, I share different ways of being in the world.

INTRODUCTION

Beginning the Right Way

Cokv Kerretv Heret Os is a Muscogee phrase that when translated means "Learning is good." I first came across this phrase when visiting the website for the College of the Muscogee Nation. It reminds me that the values of the Muscogee people are an important part of the learning process and, as such, there is a right way—a respectful way—to introduce the topic of this book to you.

My name is Andrea Sullivan-Clarke and I am from the Wind Clan of the Muscogee Nation of Oklahoma. My ancestors were originally in Alabama, but they were forcibly removed by the US government to Indian Territory, which later became the state of Oklahoma. I am here only because they survived. Many did not. I am not a knowledge keeper, nor am I an elder. I come to this project as an Indigenous person, more specifically a Muscogee, and as a philosopher. It is important that you know I am not speaking for any group or from any special perspective beyond that of a Muscogee person who is a philosopher.

I teach at the University of Windsor in Ontario, Canada. As such, I am a settler on the traditional territory of the Three Fires Confederacy, which comprises the Ojibwa, Odawa, and Potawatomi. I recognize my privilege and strive to maintain a respectful relationship with the Indigenous people where I live and work. Do you know whose land you are on? I invite you to learn about the people who lived or continue to live in the place that you occupy.

What's in a Name?

When first naming this book, I had to address some of the issues that result from colonialism and its impact on the Indigenous people of Turtle Island. For example, I must explain why I have chosen the title of the book as well as why I chose to use the terms that I have used, like 'Turtle Island.' 'Ways of being in the world' refers to the different worldviews held by Indigenous communities all over the world.

Worldviews address what is real, what we know or can come to know, and what is valued; simply put, worldviews are the philosophy of a people.

'Indigenous' is another term whose use must be addressed as well. It generally refers to the original people/s of countries all over the world. Given that I wanted the focus to be on the philosophy of those living in North America, I chose to limit the selections for each chapter to the worldviews of those living on Turtle Island. In this way, the articles provided would include the philosophies of Native American/First Nations/American Indians, Métis, and Inuit. Of course, if I wanted to be more precise, I would list every individual nation and not the broader categories of Native American/First Nations/American Indians, Métis, and Inuit. These terms, however, are used for convenience and the reader should bear this in mind. When addressing an Indigenous person, it is much more respectful to use the name of their people, and to pronounce that name as it is spoken by their people.

As mentioned earlier, I qualified the term 'Indigenous' by limiting it to the people living on Turtle Island. However, this is an issue because many Indigenous communities in North America do not use the term 'Turtle Island' and the story of how North America came to be is not part of their worldview. I opted to use the term not to privilege one worldview over another. Rather, my decision to use 'Turtle Island' resulted from my preference to use an Indigenous term instead of one that stemmed from colonialism. A second reason was that I wished to challenge the presupposition that the Americas were discovered, and named, by Europeans. If Indigenous people have existed here since time immemorial, then the term 'discovery' is not apt. 'Turtle Island' serves the purpose of providing a boundary for the referent, but it may be replaced in the future for a term that is more inclusive.

Given that the selections for this book span across time, they will contain outdated language. Consider this as you read: you are getting a glimpse into the history of social change as it pertains to Indigenous people of Turtle Island. It may prove useful to examine and critically reflect on the use of such language, and even consider that some language we use today may be outdated in the future.

One last remark regarding names. Given that every community has its own worldview, there is a danger in using the singular term 'Indigenous philosophy.' The primary concern is that the reader may conflate the views of some communities with the views of all. There is no single, complete Indigenous philosophy of Turtle Island. There are, of course, some shared similarities among worldviews, but it is more appropriate to think of each worldview individually. To counter the concern of lumping all groups together, I have included the name of the community associated with each author. Context is extremely important to understanding the philosophies of the Indigenous people of Turtle Island. It would be a grave error to assume that we are all the same. It is our differences that make us who we are.

How to Use This Book

In keeping with the Calls to Action of the Truth and Reconciliation Commission's Final Report (2015), many universities across Canada are looking to "Indigenize" their curriculum, and the trend is catching on in the United States as well. What does that mean for the humanities? In the discipline of philosophy, it not only means increasing representation in the classroom by hiring Indigenous faculty and encouraging the inclusion of Indigenous materials on the syllabus, but it also means developing courses on Indigenous philosophy in general.

In this book, I provide sections that contain readings in the Indigenous philosophies of Turtle Island (Native American/American Indian/First Nations, Métis, Inuit, and Aztec philosophy) as they relate to the divisions—metaphysics, epistemology, and value theory—found in a typical 'Introduction to Philosophy' text. Admittedly, this is not an Indigenous way of approaching philosophy. Although Indigenous philosophical thought does contain the Western categories of philosophy, my decision to divide the book in this manner was made to support the uncertain instructor and the student who is new to philosophy; the standard divisions are an artificial attempt at uniformity. Even so, it is good to realize that these divisions, in the case of Indigenous thought, are artificial.

Although this text is by no means comprehensive, it provides the instructor and the student with an introduction to the philosophical thought of the Indigenous people of Turtle Island. Throughout this undertaking, my aim was to provide materials on Indigenous philosophy for the instructor who is unfamiliar with Indigenous philosophy and seeks to include Indigenous philosophical thought on their syllabus. I also intended this book to serve as a resource for any instructor who may be apprehensive or hesitant to present material that seems so foreign to them. Many colleagues have admitted to me that they do not teach Indigenous philosophy in their courses because they are unsure where to begin, and some are especially worried that they may make mistakes. Given my conversations with many of my fellow academics, I would say that, overall, most instructors do not wish to cause offense and are unsure of how to begin in the right way. Their hesitation, however, prevents them from having the opportunity to engage with philosophical thought not found in the traditional canon (and it prevents their students from benefiting from these distinct philosophies as well).

After several conversations and even a few invitations to speak about teaching Indigenous philosophy in general, I decided that the best course would be to provide materials to support my fellow professors as they begin their journey with Indigenous philosophies. While this book could, with a few additional resources, provide a foundation for a stand-alone course, its primary purpose is to supplement the texts that are normally assigned in an undergraduate Introduction to Philosophy course. While working with Broadview Press, I constructed my manuscript, drawing on Andrew Bailey's *The Broadview Introduction to Philosophy* as a template for creating the format, as Bailey's text is well organized and accessible for students taking initial courses in philosophy. As a result, instructors have the flexibility to work from this text to meet the needs of their instruction.

Each of the readings is introduced in the chapter to help the student recognize the context in which the philosophical thought developed. Additional materials, such as discussion questions and pedagogical/cultural sources, are included after each article to serve as resources for instruction.

Cokv Kerretv Heret Os

Teaching others has a normative dimension: there is a right way, a respectful way. I have provided some tips for teaching the Indigenous philosophies in this text:

1. Get to know the local Indigenous people. Recognize there is a difference between ancestral lands and those who occupy that land today.
2. Invest in learning the history of Indigenous people.
3. Teach with humility. Be willing to admit that you are not a knowledge keeper, elder, or community member.
4. Focus on the philosophical thought instead of attempting to explain or practice the culture.
5. Acknowledge your sources and seek permission to use Indigenous materials and stories.
6. Remember that an Indigenous student is a person and not a source of examples.
7. Note that some publishers specialize in Indigenous Studies, that some libraries online have research guides on Indigenous philosophy, and that professional organizations like the American Philosophical Association and the Native American and Indigenous Studies Association have publications as well.
8. Attend sessions, talks, and cultural events that are open to the public.
9. Indigenous philosophical thought is not to be used as a tool to understand or support Western philosophy.
10. While we refer to Indigenous philosophy in the general sense, the thought of each community remains distinct. Do not overgeneralize.
11. Stories are not like Aesop's fables.
12. Some stories have been recorded and preserved by non-Indigenous people. Whether they are a missionary or an academic, it is good to keep in mind that a non-Indigenous perspective may be woven into their materials.

13. It would be very useful to read critical pieces, such as Eve Tuck and K. Wayne Yang's "Decolonization Is Not a Metaphor" and Leanne Simpson's "Anticolonial Strategies for the Recovery and Maintenance of Indigenous Knowledge."
14. Enjoy the scholarship and the relations you will encounter.

PART I

The Indigenous Philosophies of Turtle Island

INTRODUCTION

What Is It?

Indigenous people exist all over the globe. According to the United Nations, "There are an estimated 476 million Indigenous peoples in the world living across 90 countries."* Can you imagine the diversity of worldviews, ways of being, and philosophical thought that exists in our world? This textbook focuses on a small but vibrant portion of global Indigenous philosophy: the philosophical thought of the Indigenous people residing on Turtle Island.

The Indigenous philosophy of Turtle Island refers to the body of philosophical thought associated with certain groups that comprise the Indigenous inhabitants of North America, or what is traditionally referred to as Turtle Island. More specifically, it includes the philosophical thought of the American Indians of the United States and Mexico, the First Nations of Canada, as well as the philosophies of Inuit, Métis, and Native Alaskans.†

The Indigenous philosophy of Turtle Island is not simply an interjection of traditional Indigenous thought into Western philosophy, nor is it solely the critique of the traditional Western canon. Rather, it distinguishes itself from other philosophies by being borne out of the historical, oral narratives, and the traditions produced and experienced by the Indigenous people of the United States, Mexico, and Canada. Described as a field "on the verge of legitimacy within the discipline of philosophy," the Indigenous philosophy of Turtle Island resides in "the deeply held belief that there is something of value in any tribal tradition that transcends mere belief and ethnic pride."‡ Notably, it entails a different way of looking at and being in the world. Occasionally referred to as a worldview, contemporary descriptions often distinguish the negotiations made by Indigenous individuals who are

* United Nations, "We Need Indigenous Communities for a Better World," https://www.un.org/en/observances/indigenous-day.

† For those wondering about the omission of Hawaiians from this classification, see Anne Keala Kelly, "Native Hawaiians to Deb Haaland: We're Not Native Americans," *Indian Country Today*, April 12, 2021.

‡ Refer to Thomas M. Norton-Smith, *The Dance of Person and Place: One Interpretation of American Indian Philosophy* (New York: State University of New York Press, 2010), 2, and Vine Deloria Jr., "Philosophy and the Tribal Peoples," in *American Indian Thought*, edited by Anne Waters (Oxford: Blackwell, 2004), 5.

described as walking in two worlds: the dominant Western society and the other, the tribal or traditional space.[§]

The need to contrast the Indigenous philosophy of Turtle Island from the Western tradition—as well as the desire to decolonize assumptions about what constitutes the philosophical thought of Turtle Island—motivates the selections of readings for this chapter. Unlike the standard practices of the discipline, this philosophy does not follow a linear time-bound progression, nor is it practiced by answering a particular set of discipline-specific questions using an approved methodology. Thus, we should be attentive to our task: "instead of developing an idea of cultural movement that has primitive at one end of the spectrum and modern at the other, great care must be taken to identify tribal societies and Western thinking as being different in their approach to the world but equal in their conclusions about the world."[¶]

The readings in this chapter were selected with the goal of specifying in more detail some of the general philosophical thought that is attributed to the Indigenous people of Turtle Island. Given the diversity of people generally, it is worth repeating that the following views are not shared by all people on Turtle Island. When attributing philosophical concepts and positions to particular people, we should learn as much as we can about the distinct communities and people of Turtle Island. In doing so, we can respectfully learn about their unique ways of being in the world.

The first article, by Vine Deloria Jr. and Daniel R. Wildcat, provides not only a general introduction to Indigenous epistemology, but speaks to how some Indigenous people understand their place in the universe. The authors not only address the metaphysics of Indigenous relations, but they also highlight the generation of knowledge that results from living in a particular location. In addition, they note the appropriate (as in ethically correct) way of living, given these relations.

Donald L. Fixico, in the second selection, builds upon the foundation of Indigenous philosophical thought by highlighting the notions of circularity and cycles. Using examples of diverse types of circularity and cycles that occur in the world, Fixico calls attention to the similarities and differences with other non-Indigenous worldviews. Cycles and circularity, according to Fixico, reinforce the Indigenous notion that all things are related. Everything—humans, rivers, stones, etc.—is affected by the circularity and cycles that occur within the universe. Thus, nature becomes a teacher to Indigenous people.

The third and final selection, by Alejandro Santana, challenges our assumptions about philosophy by asking whether the thought of the Aztecs can, or should, be included in our determination to do philosophy. Santana not only asks the reader to answer the question in relation to the reasoning of the Aztecs, but he motivates critical self-reflection, which is often believed to be a hallmark of the discipline.

§ For information on worldviews, see Dennis McPherson and J. Douglas Rabb, *Indian from the Inside* (Jefferson, NC: McFarland and Company, 2011).

¶ Deloria Jr., "Philosophy and the Tribal Peoples," 5.

What do we think philosophy should be? And, once we settle on that description, is it identifiable in Aztec thought?

After reading the three articles in this section, you may find it beneficial to consider the standard assumptions about philosophy and ask yourself if there are any shared ideas regarding the doing of philosophy. Likewise, you may wish to compare your findings with the readings in the other sections.

1.1
"Power and Place Equal Personality"*

Vine Deloria Jr. (Standing Rock Sioux)
Daniel R. Wildcat (Yuchi member of the Muscogee Nation of Oklahoma)

ABOUT THE AUTHORS

Vine Deloria Jr. (1933–2005) was arguably the first contemporary Indigenous philosopher of Turtle Island. His book *Custer Died for Your Sins* (1969) highlighted the experience of American Indians in the United States and was foundational to the Red Power Movement. Deloria earned a degree in theology from the Lutheran School of Theology at Chicago (1963) and a JD degree from the University of Colorado Law School (1970), and was a professor in the Political Science Department at the University of Arizona, where he developed the first MA program in American Indian Studies in the United States. He later taught at the University of Colorado Boulder and served as the executive director of the National Congress of American Indians (NCAI).

Daniel R. Wildcat is an established scholar of Environmental Studies. He is currently the director of the Haskell Environmental Research Studies (HERS) Institute and a member of the Indigenous and American Indian Studies Program at Haskell Indian Nations University in Lawrence, Kansas. Wildcat earned his BA and MA degrees in sociology from the University of Kansas and an interdisciplinary PhD (2006) from the University of Missouri at Kansas City. He has taught at Haskell Indian Nations University for over 30 years. Well known for his work on environmental policy, Wildcat proposes the use of Indigenous ingenuity, referred to as indigenuity, in his book, *Red Alert! Saving the Planet with Indigenous Knowledge.*

KEY TERMS

Respect, Memory, Relationships, Knowledge, Astronomy, Experience, Predictability, Cause & Effect, Science

> Western science resolves itself into certain "laws" that describe the natural world. These laws are makeshift descriptions of the manner in which physical reality appears to operate, but they are often regarded by Western scientists as inviolable. Phenomena that fall outside the prescribed patterns of behavior

* Chapter 3 of Vine Deloria Jr. and Daniel R. Wildcat, *Power and Place* (Golden, CO: Fulcrum Resources, 2001), 21–28.

are said to be "anomalies," which can be disregarded when explaining how the physical universe functions. Eventually, of course, the Western scientist must deal with the so-called anomalies. These phenomena form an increasingly large body of knowledge and facts that cannot be explained using the acceptable paradigm into which the rest of scientific knowledge is deposited.

American Indian knowledge of the world does not suffer this structural handicap. While tribal peoples did not have a detailed conception of the whole planet in the sense that Western scientists presently do, they did have a very accurate knowledge of the lands they inhabited and the plants, animals, and other life-forms that shared their environment. It is also becoming increasingly clear that they had a fairly comprehensive knowledge of the heavens, with their own sets of constellations and stories.

The boundaries of American Indian knowledge were those of respect, not of orthodoxy. For instance, certain stories about the stars could not be told when the constellations in question were overhead. Some other kinds of stories involving animals, plants, and spirits could only be told at a particular time of year or in a specific place. There were no anomalies because Indians retained the ability to wonder at the behavior of nature, and they remembered even the most abstruse things with the hope that one day the relationship of these things to existing knowledge would become clear.

The key to understanding Indian knowledge of the world is to remember that the emphasis was on the particular, not on general laws and explanations of how things worked. Consequently, when we hear the elders tell about things, we must remember that they are basically reporting on their experiences or on the experiences of their elders. Indians as a rule do not try to bring existing bits of knowledge into categories and rubrics that can be used to do further investigation and experimentation with nature. The Indian system requires a prodigious memory and a willingness to remain humble in spite of one's great knowledge.

Although the rank-and-file professors may reject this rather cumbersome method of obtaining knowledge, it has been recognized by some important thinkers as being equal to the reductionist procedure. Percy W. Bridgman, one of the giants in physics in this century, made this remark in his book *The Way Things Are*:

> I may have observed all men, including Socrates, and found that they were mortal, and summarized by researchers in the statement "all men are mortal;" which I then filed away in my mind for future use. Later when I may have forgotten all the details of my former research, I may find a rational basis for charging Socrates for annuity which I am selling him, and my assurance that Socrates is mortal, which I get from my mental file, guides

me in setting my price. The syllogism thus has economic value for me in this situation. The unlettered American Indian, however, confronted by the same situation, would doubtless meet it by recalling that he had once verified that Socrates in particular was mortal. [Percy Williams Bridgman, *The Way Things Are* (Harvard UP, 1959), p. 91]

So we have different paths to the same conclusions.

Keeping the particular in mind as the ultimate reference point of Indian knowledge, we can pass into a discussion of some of the principles of the Indian forms of knowledge. Here power and place are dominant concepts—power being the living energy that inhabits and/or composes the universe, and place being the relationship of things to each other. It is much easier, in discussing Indian principles, to put these basic ideas into a simple equation: Power and place produce personality. This equation simply means that the universe is alive, but it also contains within it the very important suggestion that the universe is personal and, therefore, must be approached in a personal manner. And this insight holds true because Indians are interested in the particular, which of necessity must be personal and incapable of expansion and projection to hold true universally.

The personal nature of the universe demands that each and every entity in it seek and sustain personal relationships. Here, the Indian theory of relativity is much more comprehensive than the corresponding theory articulated by Einstein and his fellow scientists. The broader Indian idea of relationship, in a universe that is very personal and particular, suggests that all relationships have a moral content. For that reason, Indian knowledge of the universe was never separated from other sacred knowledge about ultimate spiritual realities.

The spiritual aspect of knowledge about the world taught the people that relationships must not be left incomplete. There are many stories about how the world came to be, and the common themes running through them are the completion of relationships and the determination of how this world should function. Such tales seem far removed from the considerations of science, particularly as Indian students are taught science in today's universities. However, when the tribal concepts are translated into scientific language, they make a good deal of sense. Completing the relationship focuses the individual's attention on the results of his or her actions. Thus, the Indian people were concerned about the products of what they did, and they sought to anticipate and consider all possible effects of their actions.

And on Appropriateness

The corresponding question faced by American Indians when contemplating action is whether or not the proposed action is appropriate. Appropriateness includes the moral dimension of respect for the part of nature that will be used or affected in our action. Thus, killing an animal or catching a fish involved paying respect to the species and the individual animal or fish that such action had disturbed. Harvesting plants also involved paying respect to the plants. These actions were necessary because of the recognition that the universe was built upon constructive and cooperative relationships that had to be maintained. Thus, ceremonies such as the First Salmon and Buffalo Dance and the Strawberry Festivals and the Corn Dances celebrated and completed relationships properly or ensured their continuance for future generations.

We can view this different perspective in yet another way that will speak more directly to Indian students studying Western science. Very early, at least beginning with Greek speculation on the nature of the world, the Western peoples seemed to have accepted a strange binary system of reasoning in which things are compared primarily according to their size and shape. Out of this perspective came the natural sciences as we have them today. Eventually distinctions were made primarily on the basis of shape, and from this tendency came the great theory of evolution that now reigns in the West. All our knowledge of the natural world within the Western framework derives from a crude comparison between skeletons of animals. Very little knowledge exists about the animals themselves except relative bone structures. We only speculate on how they see the world, think, and understand emotional experiences. Increasingly, studies show them to have as complete an emotional/intellectual life as we do.

American Indians seem to have considered this kind of thinking at one time because there are tribal stories comparing humans to various animals. The stories always emphasized that while humans cannot see as well as hawks, they can see; they are not as strong as the bear, but they are strong; not as fast as the deer, but they can run; and so forth. However, when these comparisons are carefully analyzed, one finds that both physical and psychological characteristics are described. Indians derived their knowledge of birds and animals from actual experiences, and therefore physical structure meant little to them as they anticipated encountering these creatures in the future and needed to know how they behaved for hunting and protection purposes. Thus Charles Eastman was taught that when approached by a bear or mountain lion, one should pick up a stick immediately so that the animal would think he was armed and dangerous.

When using plants as both medicines and foods, Indians were very careful to use the plant appropriately. By maintaining the integrity of the plant within the relationship, Indians discovered many important facts about the natural world that non-Indians only came upon later. The Senecas, for example, knew that corn, squash, and beans were the three Sisters of the Earth, and because they had a place in the world and were compatible spirits, the Indians always planted them together. Only recently have non-Indians, after decades of laboratory research, discovered that the three plants make a natural nitrogen cycle that keeps land fertile and productive.

Plants, because they have their own life cycles, taught Indians about time. George Will and George Hyde, in their book *Corn Among the Indians of the Upper Missouri*, point out that it was the practice of the agricultural tribes to plant their corn, hoe it a few times, and then depart for the western mountains on their summer buffalo hunt. When a certain plant in the west began to change its color, the hunters knew it was time to return home to harvest their corn. This knowledge about corn and the manner in which its growth cycle correlated with that of the plants of the mountains some 500 miles away was very sophisticated and involved the idea of time as something more complex than mere chronology. Time was also growth of all beings toward maturity.

Star Knowledge

Much Indian knowledge involved the technique of reproducing the cosmos in miniature and invoking spiritual change, which would be followed by physical change. Hardly a tribe exists that did not construct its dwellings after some particular model of the universe. The principle involved was that whatever is above must be reflected below. This principle enabled the people to correlate their actions with the larger movements of the universe. Wherever possible the larger cosmos was represented and reproduced to provide a context in which ceremonies could occur. Thus, people did not feel alone; they participated in cosmic rhythms.

Star knowledge was among the most secretive and sophisticated of all the information that the Indians possessed. Today archeoastronomers are finding all kinds of correlations between Indian practices and modern astronomical knowledge. Very complex star maps painted on buckskin hides or chiseled on canyon walls give evidence that Indians were astute observers of the heavens, and their ceremonial activities were often based on the movement of the heavens. A good deal of Indian star knowledge continues to exist, but religious prohibitions and restrictions still limit the propagation of this information. Some star knowledge goes very far back into the past when the sky looked different. The Sioux said there was once a bright star in the middle of the Big Dipper. Today we can suggest that a black hole does properly exist there.

The Principle of Correlation

Star knowledge gives us an additional principle of Indian information gathering. That principle is correspondence, or correlation. Being interested in the psychological behavior of things in the world and attributing personality to all things, Indians began to observe and remember how and when things happened together. The result was that they made connections between things that had no sequential relationships. There was, consequently, no firm belief in cause and effect, which plays such an important role in Western science and thinking. But Indians were well aware that when a certain sequence of things began, certain other elements or events would also occur.

A kind of predictability was present in Indian knowledge of the natural world. Many ceremonies that are used to find things, heal, or predict the future rely upon this kind of correlation between and among entities in the world. The so-called medicine powers and medicine bundles represented this kind of correlative understanding of how different things were related to each other. Correlation is responsible, for example, for designating the bear as a medicine animal, owls as forecasting death or illness, and snakes as anticipating thunderstorms.

This kind of knowledge is both tribal- and environmental specific. In diagnosing illness, for example, medicine people might search for the cause of sickness by questioning their patients on a variety of apparently unrelated experiences. They would be searching for the linkages that experience had taught them existed in these situations. Here again, there was considerable emphasis on the heavens. One need only examine the admonitions of different tribes with respect to shooting stars, different configurations of the moon, eclipses, and unusual cloud formations to understand how correlational knowledge provided unique ways of adjusting to the natural world.

A More Realistic Knowledge

The Indian method of observation produces a more realistic knowledge in the sense that, given the anticipated customary course of events, the Indian knowledge can predict what will probably occur. Western science seeks to harness nature to perform certain tasks. But there are limited resources in the natural world, and artificial and wasteful use depletes the resources more rapidly than would otherwise occur naturally. The acknowledgment that power and place produce personality means not only that the natural world is personal but that its perceived relationships are always ethical. For that reason, Indian accumulation of information is directly opposed to the Western scientific method of investigation, because it is primarily observation. Indians look for messages in nature, but they do not force nature to perform functions that it does not naturally do.

Indian students can expect to have a certain amount of difficulty in adjusting to the scientific way of doing things. They will most certainly miss the Indian concern with ethical questions and the sense of being personally involved in the functioning of the natural world. But they can overcome this feeling and bring to science a great variety of insights about the world derived from their own tribal backgrounds and traditions. They must always keep in mind that traditional knowledge of their people was derived from centuries, perhaps millennia, of experience. Thus, stories that seem incredible when compared with scientific findings may indeed represent that unique event that occurs once a century and is not likely to be repeated. Western knowledge, on the other hand, is so well controlled by doctrine that it often denies experiences that could provide important data for consideration.

By adopting the old Indian concern with the products of actions, students can get a much better perspective on what they are doing and how best to accomplish their goals. By maintaining a continuing respect for the beliefs and practices of their tribes, students can begin to see the world through the eyes of their ancestors and translate the best knowledge of the world into acceptable modern scientific terminology.

Most important, however, are the contributions being made by American Indian scientists. With their expertise, we can better frame our own ethical and religious concerns and make more constructive choices in the use of existing Indian physical and human resources. It is this linkage between science and the community that we must nurture and encourage. We must carry the message that the universe is indeed a personal one. It may, indeed, be a spiritual universe that has taken on physical form and not a universe of matter that has accidentally produced personality.

Suggestions for Critical Reflection

1. How does having a relationship with something like a river entail obligations to it?
2. What does the title of the reading ("Power and Place Equal Personality") mean?
3. Compare the Western version of science (creation of generalities, laws) with Indigenous science (experience of the particular).

4. How might colonial policies (like assimilation or removal) affect Indigenous knowledge and Indigenous people's understandings of themselves?
5. What is the benefit of having knowledge from the science of both worldviews (Indigenous and Western)?

Additional Resources

For additional resources relating to this reading and its themes, visit sites.broadviewpress.com/waysofbeing/1-1

1.2

"American Indian Circular Philosophy"*

Donald L. Fixico (Shawnee, Sac and Fox, Muscogee, Seminole)

ABOUT THE AUTHOR

Donald L. Fixico is a Regents' and Distinguished Foundation Professor of History at Arizona State University. He is a prolific researcher who has written 15 books on topics such as Native American oral history, the experience of the Urban Indian, and policies affecting Native Americans in the United States. He has also served as a consultant or interviewee on 25 historical documentaries. Fixico attended Bacone College in Muscogee, Oklahoma, and earned his BA (1974), MA (1976), and PhD (1980) in history at the University of Oklahoma. In addition to teaching internationally, Fixico served as a member of the Advisory Council of the National Endowment for the Humanities during the Clinton administration.

KEY TERMS

Beliefs, The Circle of Life, Ethos, Finite, Renewal, Medicine Wheel, Environment, Patterns, Cycles, Change, Logic, Metaphysics, Harmony, Unity, Group identity, Kinship, Connectedness, Equilibrium, Balance

> *"Originally the Rabbit was not regarded as a [Muscogee Creek] trickster but as a member of the little animal world. Rabbit came to the ceremonial ground and asked the people to join their circle around a fire. However, suddenly the fire seemed to go out and it became very dark. There was some confusion and people sensed that Rabbit was running away with a large bag. They caught Rabbit, and in that process Rabbit stumbled. When Rabbit stumbled, first the moon came out again, followed by the sun. People from that time on regarded Rabbit as a trickster and his stumbling created the broken, separate rhythms of the lunar and solar cycles which are connected with new energies every eighteen years. But since then, we always have to be aware of the tricky Rabbit when trying to understand the regularities and the intervals in the cosmos."[1]*
> *Jean Chaudhuri (Creek) and Joyotpaul Chaudhuri, 2001*

* From Donald L. Fixico, *The American Indian Mind in a Linear World: American Indian Studies and Traditional Knowledge* (New York: Routledge, 2003), 41–48, 49–52.

***

The circle is a fundamental part of the universe and it is a permanent geometric fixture in beliefs and philosophies throughout the history of cultures.[2] Stonehenge, constructed between 8500 B.C.E.–1100 B.C.E., in Wessex on Salisbury Plain in southern England lies in the form of a circle as its builders studied the universe or used it for religious purposes. Born approximately 582 B.C.E., Pythagoras rejected the idea that the Earth was flat and thought that the Earth and celestial bodies of the sky had a spherical shape. Aristotle hypothesized that the Earth was a sphere due to the nature of gravity and the Earth's shadow eclipsing the Moon helped to prove his beliefs. The Hindus use a mandala, or sacred circle. Jews and Christians incorporate praying circles for healing. Plato wrote "the soul is a circle."[3] Ancient Native American mounds had their bases in the forms of circles and medicine wheels in the West formed a variety of circles to explain the secrets of the universe to native peoples of North America and Canada.

The Circle of Life includes all things and they consist of spiritual energy. All around us are circles and cycles. The migration patterns of animals and cycles of seasons are a part of the Natural Order of Life. The four elements of fire, water, wind, and Earth are a part of the Muscogee Creek ethos and the same four elements are a part of many tribes. From these concepts derives American Indian thought for those Native Americans who believe in their traditions.

The depth of American Indian philosophy has yet to be explored sufficiently by the rest of the world. While most literature about Native Americans attempts to "describe" Indian life, books record the battles of Indian wars, and limited literature focuses on the "thinking" of American Indians and their various tribal philosophies. In order to understand Indian people and their ways of life, it is evident that the "circle" occupies an integral role in the beliefs of American Indians. Patterns and daily norms of American Indian groups involve the circle as a part of their many cultures. In this way, all things are related and they are a part of nature's system that might be called the "Natural Democracy" based on respect for the world and the universe.

Oglala author Ed McGaa described the inner human perspective and the significance of the circle on influencing life. "Inside of us," says McGaa, "within this great Disk of Life that each and every one of us has been bestowed with; within that creation, therein lies our character, our record, our background, our reputation, our knowledge; this mysterious spirit that the dominant culture refers to as the soul ... You expand, alter and transform this disk, this circle of growing knowledge and related experience."[4] It is a living circle of energy like the Circle of Life that is external to us.

In circular philosophy, all things are related and involved in the broad scope of Indian life. As a part of their life ways, the indigenous peoples of the Americas have studied the Earth, observed the heavenly bodies and contemplated the stars of the universe. The Mayans recorded a calendar based on the number of new moons in a year. The Lakota completed an astronomy about the heavenly bodies, and the Muscogee Creeks incorporated the stars and galaxies into their ethos of the universe. All such things are in a vast continuum that Albert Einstein referred to as circular in form.

A "circular" approach toward life is inherent in Indian cultures since time immemorial. The native world is one of cycles, and observing the cycles provides an order to life and community. Medicine makers, prophets, and wise elders studied the moving world of circularity. Black Elk of the Oglala Sioux reminds all of us about the circularity all around us. He stated, "You have noticed that everything an Indian does is in a circle, and that is because the Power of the World always works in circles, and everything tries to be round." He continued, saying, "Everything the Power of the World does is done in a circle. The sky is round ... and so are all the stars. The wind, in its greatest power whirls. Birds make their nests in circles, for theirs is the same religion as ours. The sun comes forth and goes down again in a circle. The moon does the same, and both are round. Even the seasons form a great circle in their changing, and always come back again to where they were. The life of a man is a circle from childhood to childhood and so it is in everything where power moves."[5]

For centuries, many indigenous peoples of North America have camped and formed their societies in circles. Indians of the eastern woodlands built their towns around a central point, and plains Indians held summer camps once a year in large camp circles. In their logical reasoning, the circle encompassed all the bands of the same tribe and recognized their presence. The Dakota of the plains is a prime example of this annual circular event of bands coming together.[6] Eastern woodland Indians formed their encampments around a central fire for worship and celebration of the Green Corn harvest.

Numbers help to determine cycles and important events that happen repeatedly. They provide a finite quality to life, and allow Indians to recognize the end of something and the start of its renewal. For example, there are 28 days in the months or moons of many tribes. Then the cycle begins again. The buffalo has 28 ribs, and with the same total days in a month, this number is important in life to many tribes. In the two hands of the human beings, there are 28 joints. Thus, the number 28 is often called sacred as well as the numbers 4 and 7. In the Bighorn Medicine Wheel, built 2,500 years ago by Aztec-Tanoans of the Bighorn Mountains in Wyoming, there are 28 spokes.

Native peoples looked for the constants in life as a part of the universe. They understood life to occur in cycles and those powers of nature formed definite patterns that occurred, repeating themselves. One of these universal constants is the climate. The climate of the world engages land forms in a complex system based on the interaction of the atmosphere, hydrosphere (oceans, lakes, and rivers), biosphere (Earth's living resources), cryosphere (particularly sea ice and polar ice caps), and lithosphere (the Earth's crust and upper mantle).[7] This systematic maze produced the seasons of the year for various parts of the world, and thus assisted in shaping the cultures of peoples and how they viewed life.

The environment and the climate influenced the lives and cultures of native peoples. American Indians seriously observed the weather and lived accordingly. One scholar noted that "Lakota camps did not remain in one spot year-round and did not always have a fixed membership. Validity of composition was due to both internecine struggle and climates. In warmer weather, groups tended to come together; in winter, large groups disbanded into smaller parties. This pattern of aggregation and dispersal reflected, appropriately enough, the exact seasonal behavior of the buffalo, the people's primary subsistence resource."[8]

Seasons and the Earth's rotation governed all life. The seasons of the year, rotation of the Earth, movement of the stars, and the movement of the universe are in flux such that all is in movement. By instinct, the animals innately know the occurrences of these patterns. Plants know this, too. In kindred spirit with the animals, native peoples developed their cultures after studying the ways of animals. Oglala holy man Black Elk observed that "there is much power in the circle, as I have often said; the birds know this for they fly in a circle, and build their homes in the form of a circle; the coyotes know also, for they live in round holes in the ground."[9] Throughout the animal world, the circle is just as fundamental to animals as it is to human beings. Indians have not forgotten its significance to their animal brethren.

Studying the cycles of the Earth and understanding the rotations of the seasons are not unique to American Indians. Other indigenous peoples in the world have done the same in shaping their cultures, according to the Earth's movements. Before the mainstream dependency on the clock, Europeans and Euro-Americans guided their lives according to nature. Many farmers and ranchers continue to live by the cycles and patterns of the Earth, in a non-linear way.

Due to their knowledge of the animals and their living patterns, Native Americans appealed to Nature as well as their great teacher. British scholar Roy Ellen observed that "[Indigenous] peoples are still part of nature, and therefore adjusted to natural cycles in ways in which animals are assumed to be. We find this echoed in Germanic conceptions of *Naturvolker*, Kropotkin's 'life in a state of nature.'"[10] Nature's way was the way of the American Indian and in his thinking, all life depended upon nature. Indian people did not believe that they were greater than nature, and they altered their cultural norms to fit the cycles of the seasons.

Nothing is transfixed. Nothing is secure or stable or permanent, and Indian people have accepted this situation. We want to believe that nothing has changed, but the reality is that all things change, even the story that we remember being told, but as long as the fabric of the truths of a story are retained, then we can accept it.

The concept of the circle is fundamental to understanding knowledge. This salient point was noted by one native scholar. "In circular thought" he wrote, "if a circle is envisioned and items are placed within it, we realize that each item or element has a relationship with each other in a fixed order within the system." Such entities or particles should be respected and treated equally since they belong to the same universe. In reality some entities are more powerful than others due to their varying strengths, and some of their powers are unknown by nature. They are ranked according to their special qualities and strengths and American Indians have learned about them. Indigenous peoples have treated the unknown with respect since it has a spiritual energy and unknown powers bestowed by the Creator and such power could endanger the people themselves. The circular concept of all things viewed equally is a native philosophy carried forward by generations studying the natural environment involving all of life.[11]

From an opposing point of view, the linear way of thinking and perceiving the world is the non-Indian way that Native Americans have had to learn in schools and while working with other Americans. Charles Eastman, Santee scholar, Luther Standing Bear, Lakota scholar, and others have testified how difficult it "was to learn the white man's linear way of thinking. His logic was foreign to their native way of thought. Other literature on Indian boarding schools account for the inhumane treatment of Indian students, but the root of the problem, besides cultural and racial differences, proved to be the difference in thinking" between Indians and whites. Their philosophies, ideologies, logic, and world views proved distinctively different due to the separate evolutions of the human mind set in the Eastern Hemisphere and Western Hemisphere during the pre-Columbia era....

One young native person concluded that "like the seasons changing in cycles every year and like the day and night in a circular change, the circle of life includes all things, according to Indian belief. The past is a part of the present such that history is a continuum without a beginning or an end in the Indian mind." The young person also said, "... the broken circle suggested to me what I felt in my heart and the feelings other people have in their hearts. Because the circle has been around for thousands of years, and now it's coming apart because people are forgetting about the ways of the spirit and the ways of kindness to people. They're greedy and money hungry and want power, and that won't do much when they get to the spirit world ... that if people's visions vanish and our way of life isn't like a growing, healthy tree, then we will all vanish ... That's the philosophy of Indian life. It is centered around the spirits and around the Creator. All of it."[12]

The Circle of Life begins with the cardinal directions. Some tribes have six such directions and some have seven. While recalling his vision, Black Elk remembered that ancient voices of several beings called to him: "Your Grandfathers all over the world are in a council, and they have called you here to teach you. His voice was very kind, but I shook all over with fear now, for I knew that these were not old men, but the Powers of the world. And the first was the Power of the West; the second, of the North; the third, of the East; the fourth of the South; the fifth, of the Sky; the Sixth of the Earth."[13] The Circle of Life also includes the metaphysical beings who influence people of the physical world. Metaphysical powers rule the world. The door to the spiritual world creaked opened, changing Black Elk's life forever.

As a part of his visionary experiences in later life, Black Elk recalled being on top of Harney Peak in the Black Hills. He said, "then I was standing on the highest mountain of them all [Harney Peak], and round about beneath me was the whole hoop of the world. And while I stood there I saw more than I can tell and I understood more that I saw; for I was seeing in a sacred manner these shapes of all things in the spirit, and the shape of all shapes as they must live together like one being. And I saw that the sacred hoop of my people was one of many hoops that made one circle, wide as daylight and as starlight, and in the center grew one mighty flowering tree to shelter all the children of one mother and one father. And I saw that it was holy."[14] Like Moses in the Bible and other religious prophets, the spiritual world allowed Black Elk to see some of its powers. It was beyond his imagination and frightened him.

Living in the sacred way of her people, Jackie Yellow Tail, a Crow woman, philosophized that "life is a circle, the world is a circle." She remarked that the linear way was a part of the Circle of Life. She said, "The Christian way of seeing the world is that within this circle there's a man called Jesus; on the outside is the trees, the rocks, the animals, all around the world are the different things that are on Mother Earth. In the center is man above all things. The Indian way of thinking is that there is this same circle, Mother Earth, and around her are the rocks, the trees, the grass, the mountains, the birds, the four-legged, and man. Man is the same as all those other things, no greater, no less. I mean, it's all so simple; people make it so hard. That's why I say we're like Mother Earth: each one of us has that ability within us to grow spiritually, we're connected with the Creator from the top of our head, our feet walk on Mother Earth. It's within us; and why should we hold that to ourselves when we know, no matter what color that person is, that he has the same spiritual yearning we have? People ... deserve to be treated with respect."[15]

People naturally want to feel connected to others, to belong to a group, yet most people in Western society have forgotten that they are also connected to nature. All people are a part of the community of life, yet some people try to exclude others.

Oglala spiritual leader of the American Indian Movement (AIM) during the 1970s, Leonard Crow Dog, explained, "we live in a sacred cycle, the sacred hoop. We are born from Mother Earth and we return to Mother Earth. We feed on the deer who, in turn, feeds on the grass which, in turn, is fed by our bodies after we die. It's the story of the biological cycle you learn in school. Everything is harmony and unity, and we fit within that harmony. And when our bodies die, our spirits are freed and will be here. You see, it's not a religion in the white man's sense, but a philosophy of living, a way of living."[16] Such a way of life cannot be rationalized as one part of life such as religion. It is the ethos of how indigenous people believe and live their lives.

The whole is greater than any one of its parts. For example, the family is more important than the individual among tribes who believe in a communal identity. It was meant to be that way for the best means to survive, especially during hard times. Group identity is more meaningful than the identity of one person. Among the Lakota, the *tiyospaye*, or extended family, is the Lakota way of understanding life. Within the family, kinship supports each family member. Yellowtail, Medicine Maker, and Sun Dance of the Crow, stated the relevance of belonging. He noted, "There are thirteen clans among the Crow tribe, and my clan is the Whistling Waters. Each person has relatives through the clan also, so all the members of the tribe can learn a great deal from their relatives both through blood and through the clans. The entire tribe worked together for the benefit of every person in the tribe, and the clan system helped to strengthen the cooperation of every person working toward the common welfare of the tribe."[17]

A Natural Democracy of respect exists in that all things are equal at creation. All things are related in the world and in the universe. Plants and animals are an important part of this Natural Democracy. Each plant and each animal has a role and responsibility. As a result, there is a strong dependency on each thing and all things. Cooperation is highly desired in such a community of togetherness. Anthropologist Irving Hallowell observed of the Ojibwas that plants and animals were integral to the Ojibwa world. Irving Hallowell's extensive, and extremely sympathetic and reflective work among the Ojibwas, an Algonkian people, provides ample evidence that the Ojibwas regarded animals, plants, and assorted other natural things and phenomena as persons with whom it was possible to enter into complex social intercourse. Animals, plants, stones, thunder, water, hills, and so on may be "persons" in the Ojibwa linguistic organization of experience.[18]

The American Indian mind thinks inclusively. By seeing and believing that all things are related, this natural order is a sociocultural kinship. It is symbolic kinship based on the ethos of totality and inclusion. It includes even the bad and evil things. Kinship is the bonding substance that holds the Natural Democracy system together. Kinships are formed by symbolic relationships and by blood relationships.

This kinship of a Natural Democracy extends to animals and plants. Navajo surgeon, Lori Alvord, described her father's relationship with animals and how he communicated with them. "Almost everywhere we went, on the reservation or off, he knew the dogs, and they recognized him and came running," she said. "Rez dogs. Chocolate and black-splotched or the color of coyote and mesa and riverbed mud. One blue eye, one brown, or two piercing green. They were everywhere on the reservation, used to watch the sheep or guard the Hogan [a traditional Navajo dwelling], and when you arrived they appeared magically, just like those annoying friends who materialize at mealtime. My father knew them. Crows also seemed to gather in groups or come and stand on a fence post whenever my father was around. Sometimes I'd turn a corner and find my father standing deep in a philosophical discussion with a crow."[19]

The Navajos believe that all things are connected. Animals are a part of the natural kinship and their presence should be recognized. By learning the ways of animals and making them feel unafraid, a kinship of communication is established with them. Through effective communication, equilibrium is better maintained in the Natural Order of things. But, balance and chaos are in conflict as a part of this continuum of natural order. Within the circle of life, a continual effort for balance is the purpose for individuals and communities. The linear person may not realize the importance of this effort as Western cultured people are often consumed by work or thoughts of getting something done during the day. What Western society does not normally do is to put things in the larger perspective of life. Nor does the linear mind prioritize what is important to him or her as a person in relationship to family and community, thus placing personal needs first.

It is the daily struggle, the moment's effort, to find a comforting state of mind and existence between the two opposites in life. Day and night, right and wrong, good and evil, life and death, man and woman, and the many other polar opposites are the extremities of the balance that constitute life.

Balance is between two things or more and it is the purpose in life for American Indians whose philosophy is inclusive of all things in the universe. At least five kinds of balance exist: (1) balance within one's self, (2) balance within the family, (3) balance within the community or tribe, (4) balance with external communities, including other tribes and the spiritual world, and (5) balance with the environment and the universe.

Balance is equilibrium discovered between opposites such as consistency and change. Both consistency and change are inertia and constants in life. Balance is the compromise when momentum rests in a euphoric state between the two opposite forces. It must always be realized that the greater the opposites, the greater the struggle for balance in this natural dichotomy of life.

An order for life is the purpose for all living things, or else chaos reigns. Disorder becomes a part of one's life or a part of a group, and then it controls the living. The continuous effort is normal, that is finding balance within one's self and within the universe. It is a part of living and evolution of human beings and the universe. When Rabbit temporarily stole the Sun and the Moon, chaos reigned and confused the Muscogee people until they realized what had happened. They captured Rabbit, and balance was restored.

The negativity of life is chaos and disorder. Chaos is frustration in life, anxiety, and disappointment. Such disorder leads to fear, distrust, and, ultimately, to self-destruction. Without effort on our part, it is easy to fall into disorder and chaos. Like evil twins, they are the negativity in the universe.

Without balance in oneself and in one's community, life is more difficult and alarming. Balance is the spiritual beauty of life as exhibited by the innocence of a child as set by nature. In the following years, the child becomes an adult and the struggle for balance is waged even in the twilight years when an elder acts like a child again. As the Muscogees learned from Rabbit's crime, without the Sun and Moon, we have lost balance.

By observing nature and the environment for many generations, American Indians developed tribal philosophies based on the circle. By studying the changes of the seasons and observing the lives of animals and plants as a part of nature, native logic became grounded in the central idea of a continuum of events that seemed familiar. Nature repeated itself in a continuous series of cycles and seasons of circular patterns. Animals and humans live the same various stages of life starting with birth, infancy, puberty, adulthood, old age, then death, and life repeated the same phases with the next generation. Cherokee elder Dhyani Ywahoo observed that "in Tsalagi (Cherokee) world view, life and death, manifestation and formlessness, are all within the circle, which spirals out through all dimensions. The teaching expresses that expansion of the spiral. The same story can be understood in various ways as one is exploring vaster dimensions of mind."[20]

In the white man's world of many kinds of businesses, including academia, people are categorized according to the box that they check on various forms. But when one goes outside the box to think, the person is within the circle of the universe where all beauty and good things exist, able to think new ideas and fresh thoughts, thereby nurturing the soul. The Muscogee Creek, Seminole, and other tribes like the Cheyenne realized that they needed to have a reverent relationship with the Sun and the Moon. They are both light and life to human beings, plants, and animals, including Rabbit.

Outside the box or office is nature and all of its beauty. Indian people viewed themselves as part of nature in a type of Natural Democracy. Because relationships are important, Native people stress the importance of kinship for building positive relationships. In this ethos, the worst that could happen to an individual is to be excluded from the group or community or tribe.

The sources of strength may be a homeland or a place, and perhaps they might be the same. Here is where a person goes for regaining perspective, resting, and giving thought to a major problem, self-examination, contemplating one's vision for leadership, thinking about resources, supporters, and thinking about the big picture to keep things in a real context. This is done in familiar surroundings, and they are a positive influence.

During this return to renewal of spiritual energy, a person asks deep questions of his or her being. One's natural surroundings become like nature's womb for security as the struggle for balance is analyzed by the individual. It is like the Sun providing balance during the day and the Moon supplying balance at night, as both are sources of light. Our original surroundings are best for our soul in providing spiritual strength and renewal to the mentally fatigued.

In addition to the powerful influence of the natural environment is the native concept of time. Native peoples' focus on events and stories about them has deemphasized the measuring of time on the clock of the linear world. To indigenous people, the hands of the white man's clock sometimes feel wrapped around the person's throat, strangling the soul from being free and dictating one's life by deadlines. Ironically many mainstream Americans feel the same way.

Native people have learned to live without the clock for many centuries and kept track of things according to the seasons. Many cultures around the world and other Americans have lived many centuries in the same way. Former Navajo tribal chairman Peter MacDonald recalled that the Bureau of Indian Affairs recorded his birthday as December 16, 1928. But he recalls his parents talking about the intense heat of the midday sun during May. He was born into the Haskonhazohl and Betani clan on that warm day. MacDonald noted that "my people did not track time the way white men did. There was no need to be aware of anything more than the changing seasons. Sometimes your birth was known because of a major event, such as a great blizzard that had made survival difficult for everyone. But when the weather was mild, your birth was marked by the seasons, the exact date remaining unknown, unimportant. We were in harmony with nature—birth, death, and the life that was led in between were all a part of the natural pattern of human existence."[21]

All tribes have their strategies regarding life and survival. It is their life's way and their tribal ethos. The Wintu Indians of California philosophized that a person belonged to the society rather than the person and society being two separate entities.[22] The Wintu people preferred to be a part of a community. In a group, they rationalized that hunting, growing foods, and protection from enemies groomed a communal feeling of security. Strength in numbers became a societal norm, thus causing cultural patterns to develop along this belief. The need for survival became the driving force and common concern, or else as individuals, mass confusion would result, proving the importance of commonality.[23]

In a natural environment, survival was the key issue to life. In community, practical needs were everyone's needs, thereby social behavior and morals of living were defined and redefined by practicality. After practical needs were met, tribal laws, ceremonies, and leadership became important for order in a successful community of cooperation. These nonelemental norms of native society were important, and they evolved as themes for cultural ceremonies, philosophies, art, music, and world view. A cultural genesis is initiated, therefore, with the process of interrelationships of the elements of people, family, and community, thus producing a balance of the themes in the community with nature.[24]

All social-kinship elements function cooperatively for the well-being of the tribe or nation. Traditionalists view an idyllic equilibrium with other nations and the environment, and with all things in their universe. This political-social equilibrium based on kinship including other tribal nations proves more difficult than perceiving one's own tribe in constant balance with nature and the entire universe. Often, one's tribe competed against another tribe for the same hunting areas. The physical reality obviously differed from the idyllic reality as all relations among tribes developed into political situations.

Relations influence reality among Indian peoples in a very deep manner. Ideally, the theory is for "all" to get along in the Natural Democracy, but the basics of life and human desire reestablish the boundaries of such an idyllic democracy where all things are brothers and sisters in a common circular experience. Because obvious size and abilities make animals different from each other, some species are stronger than others, whereas others are faster running or flying, and others have special talents. In the American Indian mind, all of the beings are recognized for their talents with respect.

In this context, American Indians have given human qualities to plants and animals and the learning to relate to all things is a task for life. In the big picture, the relationship of people with all the universe is the most significant, and indigenous peoples have learned how humans view themselves in this role. Thus, it is important for all peoples to comprehend that the essence of life begins with "belief" and understanding "the natural order of things."[25]

Endnotes

1 Jean Chaudhuri and Joyotpaul Chaudhuri, *A Sacred Path: The Way of the Muscogee Creeks* (Los Angeles: UCLA American Indian Studies Center, 2001), 11.

2 For more information on the fundamental quality of the circle in cultures, see J.L. Coolidge, *A Treatise on the Geometry of the Circle and Sphere* (New York: Chelsea, 1971).

3 For Plato's quote, see http://www.crystlinks.com/healingcircle.html, no date.

4 Ed McGaa, *Native Wisdom: Perceptions of the Natural Way* (Minneapolis: Four Directions Publishing, 1995), 29.

5 Quote of Black Elk, 1933, in Norbert S. Hill, Jr., ed., *Words of Power: Voices from Indian America* (Golden, CO: Fulcrum Publishing, 1994), xi.

6 Ernest L. Schusky, "The Evolution of Indian Leadership of the Great Plains, 1750–1950," *American Indian Quarterly*, Vol. 10, No. 1, Winter 1986, 71.

7 *The Times Atlas of the World*, tenth comprehensive edition (New York: Random House, 1999), 34.

8 Michael E. Steltenkamp, *Black Elk Holy Man of the Oglala* (Norman: University of Oklahoma Press, 1993), 7.

9 Joseph Epes Brown, ed., *The Sacred Pipe: Black Elk's Account of the Seven Rites of the Oglala Sioux* (New York: Penguin Books, 1971), 92, originally published by University of Oklahoma Press, Norman, 1953.

10 Roy F. Ellen, "What Black Elk Left Unsaid: On the Illusory Images of Green Primitivism," *Anthropology Today*, Vol. 2, No. 6, December 1986, 9.

11 Donald L. Fixico, "American Indians (The Minority of Minorities) and Higher Education," in Benjamin P. Bowers, Terry Jones, and Gale Auletta Young, eds., *Toward the Multicultural University* (Westport, CT: Praeger, 1995), 115.

12 Norman Guardipee, "Mending the Broken Circle," in E.K. Caldwell, ed., *Dreaming the Dawn: Conversations with Native Artists and Activists* (Lincoln: University of Nebraska Press, 1999), 28.

13 John G. Neihardt, *Black Elk Speaks: Being the Life Story of a Holy Man of the Oglala Sioux* (Lincoln: University of Nebraska Press, 1973), 21–22.

14 Ibid., 36.

15 Mark St. Pierre and Tilda Long Soldier, *Walking in the Sacred Manner: Healers, Dreamers, and Pipe Carriers—Medicine Women of the Plains Indians* (New York, London, Toronto, Sydney, Tokyo, and Singapore: Touchstone Book, 1995), 14.

16 James Mencarelli and Steven Severin, *Protest 3: Red, Black, Brown Experience in America* (Grand Rapids, MI: William B. Eerdmans Publishing Company, 1975), 150–51.

17 Yellowtail, *Yellowtail Crow Medicine Man and Sun Dance Chief: An Autobiography as Told to Michael Oren Fitzgerald* (Norman: University of Oklahoma Press, 1991), 21.

18 J. Baird Callicott, "American Indian Land Wisdom," in Paul A. Olson, ed., *The Struggle for the Land: Indigenous Insight and Industrial Empire in the Semiarid World* (Lincoln: University of Nebraska Press, 1990), 255–72.

19 Lori Arviso Alvord and Elizabeth Cohen Van Pelt, *The Scalpel and the Silver Bear* (New York: Bantam Books, 1999), 84.

20 Dhyani Ywahoo and Barbara Du Boir, eds., *Voices of Our Ancestors: Cherokee Teachings from the Wisdom Fire* (Boston: Shambhala, 1987), xiii.

21 Peter MacDonald with Ted Schwarz, *The Last Warrior: Peter MacDonald and the Navajo Nation* (New York: Orion Books, 1993), 1–2.

22 Michael Kearney, *World View* (Novato, CA: Chandler & Sharp Publications in Anthropology and Related Fields, 1984), 150–55.

23 See Emile Durkheim, *The Elementary Forms of the Religious Life* (New York: The Free Press, 1967).

24 Morris Oppier also referred to "themes" in cultural development as "affirmations" of cultural practice. Morris Oppier, "Themes as Dynamic Forces in Culture," *The American Journal of Sociology*, Vol. 51, No. 31, November 1945, 198, 199, 202.

25 Durkheim, *Forms of Religious Life*, 41.

Suggestions for Critical Reflection

1. Fixico notes that "[a]t least five kinds of balance exist: (1) balance within one's self, (2) balance within the family, (3) balance within the community or tribe, (4) balance with external communities, including other tribes and the spiritual world, and (5) balance with the environment and the universe." What other categories of balance might exist?
2. Is an "idyllic equilibrium" plausible? Why or why not?
3. Describe the differences between the "linear person" and those who exist within the circle of life.
4. Why is life more difficult without balance?
5. Why is balance difficult to maintain in circular philosophy?

Additional Resources

For additional resources relating to this reading and its themes, visit **sites.broadviewpress.com/waysofbeing/1-2**

1.3
"Did the Aztecs Do Philosophy?"*

Alejandro Santana (Mexican American)

ABOUT THE AUTHOR

Alejandro Santana is Associate Professor of Philosophy and E. John Rumpakis Professor of Hellenic Studies at the University of Portland. His research interests include Ancient Greek philosophy, Indigenous Mesoamerican philosophy, and Latin American socio-political issues related to colonialism and imperialism. Santana earned his AA (1988) from Los Angeles Pierce College and his BA (1992) from California State University Fresno. Later, he earned his PhD (2003) from University of California, Irvine. His publications appear in *Ancient Philosophy*, *Philosophical Inquiry*, the *Inter-American Journal of Philosophy*, the *American Philosophical Association Newsletter on Hispanic/Latino Issues in Philosophy*, and the *American Philosophical Association Newsletter on Native American and Indigenous Philosophy*. He is a first-generation Mexican American who works closely with Danza Azteca and other Indigenous communities in the Pacific Northwest.

KEY TERMS

Aztecs, Nahuas, Characteristics of philosophy, Explain, Meaning, Rational, Metaphysics, Epistemology, Ethics, Origins, Methods, Reflective activity, Gatekeeping

Introduction

In *Aztec Thought and Culture*, Miguel León-Portilla argues that the Aztecs, or Nahuas, addressed traditional problems in philosophy.[1] In this paper, I will present and evaluate León-Portilla's argument for his view. This is important for two main reasons. First, it will help determine how we approach the philosophical study of the Nahuatl people and their thought. León-Portilla presents the most sustained argument for the idea that the Nahuas did philosophy. If his argument is adequate, then we may engage the Nahuas as partners in philosophical inquiry. However, if his argument is inadequate, then we must either correct its mistakes or find other reasons to support

* Alejandro Santana, "Did the Aztecs Do Philosophy?" *The American Philosophical Association Newsletter on Hispanic/Latino Issues in Philosophy* 8, no. 1 (Fall 2008): 2–9.

his conclusion. But if his conclusion is simply false, then we would be mistaken to engage the Nahuas as philosophical thinkers, as we do the ancient Greeks. Although it would still be true that the Nahuas *had* a philosophy, which they certainly did, determining that philosophy would be primarily an interpretive historical and anthropological matter.[2] We wouldn't have to engage them as philosophical thinkers, but only as informants in our own philosophical quest to interpret, understand, and evaluate their thought. In this paper, I will argue that León-Portilla's argument is inadequate, but despite the problems with his argument, it is still plausible to think the Nahuas did philosophy. More specifically, I will argue the Nahuatl texts bear significant similarities to characteristics that we philosophers commonly associate with genuine philosophizing. In what follows, I will first present León-Portilla's argument, including all of the texts that he cites. Second, I will pose my main objections to his argument. Third, I will give my argument that the Nahuas did philosophy.

I. León-Portilla's Argument

To begin with, León-Portilla asks, "Did the Nahuas concern themselves with the traditional problems of philosophy? Did they experience, in addition to a religious-mythical *Weltanschauung*, that human restlessness resulting from doubt and a sense of awe which gives rise to rational inquiry into the origin, essence, and destiny of man and the world?"[3] To answer this question, he first offers a definition of philosophy. Although León-Portilla acknowledges that his definition might not be universally accepted, he takes it to be at least a *non-controversial* definition:

> Genuine philosophy arises from the explicit perception that problems are innately involved in the essence of things. A sense of wonder and mistrust of solutions derived from tradition or custom are requisite to the formulation of rational questions about the origin, the true nature, and the destiny of man in the universe. The philosopher must experience the need to explain to himself why things happen as they do. He directs himself to the meaning and true value of things, seeking the truth about life and life after death, even speculating about the possibility of knowing anything at all of that afterlife where myths and beliefs find their final answers.[4]

With this definition, León-Portilla then gives an affirmative answer to his main question. As evidence for his answer, he cites the following Nahuatl poetry from the *Colección de Cantares Mexicanos*.[5]

Text 1:
What does your mind seek?
Where is your heart?
If you give your heart to each and every thing, you lead it nowhere: you destroy your heart. Can anything be found on earth?[6]

Text 2:
Where are we going?
We came only to be born.
Our home is beyond:
In the realm of the defleshed ones.[7]
I suffer:
Happiness, good fortune never comes my way. Have I come here to struggle in vain?
This is not the place to accomplish things. Certainly nothing grows green here:
Misfortune opens its blossoms.

Text 3:
Do flowers go to the region of the dead?
In the beyond, are we dead or do we still live?
Where is the source of light, since that which gives life hides itself?

Text 4:
Truly do we live on earth?
Not forever on earth; only a little while here. Although it be jade, it will be broken.
Although it be gold, it is crushed,
Although it be quetzal feather, it is torn asunder. Not forever on earth; only a little while here.

Text 5:
Do we speak the truth here, oh Giver of life? We merely dream, we only rise from a dream. All is like a dream ...
No one speaks here of truth ...

Text 6:
Does man possess any truth?[8]
If not, our song is no longer true. Is anything stable and lasting? What reaches its aim?

According to León-Portilla, these texts provide evidence that the Nahuas indeed took the appropriate philosophical attitude expressed in his definition of philosophy: they attempted to formulate abstract philosophical questions about humanity and the world; they came to appreciate the difficulty of providing answers to these fundamental questions; and since their traditional beliefs offered answers to these questions, they questioned their traditional beliefs. Text 1 shows the author to question whether one could find satisfaction on earth. The poet also supposes that one could not give one's heart to everything, for doing so would eventually lead nowhere. Given this, the author seeks something real and of lasting value. Text 2 shows the author to address the meaning of human life and the struggle it involves; text 3 questions what happens after death. Since Nahuatl religion and mythology offered answers to these questions, León-Portilla takes these texts to be evidence that their authors were unsatisfied with the answers their traditional beliefs provided. "They doubted; they admitted that much had not been adequately explained. They longed to see with greater clarity the real outcome of our lives, and, through this, to learn what importance there might be in this struggle."[9] Texts 4 – 6 show awareness of the difficulty of establishing objective truths in a world in constant flux. The author(s) of these texts question(s) the possibility of ever establishing truth in a world that seems more like an ephemeral dream than an experience of a durable and stable reality. The texts reveal an attempt to discover foundations or "true basic principles" with which to interpret life and the ever-changing world.[10]

León-Portilla therefore concludes, "The Nahuatl enunciation of such questions is sufficient evidence that they were not satisfied by myths or religious doctrines. Their writings evince a vigorous mental development, and interest in the value, stability, or evanescence of things, and a rational vision of man himself as a problem."[11]

II. Objections to León-Portilla's Argument

Regarding León-Portilla's argument, one could raise objections about the authenticity and historicity of the texts that are cited.[12] One might also object that the term "philosophy" cannot be appropriately applied to what the Nahuas did.[13] León-Portilla has offered responses these objections, but discussing them is beyond the scope of this paper.[14] For this paper, I would like to focus on problems with his definition of philosophy. We have seen that León-Portilla offers what he takes to be a *non-controversial* definition and then argues that the Nahuatl texts fit his definition.

The problem with the argument is two-fold. To begin with, León-Portilla's definition is far from non-controversial because many would find it unacceptably imprecise and broad. One might concede that his definition identifies several qualities that are associated with philosophy, but nonetheless object that it ignores many important qualities that philosophy involves. For example, philosophy involves the systematic attempt to answer fundamental questions by giving reasons for those answers; it also involves addressing objections, clarifying concepts, making distinctions, among other things. One could also object that León-Portilla's definition is so broadly formulated that it would include poetry, theology, various forms of fictional literature, and perhaps visual art. The problem is *not* that philosophy cannot somehow overlap into these areas; instead, it is that the definition is so broad that it *ex hypothesi* includes the Nahuatl texts.

This raises another problem because León-Portilla offers no argument for his definition. This consequently reveals León-Portilla's argument to be deeply question-begging, for it leads one to ask *why* one should accept this definition of philosophy. Thus, León-Portilla's argument does not establish that we can regard the Nahuatl texts as genuine philosophy; instead, his argument seems problematic from the very start.

Now, we might agree that these song-poems are "philosophical" or "philosophically-inclined" insofar as they pose philosophical questions and sometimes give speculative answers. But we might also think it more appropriate to say that the Nahuas did something only slightly resembling philosophy, for the texts leave out much of what philosophy involves. This issue is important because it determines how we approach the Nahuas and their thought: Should we approach them as philosophical amateurs who arbitrarily painted quasi-philosophical lines of thought, or should we approach them as having done something more intentional and philosophically sophisticated?

III. My Argument That the Nahuas Did Philosophy

I submit that it is plausible to think the Nahuas did philosophy. Let me begin with characteristics that we philosophers often use to *describe* the *subject matter*, *origins*, *aims*, and *methods* of philosophy.[15]

Regarding *subject matter*, we might note that (1) philosophy addresses, but is not limited to, the various problems or questions that make up the generally-recognized areas of philosophical investigation: metaphysics, epistemology, ethics, etc.[16] Alternatively, we might note that philosophy is primarily concerned with (2) living a worthwhile, meaningful life or living in the right way.[17]

Regarding *origins*, we might say that philosophy begins with (3) wonder, (4) reflection, or (5) the clash between traditional beliefs and the need for justification.[18]

Regarding *aims*, we might mention that philosophy seeks (6) wisdom, (7) knowledge, (8) a clear, comprehensive, and plausible world-view, (9) the elimination of doubt, confusion, or nonsense, (10) intellectual liberation and autonomy.[19]

Regarding *methods*, we might note that philosophy proceeds by (11) formulating and answering fundamental questions, (12) critically examining and evaluating fundamental assumptions, (13) giving justification, (14) raising and addressing objections, (15) analysis, (16) clarifying concepts, or (17) synthesizing ideas.[20]

Given that philosophers use these characteristics to describe genuine philosophical thinking, then I submit that the Nahuatl texts can be plausibly seen as philosophy. In my view, a straight-forward reading of the Nahuatl texts shows that they have many of the characteristics listed above.[21] They certainly (1) address what we generally recognize to be philosophical issues (i.e., value, the meaning of life, life after death, knowledge, and truth). All of the texts (2) show a concern with living a worthwhile or meaningful life, and text 1 shows a concern for living in the right way. Insofar as they address these issues, they also exhibit a sense of (3) wonder and (4) reflection about them. Since these questions are raised despite the fact that Nahuatl traditional beliefs provided answers to them, there seems to be (5) a clash between traditional beliefs and the need for some kind of justification. Since the author(s) of text 5 and 6 sought fixed truths about the world, the author(s) sought some kind of (7) knowledge, at least (8) a comprehensive and plausible world view, or at the very least (9) the elimination of doubt, confusion, or nonsense.[22] Given this, one could argue that the author(s) sought to obtain a degree of (10) intellectual liberation and autonomy from their traditional beliefs. All of the texts (11) formulate and attempt to answer fundamental questions. Given the nature of their questions, they (12) attempt to critically examine and evaluate fundamental assumptions. Thus, the Nahuatl texts seem to have many of the characteristics that we generally associate with philosophical thought in terms of subject matter, origins, aims, and *some* philosophical method.

Granted, the texts do not show much in the way of (13) giving justification, (14) raising and addressing objections, (15) analysis, (16) concept clarification, or (17) synthesis of ideas. Aside from their use of poetic verse to express their philosophical thought, it is hard to determine what other methods the Nahuas might have used. But this observation should not lead us to exclude the Nahuatl texts from philosophy. Many of the Pre-Socratics are lacking in one or more of these characteristics as well, but we still include them in the philosophical canon. Given this, then consistency requires that we treat the Nahuatl texts similarly. And we have seen that the Nahuatl texts bear a substantial resemblance to a number of *other* characteristics that we associate with genuine philosophizing. If so, then consistency requires that we include them in the domain of philosophy on these grounds. We therefore have reason to regard these texts as philosophy and their authors as having done philosophy.

I should note that the catalogue I have presented is largely drawn from philosophers who are firmly within the Western philosophical tradition. But I should also emphasize that I do *not* intend to suggest that Western philosophers have or should have a privileged place in determining what is or is not philosophy. Instead, I intend to provide a sampling of views expressed by a variety of philosophers who view philosophy from a variety of perspectives. To this end, I have included feminist, Native American, and Latin American perspectives in the catalogue. I have also included perspectives of philosophers who have pluralistic views on the nature of philosophy. So, I have worked to make the catalogue substantial and reflect a diversity of views on philosophy, but I recognize that it can be improved by being made more comprehensive and exhaustive. For example, the catalogue could include critical post-modernist perspectives. It could also include South and East Asian perspectives, as well as African American, African, and Middle Eastern perspectives. With this, I recognize that the generality with which I draw my conclusion is limited by the standard I used to draw it, but I think it is safe to say that many philosophers would not take issue with the characteristics that I have provided above, although they might take issue with the fact that various other perspectives have not been included.

Yet others might take issue with my inclusion of feminist, Native American, and Latin American perspectives, as well as my suggestion that the other world perspectives should also be included. To some, one or more of these areas of thought do not do philosophy either. It is beyond the scope of this essay to address this issue,[23] but it is important to note that this, once again, raises the issue of what should or should not be included in philosophy. Ultimately, it raises the latter question about what grounds, if any, distinguish philosophy from non- philosophy, a question to which I will now turn.

Now, by giving my argument, I do not intend to argue that the Nahuatl texts can now be construed as on the philosophy side of a *distinct boundary* outside of which is non-philosophy. Indeed, I should make clear my denial of a sharp distinction between philosophy and non-philosophy.

I say this in response to what seems to be a common inclination to think in terms of sharp boundaries when considering whether a text is or is not philosophy. For example, we might say that philosophy is essentially a reflective activity grounded in wonder and thereby *include* the Nahuatl texts into the domain of philosophy; or we might say that philosophy is essentially concerned with giving justification and thereby *exclude* the Nahuatl texts. Indeed, one is especially prone to think this way when attempting to *exclude* a particular text from the domain of philosophy or a group of people from the domain of philosophical thinkers. If so, one might be inclined to think of philosophy as having an "essence" definable by one or more of the characteristics above or by some other hitherto unmentioned set of characteristics.

Nevertheless, I suggest that we resist this way of thinking. It is beyond the scope of this paper to fully argue this point, except to say the following. To think in this way implies that the "essence" of philosophy is definable in terms of necessary and sufficient conditions, for it assumes that a specific set of characteristics are all that are required to determine whether a particular text is philosophy.

But I think that it is unlikely that philosophy can be adequately defined in this way. As we have seen, philosophy can be described along several main categories: its subject matter, origins, aims, and methods. Within each category, we can mention a number of characteristics. But again neither these categories nor characteristics should be construed as exhaustive, for there is much more that can be said for each. For example, regarding main categories, we might include the practical consequences of philosophy, that is, we might say that philosophy is a pleasurable intellectual exercise done for its own sake[24] or that it helps us navigate through life more effectively and efficiently.[25] Regarding characteristics, we might say that philosophy aims at a theory of life[26] or that it examines the actions of people within the context of the concrete situations in which they live[27] or that it examines the ideas of people understood within the context of their lived experience.[28] We might also say that philosophy aims at some kind of knowledge of the world so that we can understand the social circumstances in which we live and thereby *change* them for the better.[29] Additionally, we might say that philosophy involves imagination, curiosity, openness, vision, and passion.[30] Thus, we can go on indefinitely about the dynamic and expansive nature of philosophy, and if so, it seems unlikely that we can adequately define it by a static and finite concept.

We might attempt to address this problem by constructing a very comprehensive and detailed definition, one that does well to characterize various important features of philosophy.[31] Such a definition might be helpful and even illuminating, but it is unlikely to be adequate, for it would also have to state necessary and sufficient conditions for each of the main concepts used to characterize philosophy. That is, we would also have to state necessary and sufficient conditions for, say, "wonder" or "reflection," which surely would have to be somehow included in any comprehensive definition of philosophy. This is because if necessary and sufficient conditions are required to define philosophy, then I don't see why we should not require the same for the concepts used in that definition. If this were not required for these concepts, then it would seem arbitrary to require such conditions for philosophy. Therefore, consistency would require that the essentialist demand necessary and sufficient conditions for concepts like "wonder" and "reflection," but it seems unlikely that we can adequately define these concepts, for they seem as difficult to define as "imagination" and "creativity." Thus, it is unlikely that we can adequately give necessary and sufficient conditions for philosophy, for it seems that we could indefinitely describe the nature of philosophy and, moreover, indefinitely describe the concepts used in that definition. If we attempted such a definition, then we could at best understand it to be a *characterization* of philosophy and one that does not fully capture all that philosophy is or could be.

Given this, I also suggest that it is more likely that philosophy is a concept without a distinct boundary, if we construe it as having a boundary at all; the challenge now is to understand philosophy in this way while also understanding it as distinguishable from non-philosophy.

Conclusion

At any rate, I hope this discussion shows that, despite the inadequacy of León-Portilla's argument, it is still plausible to think that the Nahuas did philosophy: the Nahuatl texts exhibit many characteristics that we philosophers use to describe genuine philosophical thinking, and on those grounds, consistency requires that we consider them as philosophy and their writers as having done philosophy. At least, I hope to have shown that it is far from obvious that we should exclude them from the domain of genuine philosophizing. It is unlikely that philosophy is the kind of thing that has a distinct boundary, because it is unlikely that one set of characteristics can serve as criteria for inclusion into its domain. Thus, it is more likely that philosophy has no distinct boundary. I have offered a family resemblance view to explain how we could understand philosophy in this way and yet distinguish it from non-philosophy, but much more work is needed to fully justify this view. Nevertheless, I hope to have shown that we should philosophically examine the Nahuatl texts and likewise engage their authors, rather than exclude them because they don't fit neatly into some rigid conception of what philosophy is.[32]

Endnotes

1 Miguel León-Portilla, *Aztec Thought and Culture: A Study of the Ancient Nahuatl Mind* [*Aztec Thought and Culture*] (Norman: University of Oklahoma Press, 1963), 3–24. Who were the Aztecs? The name "Aztecs" refers to a native group who called themselves the "Mexica." This group migrated from its origins probably in northwestern Mexico to what is now the Valley of Mexico. The Mexica established their capital, Tenochtitlan, on a marshy island off the western shore of Lake Tetzcoco. From it, they built an empire that stretched from what is now the Gulf of Mexico to the Pacific Ocean. The Mexica, however, were not the only native group in the Valley of Mexico. There were many others: Tetzcocans, Acolhua, Tlaxcatecs, Cholulans, Chalcans, to name a few. These groups shared a common language, *Nahuatl*, which is a member of the Uto-Aztecan linguistic family and related to the Ute, Hopi, and Comanche languages. They also shared strong cultural influences from the earlier Toltec and Teotihauacan civilizations (Townsend, Richard F., *The Aztecs* (London: Thames & Hudson, 2000), 44–53). This larger group is called the *Nahuas*, and it is this broader population—with the Mexica as its most dominant group—that is the focus of my study. So instead of using the name "Aztecs," I will use "Nahuas."

2 Thus I am *not* asking here whether or not the Nahuas *had* a philosophy: that question has already been answered affirmatively by ample textual evidence from which we can piece together an interpretation of their philosophy. Instead, I am asking whether or not that Nahuas explicitly *did* philosophy, as, say, the Pre-Socratics explicitly *did* philosophy. This is an important question, for it is certainly possible that the Nahuas could have a philosophy without doing it in this explicit way.

3 León-Portilla, *Aztec Thought and Culture*, xxiii.

4 Ibid., 3–4.

5 Ibid., 4–7 for texts 1–6. For all these texts, León-Portilla notes the following: "*Coleccion de Canatares Mexicanos* [*Cantares Mexicanos*] (ed. by Antonio Peñafiel), fol. 2, v. The original manuscript of this work is found in the National Library of Mexico."

6 This text seems to express an insight similar (but not identical) to the one Aristotle expresses in the *Nicomachean Ethics* (1094a20–23): "… we do not choose everything because of something else—for if we do, it will go on without limit, so that desire will prove to be empty and futile." Here, Aristotle argues that there must be a highest good that is the ultimate end for all our desires; without this ultimate end, desire is empty and futile. The similarity between text 1 and Aristotle's view has to do with the nature of desire rather than the nature of the good. Both seem to agree that desire without an ultimate end is empty and futile. There are differences, however: text 1 seems to question whether there is an ultimate end to desire and whether such an end could be discovered; Aristotle thinks there *must* be such an end, and that it can be discovered. Indeed, Aristotle later settles on an answer: the ultimate end of human desire is happiness (*NE* 1097b22–24).

7 León-Portilla notes: "The term Ximoayan, 'the abode of the defleshed ones,' was one of the Nahuatl expressions for the hereafter" (*Aztec Thought and Culture*, 6).

8 Regarding the word "truth," León-Portilla states:

> The word "truth" in Nahuatl, *neltiliztli*, is derived from the same radical as "root," *tla-nél-huatl*, from which, in turn, comes *nel-huáyotl*, "base" or "foundation." The stem syllable *nel* has the original connotation of solid firmness or deeply rooted. With this etymology "truth," for the Nahuas, was to be identified with well-grounded stability (*Aztec Thought and Culture*, 8).

9 León-Portilla, *Aztec Thought and Culture*, 6.

10 Ibid., 8.

11 Ibid., 8–9.

12 More specifically, one might question the extent to which the texts were corrupted by the Indian informants from whom these texts were secured. As León-Portilla notes, contamination may have occurred in a variety of ways, some of which are as follows (Miguel León-Portilla, "Have We Really Translated the Mesoamerican 'Ancient Word?'" ["Translated?"] in *On the Translation of Native American Literatures*, ed. Brian Swann [Washington: Smithsonian Institution, 1992], 314–15). First, the original meaning of the content of oral tradition may have been lost simply by the act of writing. As León-Portilla says, "Orality, open always to enrichment and adaptations within changing circumstances, cannot be incarcerated, reduced to linear alphabetic writing, transformed into something totally alien to the native culture" ("Translated?", 315). Second, contamination may have occurred due to self-censure: the Nahuatl informant may have provided answers that he thought would have pleased his interrogator, or he may have concealed information that he thought to be most sacred. Third, the Nahuatl informant may have answered a question to fit what his interrogator was looking for, so contamination may have occurred by emphasis. Fourth, the native informant may also have misunderstood the question that was asked and thereby provided the wrong answer.

13 Walter Mignolo notes some of the ways in which this objection has been raised (Walter Mignolo, "Philosophy and the Colonial Difference," in *Latin American Philosophy: Currents, Issues, Debates*, edited by Eduardo Mendieta [Bloomington: Indiana University Press, 2003], 80). According to Mignolo, some regarded the application of the term "philosophy" to the Nahuatl texts as "imprudent." The Nahuas may not have done anything resembling philosophical discourse; instead, they simply may have been doing something entirely different. This need not be construed as a "lack" but simply a difference. Just as the Nahuas may have "lacked" philosophy, they may have been doing something that the Europeans "lacked."

14 Regarding the first set of objections, León-Portilla argues that we can be confident that we have translated *at least part* of the Mesoamerican 'Ancient word' ("Translated?", 313–38). To begin with, the ancient Mesoamericans had an oral tradition that was formally taught but was used in conjunction with written codices so that the oral teachings enable the student to "follow" the pictorial representations in the codices. The native Mesoamericans thus used books, and they had a deep appreciation for them, which is exemplified by texts expressing reverence for wise men, "to whom the books belong." Moreover, there are texts that read as though the writer is taking dictation from someone who is "reading" a codex. For example, the text of the *Legend of the Suns* strongly suggest that the speaker is referring to a codex, for the speaker says things like, "Here is … ," "There is … ," and "of this, his appearance is here." Lastly, there exist several copies of the same transliterated indigenous text, copies that were independently collected and could be demonstrated to have its source in an indigenous codex.

Regarding the second objection, León-Portilla argues that the term "philosophy" can be applied to Nahuatl thought provided that we properly understand its application (Miguel León-Portilla, "Pre-Hispanic Thought," in *Major Trends in Mexican Philosophy*, by Universidad Nacional Autónoma de México: Consejo Técnico de Humanidades [Notre Dame: Notre Dame Press, 1966] 6–11). According to León-Portilla, when investigators of Nahuatl culture apply the term "philosophy" to Nahuatl thought, they are in no way describing Nahuatl thought *in itself*, for they cannot escape the conceptual machinery that they bring to the investigation. Instead, they apply this term to their own *historical invention* of Nahuatl thought, which results from the process of working to understand Nahuatl thought in its own proper context and then determining whether the concept of philosophy applies. When doing this, investigators might extend the original connotation of the term "philosophy" and thereby widen its applicability; however, they apply the term only when features in their reconstruction of Nahuatl thought are found to be analogous to those which are found in the concept of philosophy. In this way, investigators can make Nahuatl thought comprehensible to themselves yet maintain an awareness of the real epistemological limitations of their investigation.

15 A few important remarks about this catalogue are in order. First, this catalogue was compiled from a sampling of views expressed by a variety of philosophers. This sampling is intended to list fairly *common* ways in which philosophers *describe* their discipline. It is *not* intended to be a definition, nor is it intended to present these characteristics as "essential" properties of philosophy. Second, this sampling of descriptors is intended to be substantial, but it is neither comprehensive nor exhaustive. For example, a more comprehensive and exhaustive list would include critical post-modernist perspectives. It would also include South and East Asian perspectives, as well as African American, African, and Middle Eastern perspectives. Moreover, it would include the views of those who argue that genuine philosophy must be *a priori*, necessary, or non-scientific. Third, the main categories, including their various characteristics, need not be construed as mutually exclusive or all-compatible. Fourth, all of these characteristics should be understood to have very broad meanings, so that they generally describe the similarities of what philosophers say about philosophy, but leave out the specific meanings that each philosopher had in mind. For example, Aristotle, Russell, and Burkhart all think that philosophy aims at knowledge (7), but there are differences in the conception of knowledge that each has in mind.

16 (1) Jorge J.E. Gracia, "The History of Philosophy and Latin American Philosophy" ["History of Philosophy"], in *The Role of History in Latin American Philosophy: Contemporary Perspectives*, eds. Arleen Salles and Elizabeth Millán-Zaibert (Albany: State University of New York Press, 2005), 23; Robert C. Solomon, *The Big Questions: A Short Introduction to Philosophy* [*Big Questions*] (Toronto: Thompson Wadsworth, 2006), 7; Risiri Frondizi, "Is There an Ibero-American Philosophy?", in *Latin American Philosophy: An Introduction with Readings*, eds. Susana Nuccetelli and Gary Seay (Upper Saddle River: Pearson Education, 2004), 294. León-Portilla, *Aztec Thought and Culture*, 3–4; Jean Grimshaw, *Philosophy and Feminist Thinking* (Minneapolis: University of Minnesota Press, 1986), 22–23.

17 (2) Plato, *Apology* 38a, *Republic* I 344e; Brian Yazzie Burkhart, "What Coyote and Thales can Teach Us: An Outline of American Indian Epistemology," in *American Indian Thought: Philosophical Essays*, edited by Anne Waters (Malden, MA: Blackwell Publishing, 2004), 17.

18 (3) Plato, *Theatetus* 155d; Aristotle, *Metaphysics* I 982b13–15; León-Portilla, *Aztec Thought and Culture*, 3–4. (4) Solomon, *Big Questions*, 5–6; Simon Blackburn, *Think* (Oxford: Oxford University Press, 1999), 4–5; León-Portilla, *Aztec Thought and Culture*, 3–4. (5) John Dewey, *Reconstruction in Philosophy* [*Reconstruction*] (Boston: Beacon Press, 1948), 7–11; León-Portilla, *Aztec Thought and Culture*, 3–4.

19 (6) Plato, *Republic* V 475b, 480a; Aristotle, *Metaphysics* I 981b30. (7) Aristotle, *Metaphysics* II 993b20; Bertrand Russell, *The Problems of Philosophy* (New York: Oxford University Press, 1981), 154–55; Jaques Maritain, *An Introduction to Philosophy*, E.I. Watkin trans. (London: Sheed & Ward, 1933), 108; Laurence BonJour and Ann Baker, *Philosophical Problems: An Annotated Anthology* [*Philosophical Problems*] (New York: Pearson, 2005), 1; Brian Yazzie Burkhart, "What Coyote and Thales can Teach Us: An Outline of American Indian Epistemology," in *American Indian Thought: Philosophical Essays*, edited by Anne Waters (Malden, MA: Blackwell Publishing, 2004), 17. (8) Wilfrid Sellars, *Science, Perception and Reality* [*Science*] (London: Routledge & Kegan Paul, 1963), 1; Gracia, "History of Philosophy," 23; J.C.C. Smart, *Philosophy and Scientific Realism* (London: Routledge & Kegan Paul, 1963), 1–2; Andrea Nye, "It's Not Philosophy," *Decentering the Center: Philosophy for a Multicultural, Postcolonial, and Feminist World*, edited by Uma Narayan & Sandra Harding (Bloomington and Indianapolis: Indiana University Press, 2000), 104. (9) C.S. Peirce, "The Fixation of Belief," in *Philosophical Writings of Peirce*, ed. Justus Buchler (New York: Dover, 1955), 10; Ludwig Wittgenstein, *Philosophical Investigations* 2nd ed., trans. G.E.M. Anscombe (New York: Macmillan, 1967), 47 (PI 109), 50 (PI 125), and 51 (PI 133); Rudolf Carnap, "Philosophy and Logical Syntax," in *What is Philosophy?*, ed. Henry W. Johnstone, Jr. (New York: Macmillan, 1965), 46–48, 51–52, 54–56; Max Black, "Linguistic Method in Philosophy" ["Linguistic Method"], in *What is Philosophy?*, ed. Henry W. Johnstone, Jr. (New York: Macmillan, 1965), 66–67. (10) Manuel Velasquez, *Philosophy: A Text with Readings* 10th edition (Belmont, CA: Thomson Wadsworth, 2008), 4.

20 (11) Sober, Elliott, *Core Questions in Philosophy: A Text with Readings* 4th ed. [*Core Questions*] (New Jersey: Pearson 2005), 4; Kessler, Gary E., *Voices of Wisdom: A Multicultural Philosophy Reader* 6th ed. (Belmont: Thompson, 2007), 4. (12) Sober, *Core Questions*, 4; Grimshaw, *Philosophy and Feminist Thinking*, 30, 32–33. (13) Solomon, *Big Questions*, 6; BonJour and Baker, *Philosophical Problems*, 8–9. (14) Ibid., 9–11. (15) Bertrand Russell, "On Scientific Method in Philosophy," in *What is Philosophy?*, ed. Henry W. Johnstone, Jr. (New York: Macmillan, 1965), 40; Solomon, *Big Questions*, 6. (16) Black, "Linguistic Method," 66–67; Dewey, *Reconstruction*, 26; BonJour and Baker, *Philosophical Problems*, 2; Solomon, *Big Questions*, 6; Sober, *Core Questions*, 4–5. (17) Solomon, *Big Questions*, 6, "gathering together different ideas into a single, unified vision."

21 Here one could raise problems with the accuracy of León-Portilla's translations, but for the purpose of this paper, I will leave these problems to the translators.

22 One might ask here: Did the Nahuas aim for wisdom (5)? Texts 1–6 do not provide evidence for this, but elsewhere León-Portilla argues that there were indeed Nahuatl wise men, or *tlamatini*. According to León-Portilla, *tlamatini* is best translated as "he who knows things" or "he who knows something" (*Aztec Thought and Culture*, 11). To give his argument, León-Portilla cites another text that gives an elaborate description of the Nahuatl wise man. This description, which is too long to quote here, defines the wise man as "a light, a torch ... the path, the true way for others." The wise man possesses "... the handed-down wisdom; he teaches it; he follows the path of truth." He is a "[t]eacher of truth, he never ceases to admonish." We are told that "[e]veryone is comforted by him, corrected, and taught. Thanks to him people humanize their will and receive a strict education" (León-Portilla, *Aztec Thought and Culture*, 10). Thus, despite the fact that texts 1–6 do not show that the Nahuas aimed at wisdom, there is *other* evidence that the Nahuas aimed at what could be construed as wisdom.

23 One place where, broadly speaking, this objection is addressed is in the fall 2001 issue of the *APA Newsletter* (vol. 1, no. 1). More specifically, see Anne Waters, "Broadening the Scope of American Philosophy at the Turn of a New Millennium"; V.F. Cordova, "What is Philosophy?"; Robert C. Solomon, "What is Philosophy? The Status of Non-Western Philosophy in the Profession"; Joseph Prabhu, "Philosophy in an Age of Global Encounter"; Yoko Arisaka, "Reflections on 'What is Philosophy? The status of Non-Western Philosophy in the Profession'"; Pieter Duvenage, "Is There a South African Philosophical Tradition?"; and Jay M. Van Hook, "The Universalist Thesis Revisited: What Direction for African Philosophy in the New Millennium?" For other interesting work on academic philosophy, see also Tracy Bowell, "Fitting In? Negotiating Our Places in the Profession," and Nancy J. Holland, "Philosophy and the Future of Women's Studies."

24 Blackburn, *Think*, 6.

25 Blackburn, *Think*, 6–7; Sellars, *Science*, 1–2.

26 José Ortega y Gasset, *What is Philosophy?* (New York: W.W. Norton Co., 1960), 240.

27 Vine Deloria, Jr., "Philosophy and the Tribal Peoples," in *American Indian Thought: Philosophical Essays*, edited by Anne Waters (Malden, MA: Blackwell Publishing, 2004), 11.

28 V.F. Cordova, "Approaches to Native American Philosophy," in *American Indian Thought: Philosophical Essays*, edited by Anne Waters (Malden, MA: Blackwell Publishing, 2004), 27.

29 Maurice Cornforth, *Science Versus Idealism: A Defense of Philosophy against Positivism and Pragmatism* (New York: International Publishers, 1962), 223.

30 Robert C. Solomon, *The Joy of Philosophy: Thinking Thin Versus the Passionate Life* (New York: Oxford University Press, 1999), vi, 3, 5, 7, 9.

31 Gracia gives perhaps the most comprehensive definition of philosophy that I have yet come across. He does so in three points.

> The first is that the aim of philosophy is to develop a view of the world, or any of its parts, which seeks to be accurate, consistent, comprehensive, and supported by sound evidence. As such, philosophy can be distinguished from other disciplines of learning in two ways: (1) It is more general insofar as all other disciplines of learning are concerned with restricted areas of knowledge involving specific methodologies, particular objects or kinds of objects, or both; and (2) it involves areas of investigation that are uniquely philosophical such as ethics, logic, and metaphysics. The second point is that philosophy concerns the solution of philosophical problems, that is, of problems that surface precisely when one tries to achieve the aim just stated, either because of conceptual inconsistencies, empirical evidence, or inadequacies of other sorts. Finally, philosophy is not merely a descriptive enterprise; it also involves interpretation and evaluation. To proceed philosophically, then, is to proceed so as to achieve the aims of the discipline; and to proceed nonphilosophically is precisely to proceed in ways that divert oneself from those aims ("History of Philosophy," 23).

32 I would like to thank James Maffie, Caery Evangelist, Rod Jenks, and Jim Baillie for their helpful comments during the construction of this paper. I would also like to thank Grant Silva, Norman Swazo, Michael Koch, and José Mendoza for their helpful comments when I presented the paper at the spring 2007 meeting of the Society of Iberian and Latin American Thought.

References

Arisaka, Yoko. "Reflections on 'What is Philosophy? The Status of Non-Western Philosophy in the Profession.'" *American Philosophical Association Newsletter on the Status of Asian & Asian-American Philosophers & Philosophies* 1, no. 1 (2001): 31–33.

Black, Max. "*Linguistic Method in Philosophy.*" In *What is Philosophy?*, edited by Henry W. Johnstone, Jr., 57–67. New York: Macmillan, 1965.

Blackburn, Simon. *Think*. Oxford: Oxford University Press, 1999.

BonJour, Laurence and Ann Baker. *Philosophical Problems: An Annotated Anthology*. New York: Pearson, 2005.

Bowell, Tracy. "Fitting In? Negotiating Our Places in the Profession." *American Philosophical Association Newsletter on Feminism and Philosophy* 1, no. 1 (2001): 67–70.

Burkhart, Brian Yazzie. "What Coyote and Thales can Teach Us: An Outline of American Indian Epistemology." In *American Indian Thought: Philosophical Essays*, edited by Anne Waters, 15–26. Malden, MA: Blackwell Publishing, 2004.

Carnap, Rudolf. "Philosophy and Logical Syntax." In *What is Philosophy?*, edited by Henry W. Johnstone, Jr., 46–56. New York: Macmillan, 1965.

Cordova, V.F. "Approaches to Native American Philosophy." In *American Indian Thought: Philosophical Essays*, edited by Anne Waters, 27–33. Malden, MA: Blackwell Publishing, 2004.

—. "What is Philosophy?" *American Philosophical Association Newsletter on American Indians in Philosophy* 1, no. 1 (2001): 14–16.

Cornforth, Maurice. *Science Versus Idealism: A Defense of Philosophy against Positivism and Pragmatism*. New York: International Publishers, 1962.

Deloria, Jr., Vine. "Philosophy and the Tribal Peoples." In *American Indian Thought: Philosophical Essays*, edited by Anne Waters, 3–11. Malden, MA: Blackwell Publishing, 2004.

Dewey, John. *Reconstruction in Philosophy*. Boston: Beacon Press, 1948.

Duvenage, Pieter. "Is There a South African Philosophical Tradition?" *American Philosophical Association Newsletter on International Cooperation* 1, no. 1 (2001): 112–17.

Frondizi, Risieri. "Is There an Ibero-American Philosophy?" In *Latin American Philosophy: An Introduction with Readings*, edited by Susana Nuccetelli and Gary Seay, 294–301. Upper Saddle River: Pearson Education, 2004.

Gracia, Jorge J.E. "The History of Philosophy and Latin American Philosophy." In *The Role of History in Latin American Philosophy: Contemporary Perspectives*, edited by Arleen Salles and Elizabeth Millán-Zaibert, 21–42. Albany: State University of New York Press, 2005.

—. *Hispanic/Latino Identity: A Philosophical Perspective*. Great Britain: Blackwell, 2000.

Grimshaw, Jean. *Philosophy and Feminist Thinking*. Minneapolis: University of Minnesota Press, 1986.

Holland, Nancy J. "Philosophy and the Future of Women's Studies." *American Philosophical Association Newsletter on Feminism and Philosophy* 1, no. 1 (2001): 71–72.

Kessler, Gary E. *Voices of Wisdom: A Multicultural Philosophy Reader* 6th ed. Belmont: Thompson, 2007.

León-Portilla, Miguel. *Fifteen Poets of the Aztec World*. Norman: University of Oklahoma Press, 1992.

—. "Have We Really Translated the Mesoamerican 'Ancient Word?'" In *On the Translation of Native American Literatures*, edited by Brian Swann, 313–38. Washington: Smithsonian Institution, 1992.

—. "Pre-Hispanic Thought." In *Major Trends in Mexican Philosophy* by Universidad Nacional Autónoma de México: Consejo Técnico de Humanidades, 2–56. Notre Dame: Notre Dame Press, 1966.

—. *Aztec Thought and Culture: A Study of the Ancient Nahuatl Mind*. Norman: University of Oklahoma Press, 1963.

Maritain, Jacques. *An Introduction to Philosophy*. E.I. Watkin trans. London: Sheed & Ward, 1933.

Mignolo, Walter. "Philosophy and the Colonial Difference." In *Latin American Philosophy: Currents, Issues, Debates*, edited by Eduardo Mendieta, 80–86. Bloomington: Indiana University Press, 2003.

Nye, Andrea. "It's Not Philosophy." In *Decentering the Center: Philosophy for a Multicultural, Postcolonial, and Feminist World*, edited by Uma Narayan & Sandra Harding, 101–09. Bloomington and Indianapolis: Indiana University Press, 2000.

Ortega y Gasset, José. *What is Philosophy?* New York: W.W. Norton Co., 1960.

Peirce, C.S. "The Fixation of Belief." In *Philosophical Writings of Peirce*, edited by Justus Buchler, 5–22. New York: Dover, 1955.

Prabhu, Joseph. "Philosophy in an Age of Global Encounter." *American Philosophical Association Newsletter on the Status of Asian & Asian-American Philosophers & Philosophies* 1, no. 1 (2001): 29–31.

Russell, Bertrand. *The Problems of Philosophy*. New York: Oxford University Press, 1981.

—. "On Scientific Method in Philosophy." In *What is Philosophy?*, edited by Henry W. Johnstone, Jr., 37–45. New York: Macmillan, 1965.

Sellars, Wilfrid. *Science, Perception and Reality*. London: Routledge & Kegan Paul, 1963.

Smart, J.C.C. *Philosophy and Scientific Realism*. London: Routledge & Kegan Paul, 1963.

Sober, Elliott. *Core Questions in Philosophy: A Text with Readings* 4th ed. Upper Saddle River, NJ: Pearson, 2005.

Solomon, Robert C. *The Big Questions: A Short Introduction to Philosophy*. Toronto: Thompson Wadsworth, 2006.

—. "What is Philosophy? The Status of Non-Western Philosophy in the Profession." *American Philosophical Association Newsletter on the Status of Asian & Asian-American Philosophers & Philosophies* 1, no. 1 (2001): 27–29.

—. *The Joy of Philosophy: Thinking Thin Versus the Passionate Life*. New York: Oxford University Press, 1999.

Townsend, Richard F. *The Aztecs*. London: Thames & Hudson, 2000.

Van Hook, Jay M. "The Universalist Thesis Revisited: What Direction for African Philosophy in the New Millennium?" *American Philosophical Association Newsletter on International Cooperation* 1, no. 1 (2001): 121–24.

Velasquez, Manuel. *Philosophy: A Text with Readings* 10th ed. Belmont, CA: Thomson Wadsworth, 2008.

Waters, Anne. "Broadening the Scope of American Philosophy at the Turn of a New Millennium." *American Philosophical Association Newsletter on American Indians in Philosophy* 1, no. 1 (2001): 10–14.

Wittgenstein, Ludwig. *Philosophical Investigations* 2nd ed., trans. G.E.M. Anscombe. New York: Macmillan, 1967.

Suggestions for Critical Reflection

1. Should we be critical about what is considered "non-philosophy" and "philosophy"? Is there a "distinct boundary" between philosophy and non-philosophy?
2. Are certain methods (i.e., argumentation) essential to doing philosophy? Why or why not?
3. The author "raises the issue of what should or should not be included in philosophy." Who gets to decide this boundary?
4. Does philosophy have to be rigorous?
5. Why might the Nahuas have been excluded from the study of philosophy previously?

Additional Resources

For additional resources relating to this reading and its themes, visit **sites.broadviewpress.com/waysofbeing/1-3**

PART II

Philosophy of Religion

INTRODUCTION

Creation, the Sacred, and the People

In the Western canon, the philosophy of religion not only examines the themes and concepts involved in religious traditions, but it also includes the investigation and assessment of alternative worldviews.* While philosophy of religion courses may entertain questions in the other general areas of philosophy (e.g., metaphysics, epistemology, and values), they most often focus on the philosophy of the Medieval period, which considers such questions as: Does a Christian God exist? Is that God all powerful? Is it better to believe in such a Being if one can never know that it exists?

Indigenous philosophy is quite different from its Western counterpart, and expectedly so. Indigenous philosophical thought prior to contact with Europeans stands in stark contrast to the worldview that develops from an organized Christian religion, such as Catholicism. This is made evident in the selections in this chapter.

The chapter opens with a collection of letters and speeches that voice the confusion and frustration from Indigenous people who are engaging with the contradiction of a religion that posits the existence of a benevolent Being whose believers are actively working to conquer Indigenous people. While the following speeches and correspondence make up only a small sample of the initial responses to contact with European settlers, missionaries, and governments, it is worth noting the similarities in the responses even though the authors come from very different communities.

The chapter continues with an excerpt from *God Is Red* by Vine Deloria Jr. Colonialism entails the eradication of the traditional Indigenous worldview. Through many governmental policies—such as the removal of Indigenous people from their land, the use of a reserve/reservation system, the mandatory attendance of Indigenous children at residential schools, and various attempts to 'civilize' Indigenous people—the war on Indigenous philosophy and particularly its metaphysics is conducted. Religion has played a critical role in the erasure of Indigenous philosophy, especially since many residential schools were overseen by various Christian denominations. The piece by Deloria highlights some of the fundamental differences between Christian and Indigenous religious worldviews.

* For a complete description of the philosophy of religion, please refer to Charles Taliaferro, "Philosophy of Religion," *The Stanford Encyclopedia of Philosophy* (Winter 2021), https://plato.stanford.edu/archives/win2021/entries/philosophy-religion/.

As a result of these differences, it is reasonable to expect some misunderstandings regarding the approaches to being in the world that each worldview endorses. One of the most misunderstood concepts in Indigenous thought is the application of the term 'sacred.' Given the different worldviews, the term is one that does not directly translate between the Western or Christian conception. Winona LaDuke illustrates the connection between the land (to include all the nonhuman relations) and an Indigenous community's epistemology using examples from Turtle Island. To be sacred is, at its most fundamental, a link between the knowledge, the obligations, and the practice of the people. It informs a way of being in the world, and in this way, the content of LaDuke's article also seems suitable as a reading in other sections of this book.

The Indigenous equivalent to the philosophy of religion is quite different from its Western counterpart. Where Western philosophy, especially that found in the Medieval period, is interested in evaluating claims—such as whether God exists or whether certain features, e.g., if God is all-powerful, can be attributed to God—the Indigenous philosophy of religion is focused on how to live in the world.

2.1
Assorted Responses to Christianity: Speeches and Letters

2.1a
1567 Letter of Francisco de Montejo Xiu*

Ah Kukum, Don Francisco de Montejo Xiu (Mayan)

ABOUT THE AUTHOR

In 1547, a member of the Mayan ruling lineage for the Mani province, Ah Kukum, was baptized as Don Francisco de Montejo Xiu.† Not much is known about this Mayan leader, and it is easy to confuse him with the Spanish conquistadors who attempted to conquer the Yucatán Peninsula: Don Francisco de Montejo Xiu the elder and the younger. It is believed that Ah Kukum's baptism was part of a Mayan strategy to secure favour with the Spanish military/government in light of the aggressive conversion program of the church.‡ The following letter was not only written in response to the policies and practices of the Spanish Inquisition that were being conducted by Friar Diego de Landa, but it was also a counter to the letters written by the Mayan leaders of other provinces that expressed support for Diego de Landa and the Church.§

KEY TERMS

Inquisition, New Spain, Diego de Landa, Slavery, Yucatán, Conquistadors, Torture

* From Friar Diego de Landa and William Gates, *Yucatan Before and After the Conquest* (New York: Dover Publications, 1978), 115–17.

† See Inga Clendinnen, *Ambivalent Conquests: Maya and Spaniard in Yucatan, 1517–1570* (New York: Cambridge University Press, 2003), 54.

‡ See Clendinnen, 54.

§ The letters of support are thought to be suspicious given their similar wording and may have been submitted by someone other than the Mayan leaders (Clendinnen, 101–02).

Letter of Francisco de Montejo Xiu.
Governor of Maní, and other prominent town governors,
To the King, April 12, 1567.

Sacred Catholic Majesty:

After we learned the good, in knowing God our Lord as the only true god, leaving our blindness and idolatries, and your majesty as temporal lord, before we could well open our eyes to the one and the other, there came upon us a persecution of the worst that can be imagined; and it was in the year '62, on the part of the Franciscan religious, who had taken us to teach the doctrine, instead of which they began to torment us, hanging us by the hands and whipping us cruelly, hanging weights of stone on our feet, torturing many of us on a windlass, giving the torture of the water, from which many died or were maimed.

Being in these tribulations and burdens, trusting in your majesty's Justice to hear and defend us, there came the Dr. Quijada to aid our tormentors, saying that we were idolaters and sacrificers of men, and many other things against all truth, which we never committed during our time of blindness and infidelity. And as we see ourselves maimed by cruel tortures, many dead of them, robbed of our property, and yet more, seeing disinterred the bones of our baptised ones, who had died as Christians, we came to despair.

Not content with this, the religious (i.e., the friars) and thy royal Justice, held at Maní a solemn auto of inquisition, where they seized many statues, disinterred many dead and burned them there in public; made slaves of many to serve Spaniards for from eight to ten years, and placed the sambenitos. The one and the other gave us great wonder and fear, because we did not know what it all was, having been recently baptised, and not informed; and when we returned to our people and told them to hear and guard justice, they seized us, put us in prison and chains, like slaves, in the monastery at Merida, where many of us died; and they told us we would be burned, without our knowing the why.

At this came the bishop whom your majesty sent, who, although he took us from prison and relieved us from death and the sambenitos, has not relieved us from the shame of the charges that were made against us, that we were idolaters, human sacrifices, and had slain many men; because, at the last, he is of the habit of San Francisco and does for them. He has consoled us by his words, saying that your majesty would render justice.

A receptor came from Mexico, and made inquiry, and we believe it went to the Audiencia, and nothing has been done.

Then came as governor don Luís de Céspedes, and instead of relieving us he has increased our burdens, taking away our daughters and wives to serve the Spaniards, against their will and ours; which we feel so greatly that the common people say that not in the time of our infidelity were we so vexed or maltreated, because our ancestors never took from one his children, nor from husbands their wives to make use of them, as today does your majesty's Justice, even to the service of the negros and mulattos.

And with all our afflictions and labors, we have loved the fathers and supplied their necessities, have built many monasteries for them, provided with ornaments and bells, all at our cost and that of our vassals and fellows; although in payment of our services they have made of us their vassals, have deprived us of the signories we inherited from our ancestors, a thing we never suffered in the time of our infidelity. And we obey your majesty's justice, hoping that you will send us remedy.

One thing that has greatly dismayed and stirred us up, is the letters written by Fray Diego de Landa, chief author of all these ills and burdens, saying that your majesty has approved the killings, robberies, tortures, slaveries and other cruelties inflicted on us; to which we wonder that such things should be said of so Catholic and upright a king as is your majesty. If it is told that we have sacrificed men after that we received baptism, it is a great and false witness invented by them to gild their cruelties.

And if there have been or are idols among us, they are but those we have gathered to send to the religious as they required of us, saying that we had confessed to their possession under the torture; but all know that we went many leagues to gather them from places where we knew that they had been kept by those before us, and which we had abandoned when we were baptised and in good conscience they should not punish us as they have done.

If your majesty wishes to learn of all, send a person to search the truth, to learn of our innocence and the great cruelty of the padres; and had not the bishop come, we should all have been brought to an end. And though we cherish well Fray Diego and the other padres who torment us, only to hear them named causes our entrails to revolt. Therefore, your majesty, send us other ministers to teach us and preach to us the law of God, for we much desire our salvation.

The religious of San Francisco of this province have written certain letters to your majesty and to the general of the order, in praise of Fray Diego de Landa and his other companions, who were those who tortured, killed and put us to scandal; and they gave certain letters written in the Castilian language to certain Indians of their familiars, and thus they signed them and sent them to your majesty. May your majesty understand that they are not ours, we who are chiefs of this land, and who did not have to write lies nor falsehoods nor contradictions. May Fray Diego de Landa and his companions suffer the penance for the evils they have done to us, and may our descendants to the fourth generation be recompensed the great persecution that came on us.

May God guard your majesty for many years in his sacred service and for our good and protection. From Yucatan, the 12 of April, 1567.

Your majesty's humble vassals kiss your royal hands and feet.

(signed by)

don Francisco de Montejo Xiu, govr. of Maní
Juan Pacab, govr. of Muna
Jorge Xiu, govr. of Panaba
Francisco Pacab, govr. of Te-Xul.

Suggestions for Critical Reflection

1. One of the goals of the Inquisition was to ensure that the converted remained so. Do you think the methods described in the letter were appropriate? Why or why not? Is torture, whether historical or contemporary, justified?
2. Why do you think the need for confessions was so critical to someone like Diego de Landa? Should the confessions, given how they were obtained, count as testimony (in the philosophical sense)?
3. Colonialism included the burning of sacred Mayan texts and the destruction of Mayan objects. Describe the difficulties encountered when researching Mayan philosophy.

Additional Resources

For additional resources relating to this reading and its themes, visit **sites.broadviewpress.com/waysofbeing/2-1a**

2.1b

SHAKÓYE:WA:THA' (Red Jacket) 1805 Speech on Religion*

SHAKÓYE:WA:THA', Red Jacket (Seneca)

ABOUT THE AUTHOR

Born into the wolf clan of the Seneca Nation, SHAKÓYE:WA:THA' (Red Jacket) negotiated with the United States after the American Revolutionary War. During the war, the Seneca were allied with the British. Once defeated, SHAKÓYE:WA:THA' oversaw the cession of their lands through the Treaty of Canandaigua (1794). Later, he took part in the War of 1812 on the side of the Americans, assisting them in the Battle of the Chippawa. He was awarded an embroidered red jacket, which provided the origin for his non-Indigenous name. The following speech, "Religion for the White Man and the Red" has been described as one of the best examples of North American oratory. It was given as a response to a Boston Missionary Society's request to proselytize among the Haudenosaunee settlements in northern New York. As a result of SHAKÓYE:WA:THA''s speech, the missionary's representative refused to shake hands, declaring that no fellowship could exist between the religion of God and the works of the Devil.

KEY TERMS

Great Spirit, God, First Contact, Early Relations, Christianity, Colonialism, Cultural Assimilation

...

"Brothers of the Six Nations: I rejoice to meet you at this time, and thank the Great Spirit that he has preserved you in health, and given me another opportunity of taking you by the hand.

"Brothers: The person who sits by me is a friend who has come a great distance to hold a talk with you. He will inform you what his business is, and it is my request that you would listen with attention to his words."

The missionary thereupon opened his business in the following terms:—

* From Daniel Drake, *Lives of Celebrated American Indians* (Boston: Bradbury, Soden & Co., 1843), 283–87.

"My Friends: I am thankful for the opportunity afforded us of uniting together at this time. I had a great desire to see you, and inquire into your state and welfare. For this purpose I have travelled a great distance, being sent by your old friends, the Boston Missionary Society. You will recollect they formerly sent missionaries among you, to instruct you in religion, and labor for your good. Although they have not heard from you for a long time, yet they have not forgotten their brothers, the Six Nations, and are still anxious to do you good.

"Brothers: I have not come to get your lands or your money, but to enlighten your minds, and to instruct you how to worship the Great Spirit agreeably to his mind and will, and to preach to you the gospel of his son Jesus Christ. There is but one religion, and but one way to serve God, and if you do not embrace the right way you cannot be happy hereafter. You have never worshipped the Great Spirit in a manner acceptable to him; but have all your lives been in great errors and darkness. To endeavor to remove these errors, and open your eyes, so that you might see clearly, is my business with you.

"Brothers: I wish to talk with you as one friend talks with another; and if you have any objections to receive the religion which I preach, I wish you to state them; and I will endeavor to satisfy your minds and remove the objections.

"Brothers: I want you to speak your minds freely: for I wish to reason with you on the subject, and, if possible, remove all doubts, if there be any on your minds. The subject is an important one, and it is of consequence that you give it an early attention while the offer is made you. Your friends the Boston Missionary Society will continue to send you good and faithful ministers, to instruct and strengthen you in religion, if, on your part, you are willing to receive them.

"Brothers: Since I have been in this part of the country, I have visited some of your small villages, and talked with your people. They appear willing to receive instruction, but as they look up to you as their older brothers in council, they want first to know your opinion on the subject. You have now heard what I have to propose at present. I hope you will take it into consideration, and give me an answer before we part."

After about two hours consultation among themselves, Red-Jacket rose and spoke as follows:

"Friend and Brother: It was the will of the Great Spirit that we should meet together this day. He orders all things, and has given us a fine day for our Council. He has taken his garment from before the sun, and caused it to shine with brightness upon us. Our eyes are opened, that we see clearly; our ears are unstopped, that we have been able to hear distinctly the words you have spoken. For all these favors we thank the Great Spirit; and HIM *only*.

"Brother: This council fire was kindled by you. It was at your request that we came together at this time. We have listened with attention to what you have said. You requested us to speak our minds freely. This gives us great joy; for we now consider that we stand upright before you, and can speak what we think. All have heard your voice, and all speak to you now as one man. Our minds are agreed.

"Brother: You say you want an answer to your talk before you leave this place. It is right you should have one, as you are a great distance from home, and we do not wish to detain you. But we will first look back a little, and tell you what our fathers have told us, and what we have heard from the white people.

"Brother: Listen to what we say. There was a time when our forefathers owned this great island. Their seats extended from the rising to the setting sun. The Great Spirit had made it for the use of Indians. HE had created the buffalo, the deer, and other animals for food. HE had made the bear and the beaver. Their skins served us for clothing. HE had scattered them over the country, and taught us how to take them. HE had caused the earth to produce corn for bread. All this HE had done for his red children, because HE loved them. If we had some disputes about our hunting ground, they were generally settled without the shedding of much blood. But an evil day came upon us. Your forefathers crossed the great water and landed on this island. Their numbers were small. They found friends and not enemies. They told us they had fled from their own country for fear of wicked men, and had come here to enjoy their religion. They asked for a small seat. We took pity on them, granted their request; and they sat down amongst us. We gave them corn and meat; they gave us poison[1] in return.

"The white people, Brother, had now found our country. Tidings were carried back, and more came amongst us. Yet we did not fear them. We took them to be friends. They called us brothers. We believed them and gave them a larger seat. At length their numbers had greatly increased. They wanted more land; they wanted our country. Our eyes were opened, and our minds became uneasy. Wars took place. Indians were hired to fight against Indians, and many of our people were destroyed. They also brought strong liquor amongst us. It was strong and powerful, and has slain thousands.

"Brother: Our seats were once large and yours were small. You have now become a great people, and we have scarcely a place left to spread our blankets. You have got our country, but are not satisfied; you want to force your religion upon us.

"Brother: Continue to listen. You say that you are sent to instruct us how to worship the Great Spirit agreeably to his mind, and, if we do not take hold of the religion which you white people teach, we shall be unhappy hereafter. You say that you are right and we are lost. How do we know this to be true? We understand that your religion is written in a book. If it was intended for us as well as you, why has not the Great Spirit given to us, and not only to us, but why did he not give to our forefathers, the knowledge of that book, with the means of understanding it rightly? We only know what you tell us about it. How shall we know when to believe, being so often deceived by the white people?

"Brother: You say there is but one way to worship and serve the Great Spirit. If there is but one religion, why do you white people differ so much about it? Why not all agreed, as you can all read the book?

"Brother: We do not understand these things. We are told that your religion was given to your forefathers, and has been handed down from father to son. We also have a religion, which was given to our forefathers, and has been handed down to us their children. We worship in that way. It teaches us to be thankful for all the favors we receive; to love each other, and to be united. We never quarrel about religion.

"Brother: The Great Spirit has made us all, but HE has made a great difference between his white and red children. HE has given us different complexions and different customs. To you HE has given the arts. To these HE has not opened our eyes. We know these things to be true. Since HE has made so great a difference between us in other things, why may we not conclude that he has given us a different religion according to our understanding? The Great Spirit does right. HE knows what is best for his children; we are satisfied.

"Brother: We do not wish to destroy your religion, or take it from you. We only want to enjoy our own.

"Brother: You say you have not come to get our land or our money, but to enlighten our minds. I will now tell you that I have been at your meetings, and saw you collect money from the meeting. I cannot tell what this money was intended for, but suppose that it was for your minister, and if we should conform to your way of thinking, perhaps you may want some from us.[2]

"Brother: We are told that you have been preaching to the white people in this place. These people are our neighbors. We are acquainted with them. We will wait a little while, and see what effect your preaching has upon them. If we find it does them good, makes them honest and less disposed to cheat Indians, we will then consider again of what you have said.

"Brother: You have now heard our answer to your talk, and this is all we have to say at present. As we are going to part, we will come and take you by the hand, and hope the Great Spirit will protect you on your journey, and return you safe to your friends."

...

Endnotes

1 Rum.

2 This paragraph is not contained in the first edition of the speech, as published by James D. Bemis, in 1811; but I find it in the speech as given by Drake, in his *Book of the Indians*, and also in Thatcher's *Indian Biography*. Still, it appears to me to be an interpolation.

Suggestions for Critical Reflection

1. What reasons does SHAKÓYE:WA:THAˀ (Red Jacket) provide for keeping the Indigenous and Christian religions separate? Do you find these reasons compelling?
2. What contradictions of the Christian religion does SHAKÓYE:WA:THAˀ (Red Jacket) identify?
3. SHAKÓYE:WA:THAˀ (Red Jacket) notes that the religion is recorded in a book (the Bible). How different is this from the religion of the Seneca? Is there a marked difference between these different sources of knowledge? Is one privileged over the other in the Western worldview?
4. Is the response of the missionary's representative (i.e., to refuse fellowship with the Seneca, or the Haudenosaunee) philosophical? What other avenues might the representative take toward establishing respectful relations and philosophical engagement?

Additional Resources

For additional resources relating to this reading and its themes, visit **sites.broadviewpress.com/waysofbeing/2-1b**

2.1C

Ma-chú-nu-zhe (Standing Bear) 1879 Landmark Civil Rights Case Testimony*

Ma-chú-nu-zhe, Standing Bear (Ponca)

ABOUT THE AUTHOR

Ma-chú-nu-zhe (Standing Bear), a Ponca Chief, is the named participant in a notable court case: *Standing Bear v. Crook.* The case ultimately determined that Native Americans in the United States were persons under the law and as such, entitled to certain rights and protections such as the right of *habeas corpus.* The following is part of his testimony regarding his religious beliefs. Ma-chú-nu-zhe went on to become a speaker on behalf of Indigenous rights and later was part of Buffalo Bill's Wild West Show.

KEY TERMS

Removal, Testimony, Missionaries, Bible, Christian Indians, Agriculture, Indian Territory, Indian Agents/Inspectors, Great Father

At eleven o'clock that night the weary editor reached his home. The first thing he did was to call for a good "square meal." Having disposed of that he sat down at his desk and wrote out the speeches of Standing Bear and Ta-zha-but, with such other matter as made a connected history of the affair up to that time and at twenty minutes past 5 A.M. retired.

At seven o'clock he was up. Gen. Crook was to hold his council with Standing Bear at ten o'clock, and procuring a conveyance, he started for Fort Omaha. The council did not really commence until twelve o'clock, and was held in Gen. Crook's office. There were present General Crook, Colonel Royall, General Williams, Lieutenants Bourke and Carpenter, and the editor, who was somewhat astonished to see Standing Bear dressed in a magnificent full costume of an Indian chief. He had a red blanket, trimmed with broad blue stripes, a wide beaded belt around his waist, and wore a necklace of bear's claws. The other Indians were dressed in citizens' clothes. Standing Bear spoke first as follows:

* From T.H. Tibbles, *The Ponca Chiefs: An Indian's Attempt to Appeal from the Tomahawk to the Courts. A Full History of the Robbery of the Ponca Tribe of Indians, with All the Papers Filed and Evidence Taken in the Standing Bear Habeas Corpus Case, and Full Text of Judge Dundy's Celebrated Decision, with Some Suggestions Towards a Solution of the Indian Question* (Lockwood, Brooks & Company, 1879), 31–33 and 72–75.

"FRIENDS AND BROTHERS,—The Almighty created us Indians. We are as he made us. The Almighty has given to the whites a book to read, and they have plenty of things to work with. The Indian has no book. He cannot read. Here is where I am weak and you are strong. I never see a book or paper of any kind, but I think it is a good thing. It lets you know all that is going on in the world. I want my children to learn to read. I want them to go to school, my friends. A great while ago we came from the great water to the east. We kept coming, coming, coming west until we got to Dakota. I made a good living there. Then some power took hold of me, as by the arm, and made me to stand up and told us to go south. They took us to a very bad place. They took our plows and all our farming utensils and locked them up. I have never seen them since. After I got to the Territory I went to see my Great Father at Washington. When I went into his office he took me by the hand. I said to the Great Father, 'My people are much wronged, and I hope you will do something for me. I am in an awful bad place.' I told him before I went to the Territory that I had a good house and barn which I had built with my own hands. I had cattle and hogs and all kinds of stock, and somebody came and took all my things away, and my Great Father stood up and said: 'How is this? I will order an inspection.' I told him I was in a bad fix. He told me to go and see if I could find some good land near where we then were. I went back. I started to look for land. I found some land that looked good. We moved onto it, but some unseen force came down upon us and crushed us to the earth. One hundred and fifty-seven of our people died right there. A few days passed by, and an inspector came from Washington. I told him I would like to move back to my old home, that he saw we were in a dreadful place. He answered in this way: 'I will do all I can. I will try what I can do for you.' He didn't say he could do anything, but that he would go back to Washington, and tell them what a bad place it was. But I was like one in haste. I wanted to save the lives of my people."

Standing Bear then asked permission to address the officers and others present, and Gen. Crook gave him permission, and turning to them, he made the following pathetic appeal:

"MY FRIENDS AND BROTHERS,—I am now with the soldiers and officers. I want to go back to my old place north. I want to save myself and my tribe.

"My brothers, it seems to me as if I stood in front of a great prairie fire. I would take up my babies and run to save their lives; or as if I stood on the bank of an overflowing river, and I would take my people and fly to higher ground. Oh! my brothers, the Almighty looks down on me, and knows what I am, and hears my words. May the Almighty send a good spirit to brood over you, my brothers, to move you to help me. If a white man had land, and some one should swindle him, that man would try to get it back, and you would not blame him. Look on me. Take pity on me, and help me to save the lives of the women and children. My brothers, a power, which I cannot resist, crowds me down to the ground. I need help. I have done."

...

As much had been said about these Poncas being savages. Standing Bear was asked to state his religious belief. Without a moment's reflection, he spoke as follows:

"There is one God, and He made both Indians and white men. We were all made out of the dust of the earth. I once thought differently. I believed there were happy hunting-grounds, where there were plenty of game, and plenty to eat, no sickness, no death, and no pain. The best of the Indians would go to these happy hunting-grounds. I thought that those who were bad would never live any more; that when they died that was the end of them. But I have learned that these things are not so, and that God wishes us to love Him and obey His commandments, follow the narrow road, work for Him on earth, and we shall have happiness after we die. I am told His Son died for us, died that we might live. I want to try and do something for Him, to be like Him, follow in His footsteps as nearly as I can. I think there is but one God. I need help to do right, and I pray to Him that he will help me for His Son's sake. I do not wish to do anything wrong. I wish to follow the narrow road. It is the road of happiness. God never does anything wrong. He knows what is best for me. No man can understand God, or know why He deals with us as He does. Sometimes what we think is the worst is the best for us. When I was arrested by the soldiers and brought down here, I thought for a little while that God had forsaken me, but now I see that, perhaps, it is the best thing for me and my people. If they would only hearken to His word, they would find that all is for their good. He sees me all the time. He watches over me, and knows all I do. He knows my thoughts. He knows when I think wicked thoughts. He knows it all. If He did not watch over me, and take care of me, I should die. I want Him to watch over me, and take care of me, and I believe He always will. He helps me. I can do nothing without His help. I love His truth. I hate lies. I wish to follow the truth always. God has control of the whole earth, and everything is in His power. He sees over all things at once, every man, woman, and child, and knows their thoughts and actions, and everything they do. He watches over me wherever I go. He sees me here to-day. He has been with me through all my wanderings, and has taken care of me. He has seen how I have been taken away from my land. Through all this He has been close to me. When I have felt that I had no friends, I remembered that He was my Father. His people have been good to me, but the people of the devil are trying to send me to hell. They have tried to make me believe that God tells them what to do, as though God would put a man where he would be destroyed, and they have destroyed many already, but they cannot deceive me. God put me here, and intends for me to live on the land they are trying to cheat me out of.

"I pray to God every day for Him to help me to regain my rights, if I am worthy of it. For His Son's sake I have asked it. He made me and the whites, and although we are of a different color, I think men's hearts are all alike. If I were to go back to my land to-day, the first thing I would do would be to fall down on my knees and thank God for it. I think in the future, as I grow in years, I will try to love Him more and more every day, do that which is right, and be afraid to do that which is wrong."

He was asked how long he had held these views, and he replied, "Since the missionary came up from Omaha Agency, about eight years ago, and told me the right way."

"How many of the tribe think the same way on this subject that you do?"

"Only a few. It is a hard thing to say, but I will tell you the truth. Some of these have died since we went down to the Territory. We had no missionary down there, and no one to talk to us about God. My boy, who died there, would get a few in a tent and talk to them sometimes and tell them the right way the best he knew how. He used to pray with me very often, and read to me out of the Testament. Some of the people who were sick prayed all the time when they were dying. They asked God to take them away from there if it was His will, or to end their sufferings speedily. When any one came to our old reservation to talk of God, I would always find a place for him to speak, and get the people to come."

...

Suggestions for Critical Reflection

1. Ma-chú-nu-zhe (Standing Bear), like SHAKÓYE:WA:THAˀ (Red Jacket), notes the differences in God's treatment of Indigenous and non-Indigenous people. Those differences made SHAKÓYE:WA:THAˀ question the benefits of religion, but it did not have the same effect for Ma-chú-nu-zhe. Do you find one's statements more compelling than the other's? Why or why not?
2. At the time of Ma-chú-nu-zhe's court case, Indigenous people were considered wards of the state and subject to the care of the federal government. Given that the Ponca were Christian farmers (with homes,

barns, livestock, and tools), what were the reasons for the continued removal to Indian Territory?

3. In describing his beliefs before and after converting, Ma-chú-nu-zhe presents a difference between Indigenous and Western religious worldviews: an emphasis on the afterlife instead of the now. What might be some of the implications associated with each?

Additional Resources

For additional resources relating to this reading and its themes, visit **sites.broadviewpress.com/waysofbeing/2-1c**

2.2
"The Problem of Creation"*

Vine Deloria Jr. (Standing Rock Sioux)

ABOUT THE AUTHOR

Described by his alma mater, the University of Colorado Law School, as being "known to many as the leading American Indian intellectual of the 20th century," Vine Deloria Jr. was a lawyer and theologian, who published over 20 influential texts, covering several topics in Indigenous philosophy.† Books like *Custer Died for Your Sins: An Indian Manifesto* (1969) and *God Is Red: A Native View of Religion* (1973) were pivotal in the Native American struggle for self-determination, prompting activism that supported Native American rights.

KEY TERMS

Theology, Religion, Creation, Reality, Creator, Interrelationships, Corruption, Good/Bad, Inherent, Dominance, Shallow, Stewardship, Humans, Nature

Indian tribal religions and Christianity differ considerably on numerous theological points, but a very major distinction that can be made between the two types of thinking concerns the idea of creation. Christianity has traditionally appeared to place its major emphasis on creation as a specific event while the Indian tribal religions could be said to consider creation as an ecosystem present in a definable place. In this distinction we have again the fundamental problem of whether we consider the reality of our experience as capable of being described in terms of space or time—as "what happened here" or "what happened then."

Both religions can be said to agree on the role and activity of a creator. Outside of that specific thing, there would appear to be little that the two views share. Tribal religions appear to be thereafter confronted with the question of the interrelationship of all things. Christians see creation as the beginning event of a linear time sequence in which a divine plan is worked out, the conclusion of the sequence being an act of destruction bringing the world to an end. The beginning and end of time are of no apparent concern for many tribal religions.

* Chapter 5 of Vine Deloria Jr.'s *God Is Red: A Native View of Religion* (Golden, CO: Fulcrum, 1973), 78–97.

† See Colorado Law, "Vine Deloria Jr. '70," https://www.colorado.edu/law/vine-deloria-jr.

The act of creation is a singularly important event for the Christian. It describes the sequence in which the tangible features of human existence are brought into being, and although some sermons have made much of the element of light that appears in the creation account of Genesis and the prologue of St. John's Gospel, the similarity of the two books and their use of light do not appear to be of crucial importance in the doctrine of creation. For the Christian it would appear that the importance of the creation event is that it sets the scene for an understanding of the entrance of sin into the world.

Intimately tied with the actual creation event in the Christian theological scheme is the appearance of the first people, Adam and Eve. They are made after the image of God. It is important that this point be recognized, as it has affected popular conceptions held by Christians and seems to have some relevance to central theological doctrines. As the Genesis story relates that the first people were made after God's image, Christians, although not necessarily their Hebrew predecessors and Jewish contemporaries, have popularly conceived God as having a human form. That is to say, God looks like a man. Paintings represent Him generally as an old man, deriving perhaps from the old Hebrew conception of the "Ancient of Days."

The first distinction between Indian tribal religions and Christianity would appear to be in the manner in which deity is popularly conceived. The overwhelming majority of American Indian tribal religions refused to represent deity anthropomorphically.[1]

To be sure, many tribes used the term *grandfather* when praying to God, but there was no effort to use that concept as the basis for a theological doctrine by which a series of complex relationships and related doctrines could be developed. While there was an acknowledgment that the Great Spirit has some resemblance to the role of a grandfather in the tribal society, there was no great demand to have a "personal relationship" with the Great Spirit in the same manner as popular Christianity has emphasized personal relationships with God.[2]

The difference between conceiving God as an anthropomorphic being and as an undefinable presence carries over into the distinction in the views of creation. Closely following the creation of the world in Christian theology comes the disobedience of man, Adam, in eating the forbidden fruit growing on a tree in the Garden of Eden. In this act as recorded in Genesis, humankind "fell" from God's grace and was driven out of the garden by the angry God. The major thesis of the Christian religion is thus contained in its creation story, because it is for the redemption of man that the atonement of Jesus of Nazareth is considered to make sense.

With the fall of Adam the rest of nature also falls out of grace with God, Adam being a surrogate for the whole of creation. This particular point has been a very difficult problem for Christian theologians. While it adequately explains the entrance of evil into the world, just how it could occur in a universe conceived as perfect has been difficult for theologians to answer. St. Augustine preferred to think that God Himself had taken the form of the snake that, in the story, talked Eve into eating the forbidden fruit.[3] St. Augustine's solution has not generally been accepted, even though it appears to explain the logical sequence.

Perhaps of more importance are two aspects of the Christian doctrine of creation bearing directly on us today. One aspect is that the natural world is thereafter considered as corrupted, and it becomes theoretically beyond redemption. Many Christian theologians have attempted to avoid this conclusion, but it appears to have been a central doctrine of the Christian religion during most of the Christian era. No less a thinker than Paul Tillich attempted to reconstruct the doctrine into more satisfying terms that would be acceptable to the modem world. In a rather complex analysis in his *Systematic Theology*, Tillich wrestled with the problem.

> Christianity must reject the idealistic separation of an innocent nature from guilty man. Such a rejection has become comparatively easy in our period because of the insights gained about the growth of man and his relation to nature within and outside himself. First, it can be shown that in the development of man there is no absolute discontinuity between animal bondage and human freedom. There are leaps between different stages, but there is also a slow and continuous transformation. It is impossible to say at which point in the process of natural evolution animal nature is replaced by the nature which, in our present experience, we know as human, a nature which is qualitatively different from animal nature.[4]
>
> And, as there are analogies to human freedom in nature, so there are also analogies to human good and evil in all parts of the universe. It is worthy of note that Isaiah prophesied peace in nature for the new eon, thereby showing that he would not call nature "innocent." Nor would the writer who, in Genesis, chapter 3, tells about the curse over the land declare nature innocent. Nor would Paul do so in Romans, chapter 8, when he speaks about the bondage to futility which is the fate of nature. Certainly, all these expressions are poetic-mythical. They could not be otherwise, since only poetic empathy opens the inner life of nature. Nevertheless, they are realistic in substance and certainly more realistic than the moral utopianism which confronts immoral man with innocent nature. Just as, within man, nature participates in the good and evil he does, so nature, outside man, shows analogies to man's good and evil doing. Man reaches

> into nature, as nature reaches into man. They participate in each other and cannot be separated from each other. This makes it possible and necessary to use the term "fallen world" and to apply the concept of existence (in contrast to essence) to the universe as well as man.[5]

Like many other Christian thinkers, Tillich cannot break the relationship between humans and the natural world in which both share a corrupt nature. Even his dependence on evolution appears to be but a temporary nod to the reflections of science, because he stands ready to label the nature of people corrupt at whatever point in the evolutionary process a human being comparable in psychological processes to ourselves emerges.

Indian tribal religions also held a fundamental relationship between human beings and the rest of nature, but the conception was radically different. For many Indian tribal religions the whole of creation was good, and because the creation event did not include a "fall," the meaning of creation was that all parts of it functioned together to sustain it. Young Chief, a Cayuse, refused to sign the Treaty of Walla Walla because he felt the rest of the creation was not represented in the transaction.

> I wonder if the ground has anything to say? I wonder if the ground is listening to what is said? I wonder if the ground would come alive and what is on it? Though I hear what the ground says. The ground says, It is the Great Spirit that placed me here. The Great Spirit tells me to take care of the Indians, to feed them aright. The Great Spirit appointed the roots to feed the Indians on. The water says the same thing. The Great Spirit directs me, Feed the Indians well. The grass says the same thing, Feed the Indians well. The ground, water and grass say, the Great Spirit has given us our names. We have these names and hold these names. The ground says, The Great Spirit placed me here to produce all that grows on me, trees and fruit. The same way the ground says, It was from me man was made. The Great Spirit, in placing men on earth, desired them to take good care of the ground and to do each other no harm.[6]

The similarity between Young Chief's conception of creation and the Genesis story is striking, but when one understands that the Genesis story is merely the starting place for theological doctrines of a rather abstract nature while Young Chief's beliefs are the practical articulations of his understanding of the relationship between the various entities of the creation, the difference becomes apparent. In the Indian tribal religions, man and the rest of creation are cooperative and respectful of the task set for them by the Great Spirit. In the Christian religion both are doomed from shortly after the creation event until the end of the world.

The second aspect of the Christian doctrine of creation that concerns us today is the idea that man receives domination over the rest of creation. Harvey Cox, a popular Protestant theologian, articulates rather precisely the attitude derived from this idea of Genesis: "Just after his creation man is given the crucial responsibility of naming the animals. He is their master and commander. It is his task to subdue the earth."[7] It is this attitude that has been adopted wholeheartedly by Western peoples in their economic exploitation of the earth. The creation becomes a mere object when this view is carried to its logical conclusion—a directly opposite result from that of the Indian religions.

Whether or not Christians wanted to carry their doctrine of human dominance as far as it has been carried, the fact remains that the modern world is just now beginning to identify the Christian religion's failure to show adequate concern for the planet as a major factor in our present ecological crisis. Among the earliest scholars to recognize the Christian responsibility for our present situation of ecological chaos was Lynn White, Jr., who gave a presentation titled "The Historical Roots of Our Ecological Crisis" in 1967 before the American Association for the Advancement of Science. White presented the same previously discussed criticism of Christian theology, emphasizing the tendency of the Christian religion to downgrade the natural world and its life forms in favor of the supernatural world of the Christian postjudgment world of eternal life.[8] But he was extremely kind for a man who had his intellectual arguments honed so fine that he could have gone for the jugular vein had he wanted. White proposed that St. Francis be made the ecological saint, elevating Francis to a pedestal he did not deserve.

A number of Christians appear to be taking up White's thesis, and one frequently hears arguments that St. Francis represents the true Christian tradition. The Franciscan tradition is not a major theme of either Christian or Western thought, however, and it would appear as if advocating St. Francis as a patron of the Christian attitude toward creation is not only historically late but uncertain. White's thesis proved unbearable to Dr. René Dubos, of New York City Rockefeller University, who gave a presentation in 1969 at the Smithsonian Institution in Washington, D.C., on "A Theology of the Earth." In it Dubos disclaimed White's charge against Christianity. Dubos contended that other societies had also created ecological disasters. He felt that Christianity was therefore not to be held accountable for the shortcomings of Westerners. He buttressed his thesis by references to St. Francis and, more particularly, to St. Benedict, founder of the Benedictine Order. Dubos found that the Benedictine work rules, which at that time included draining swamps and filling in lowlands, were more suitable for modern man than St. Francis' ideas of nature worship.[9]

Dubos's valiant defense of Christian thought lacks a number of substantial considerations. While other societies did create ecological disasters, Dubos would be hard put to find in the theologies of many other religions either a command to subdue the earth or the doctrine that the creation had "fallen" and shared responsibility for a man's direct violation of divine commands. There is also little evidence that destroying wetlands is ecologically sound, a fact the Bush administration ignores as it proposes to weaken federal law against tampering with the wetlands.

Further indications of Dubos's miscalculation of Christian sincerity—and evidence, perhaps, that Christians have not yet understood the complexity of the ecological crisis—were evidenced by the liturgy of the earth created by the National Cathedral in Washington, D.C. The confession used in this liturgy exemplifies the extent to which even concerned Christians have misunderstood the seriousness of the ecological problem.

> Lord God, we say here in Your presence and before each other that we, both individually and collectively, have not been good stewards of Your earth. We have fouled the air, spoiled the water, poisoned the land, and by these acts have gravely hurt each other. We know now that this has and will cost us, and for these and all other sins we are truly sorry. Give us, we pray, the strength and guidance to undo what we have done and grant us inspiration for a new style of living.[10]

Even in this attempt to bring religious sensitivity to the problem of ecological destruction, one can see the shallow understanding of the basis of the religious attitude that has been largely responsible for the crisis. No effort is made to begin a new theory of the meaning of creation. Indeed, the popular attitude of stewardship is invoked, as if it had no relationship to the cause of the ecological crisis whatsoever. Perhaps the best summary of the attitude inherent in the liturgy is, "Please, God, help us cut the cost, and we'll try to find a new life-style that won't be quite as destructive." The response is inadequate because it has not reached any fundamental problem; it is only a patch job over a serious theological problem. But at least in this liturgy we humans are bad and nature is good—a marked advance over earlier conceptions.

Endnotes

1 Frederick Webb Hodge, *Handbook of American Indians North of Mexico*, vol. II (Lanham, MD: Rowman & Littlefield, 1965), 366.

Something more needs to be said about anthropomorphic images. Medicine men report the existence of spiritual beings that have or take on human forms. Thus Black Elk and other Sioux mystics report that they have sat with the Six Grandfathers and counseled with them. Much more thought needs to be given to the question of whether the Indians had "gods" in the same sense as Near Eastern peoples. Was the mysterious power—*wakan tanka* in the Dakota language—the same as the spiritual power that provided life and was superior to any specific personifications of itself? If so, the ultimate representation of this sacred universe—and other sacred Indian universes—was without a deity in the Near Eastern sense.

2 For example, see Joseph Epes Brown, *The Sacred Pipe* (Norman: University of Oklahoma Press, 1953, 3–6) for Black Elk's discussion of this relationship.

3 In *The Confessions* by St. Augustine (London: Burns & Oates, 1954), the solution to the problem of evil seems to be completing the circle and suggesting that the deity himself is the tempter. Carl Jung also folds back the problem of good and evil to make a complete circle or circuit. The Plains Indian concept is considerably more complex and seems to involve the related question of the structure of conscious life—the difference between probable future events and the realization of existing possibilities. It is too complicated to deal with here except to note that there is a considerable difference between the two traditions.

4 Paul Tillich, *Systematic Theology*, vol. II (Chicago: University of Chicago Press, 1957), 41–42.

5 Ibid. In all of North American Indian traditions there is, of course, no sense of "animal bondage" but rather relationships with the specific peoples of creation; hence, creation is ultimately good and humans are a part of it.

6 T.C. McLuhan, *Touch the Earth* (New York: Outerbridge & Dienstfrey, 1971), 8.

7 Harvey Cox, *The Secular City* (New York: Macmillan, 1965), 20.

8 Lynne White, Jr., "The Historical Roots of Our Ecological Crisis," paper. American Association for the Advancement of Science, 1967.

9 René Dubos's address is published as a small booklet by the Smithsonian Institution, Washington, D.C. It is singularly instructive, however, to note that filling in marshes and wetlands destroys habitat for a significant number of species and moves the planet toward ecological unbalance. Thus, White's thesis holds even when applied to what Christians believe is their most benign behavior.

10 Quoted in an article by Louis Cassels in the Religion Section, *The Denver Post* (March 7, 1970).

Suggestions for Critical Reflection

1. What implications does the Christian concept of domination over the natural world have for life today? Contrast this with an Indigenous worldview.
2. Is the Christian concept of human nature being inherently corrupt damaging? Why or why not?
3. Deloria Jr. notes the use of 'grandfather' by Native Americans to denote that God is not intended to underwrite the relationship between God and the people, nor serve as "the basis for theological doctrine."‡ What are the similarities and differences between it and the use of 'Great Father' to denote the president of the United States?

‡ See page 67 above.

4. Deloria Jr. states that the "majority of American tribal religions refused to represent deity anthropomorphically."[§] However, most Christians conceive God as having a human form. State the consequences/implications of this contrast.

Additional Resources

For additional resources relating to this reading and its themes, visit **sites.broadviewpress.com/waysofbeing/2-2**

§ Ibid.

2.3
"In the Time of the Sacred Places"*

Winona LaDuke (Ojibwe)

ABOUT THE AUTHOR

"Winona LaDuke, a Native American activist, economist, and author, has devoted her life to advocating for Indigenous control of their homelands, natural resources, and cultural practices."† An Ojibwe, LaDuke has tirelessly worked on behalf of Indigenous communities on Turtle Island and beyond. Graduating from Harvard in 1982, LaDuke served as a high school principal on the White Earth Ojibwe Reservation. She has also played a key role in grass roots organizing, helping to establish non-profit advocacy groups like the White Earth Land Recovery Project (WELRP) and Honor the Earth. LaDuke served as running mate to Ralph Nader on the Green Party's presidential ticket in 1996 and 2000. She continues to defend Indigenous communities, participating in 2016 Dakota Access Pipeline protests, writing several books, and providing public outreach.

KEY TERMS

Sacred Stories, Balance, Anishinaabe, Original Instructions, Manifest Destiny, Utilitarian, Transience, Relationships, Desecration

> *It's not like a church where you have everything in one place. We could describe how sacred sites are the teachers ... We don't want the American Dream ... We want our prayer rocks.*
>
> Caleen Sisk, Interview, August 15, 2013, Winnemun Wintu Territory

Minwenzha

For as long as there are memories, the traditional peoples of Turtle Island have narrated sacred stories and lived in sacred places. The stories guided our lives, reinforced our values of community wellbeing and respect for our sacred Mother Earth, and fostered our spirituality. The places provided us with sites for our homes, for our agriculture and fishing, and for engaging with the Creator Spirit and other spirits. Turtle Island is now called "America" by

* Winona LaDuke, "In the Time of the Sacred Places," in *The Wiley Blackwell Companion to Religion and Ecology*, ed. J. Hart (Oxford: John Wiley and Sons, 2017), 71–84.

† Mariana Brandman, "Winona LaDuke," National Women's History Museum, 2021.

descendants of the aggressive immigrants who began to trespass on these shores shortly after Christopher Columbus was discovered by indigenous peoples as he disembarked from his foreign ship and trespassed on native peoples' land. Despite this foreign invasion, resulting in the aliens' oppression of native peoples, seizure of our lands, and degradation of the natural world, the sacred stories continue to be told. We dream of the time foretold by our ancestors when the Earth will be made whole and known by all people to be holy.

Sacred Stories

In the time of Thunderbeings and Underwater Serpents the humans, animals, and plants conversed, carried on lives of mischief and wonder, and fulfilled everyday tasks. The prophets told of trying times ahead, explained the causes of the deluge of the past, and predicted two possible paths of the future—one scorched, one green—from which the Anishinaabeg would have to choose.

In the time of Thunderbeings and Underwater Serpents it was understood that a perpetual balance with the universe beyond this material world, a universe to whom we would belong always, needed to be maintained.

The Anishinaabe people live within distinct, land-based universes, and oscillate between these worlds. The light of day and the deepness of night remain; the parallel planes of spirit world and material world coexist in perpetuity. All remains, despite the jackhammer of industrial civilization, the rumble of combustion engines, and the sanitized white of a dioxin-bleached day. That was then, but it is also now. Teachings, ancient as the people who have lived on a land for five millennia, speak of a set of relationships to all that is around, predicated on respect, recognition of the interdependence of all beings, understanding of humans' absolute need to be reverent and to manage our behavior, and awareness that this relationship must be reaffirmed through lifeways and acknowledgment of the sacred.

A millennium after that time of the Thunderbeings and Underwater Serpents, those beings still emerge: lightning strikes unexpectedly, seemingly unending fires of climate change scorch Mother Earth, frequent tornadoes flatten buildings, King Tides and river deluges flood the land, and copper beings abound in the midst of industrial society. So it is that we come to face our smallness in a world of mystery and our responsibilities to all life that surrounds us.

> We are a part of everything that is beneath us, above us and around us. Our past is our present, our present is our future, and our future is seven generations past and present.
>
> Oren Lyons, Haudenosaunee oral history

In the midst of the now-time, land-based peoples work to continue a lifeway, or follow simply the original instructions passed on by Gichi Manidoo, the Creator, and others who instruct us. This path often is littered with the remnants or threat of a fossil fuel and nuclear economy—a uranium mine, a big dam project, or tar sands oil extraction. People still work, however, to restore or retain their relationship to a sacred place and to a world, and to tell and retell sacred stories. In many places, for instance, people hold Earth renewal ceremonies or water-healing ceremonies; perhaps these are how, in an indigenous philosophical view, people are able to continue to exist....

This is also a story of a different society, one based on the notion of "frontier." America is that society. It was born of a fifteenth-century-origin Doctrine of Discovery, a papal-justified European claim to entitlement to vanquish and destroy that which was indigenous, and an accompanying assertion that indigenous territories were *terra nullius* ("empty land") because no Europe-like civilization existed there.[1] America was framed in the mantra of Manifest Destiny. This settler relationship to this North American continent has been historically one of conquest, of utilitarian relationship—an anthropocentric taking of Mother Earth's and native peoples' wealth to make more things for empire. That society has named and claimed for its empire one mountain after another: Mount Rainier, Washington; Harney Peak, South Dakota; Mount McKinley, Alaska; Mount Lassen, California; Pikes Peak, Colorado. But naming and claiming with a flag does not mean relationship, it means only naming and claiming.[2]

This process denudes relationship, particularly when it names sacred mountain spirits after mortal men, who trample through for a few decades. Americans have developed a sense of place related to empire, with no understanding that for indigenous peoples the Holy Land is not Israel: it is here.

Americans are also, by the social norm of the country, transient. This attitude and practice teach them the notion and enduring illusion of an American dream of greener pastures, always elsewhere. This, too, belittles a relationship to place. It does not teach responsibility, only entitlement: mineral rights, water rights, and private property, as enshrined in the Constitution.

In the times in which we find ourselves, with ecosystems crashing, bees, fish, and trees dying, climate change rampant, and consequently, destabilization continuing, our relationship to place and to our relatives—whether they have wings, fins, paws, or roots—merits reconsideration.

Sacred Places

Since the beginning of time, the Creator and Mother Earth have given our peoples places to learn the teachings that will allow us to continue to be, and to reaffirm our responsibilities and ways to be on the lands from which we have come. Indigenous peoples are place-based societies,[3] and at the center of those places are the most sacred of our sites, where we reaffirm our relationships.

Everywhere there are indigenous people, there are sacred sites, there are ways of knowing, there are *relationships*. The people, the rivers, the mountains, the lakes, the animals, and the fish are all related. In recent years, the US courts have challenged our right to be in these places, and indeed our ability to protect them. In many cases, we are asked to quantify "how sacred it is" or "how often it is sacred," baffling concepts in the spiritual realm. Yet we do not relent, we are not capable of becoming subsumed.

Related Peoples: Nur and Human

In northern California, the Winnemem Wintu people have known since time immemorial of their relationship to the *Nur*, the salmon people. They have known that they have a sacred responsibility to protect and care for the salmon that have sustained them on the slope of *Boyum Patuk*, the sacred mountain now known as Mount Shasta. The *Nur* gave the Winnemem their voice and taught them to sing. The Winnemem were told long ago that if the salmon disappeared so, too, would they.

Legends tell of the time when the *Nur* people took pity on the Wintu people and gave them their voice. In return, the salmon only sing as they course the rivers of the northwest, and only the Wintu can hear them. The Wintu, in turn, are to care for the *Nur* always and to sing. And so they try to fulfill this responsibility a millennium later. The people believe that "when the last salmon is gone, humans will be gone too," Caleen Sisk, traditional spiritual leader of the Winnemem Wintu, explains (2013 interview, as cited above):

A millennium on the river did well for both the people and the salmon, who inhabited an area whose remoteness from white civilization was its protection.

Although they were signatories in good faith to what would be an unratified 1851 treaty, and later identified as the tribe many of whose members would be drowned in the aftermath of the 1941 Federal Act which created the Shasta Dam, the Winnemem Wintu ceased to exist as "Indians" under federal law. This strange irony, that the government created by the settlers and intruders who took your land and killed your people gets to determine if you are still an Indian, even if you exist, remains particularly bitter to many tribes. The Winnemem Wintu are particularly caught in this quagmire.

In 1941, the Shasta dam drowned more than 26 miles of the lower McCloud River system. It submerged sacred sites, villages, and history under a deep pool of water destined to benefit cities far away, provided agriculture for the world, and invited to this altered land new occupants and transient tourists who could afford the new way of life. The dam drowned much of the history of the Winnemem Wintu; the dam blocked the passage of the salmon people—the McCloud River *Nur*. The *Nur* either interbred with the Sacramento River salmon or died out in California.

Fish Rock was blown up to make room for a railroad track in 1914, which was, like so much else, drowned by the waters that would become known as Lake Shasta. What is left of Dekkas Rock, a prayer site, now protrudes from the reservoir as, one reporter notes, "a malformed atoll." It was here, on the banks of the river, that the Winnemem held what other native peoples in the region call "Big Times," where disputes were adjudicated, songs were sung, ceremonies were held, and marriages were arranged.

The Wintu grieved the loss of their salmon, their sacred doctoring rocks, and their river. Yet, "Our old people said that the salmon would be hidden behind a river of ice. Indian doctors and prophets had been with the Wintu long ago, and prophesied the time when the salmon would disappear," Caleen Sisk tells me. That was almost unimaginable to the Wintu or to those who had "discovered the salmon" of the McLeod or Middle River.

More than a century ago Livingston Stone, a fish culturist, arrived in Wintu territory. He said that the spawning Chinook were so plentiful he could have walked across their backs from one side of the river to the other. In the 1870s, he established the Baird Hatchery on the McCloud, originally in an attempt to breed a Pacific salmon to replenish the now dwindling and overfished Atlantic salmon stocks. The Winnemem Wintu were initially opposed to the fishery, but made peace with the White men of the fisheries on the condition that the salmon would always be able to come home.

In a strange turn of events, in 1890 Stone decided to attempt to transplant the Wintu *Nur* to another world, Aotearoa (now called New Zealand). There, in the Rakaia River on the South Island, moved over a vast ocean to be among sphagnum moss, the *Nur* salmon people came to live.

So it was that the salmon of the McLeod, the *Nur*, disappeared from the Wintu world. However, just as had been prophesied, they returned—but elsewhere. The Rakaia River is a River of Ice, emerging from a glacial mountain in the south of Aotearoa. In 2008, the Wintu went to Aotearoa to visit their salmon for the first time since the dams destroyed their relatives. And the Wintu sang once again for the *Nur*. It is 50 years since the dam destroyed the homeland of the salmon and much of the sacred world of the Wintu, but the Wintu believe that through prayer, prophecy, and hard work, the *Nur* will return....

Doko'oosliid, *Kachinas Mountain, and Recycled Ski Areas*

To the far south, in the realm of the sacred mountains of the Diné (Navajo) people, *Dine Bii Kaya*, four sacred mountains are again facing threats. Mount Taylor is once again proposed as a site for uranium mining, and *Doko'oosliid*, the Navajos' Sacred Mountain of the West, is being desecrated for the pleasure of skiers.

This volcanic highland area of Arizona began to form over 6 million years ago with the eruption of nearly 600 volcanoes. The most dramatic of those eruptions created a place sacred to 13 tribes, a cluster of three 12,000-ft mountain peaks, known as a place where the Kachina spirits emerge, and the sacred Mountain of the West, one of four cornerstones marking the borders of *Dine Bii Kaya*, the land of the Diné. In the vain vernacular of American empire, the sacred mountains are called the San Francisco Peaks.

On the highest point in Arizona, the only arctic-alpine vegetation in the state grows in a fragile 2-square-mile zone. Arizona's best examples of Ice Age glaciation can be found here. It is here that sacred herbs have been gathered and religious ceremonies held since the dawn of time.

In 1984, the US Congress recognized the fragile ecosystem and cultural significance of the area and designated the Kachina Peaks a wilderness. Yet, in this unlikely place, in an ostensibly protected wilderness in the desert, the current conflict is over a ski resort. Its developers plan to pipe treated sewage water from Flagstaff to make and spray artificial snow on the sacred mountain. There is no water source on the mountain other than what falls from the sky.

Ironically, on the Navajo Reservation, "water is so scarce and inaccessible that some 40 percent of the tribe's 190,000 residents have no potable supply, and many receive their water out of the back of trucks ... A 2006 water-pricing analysis by the tribe found that 3,800 liters (1,000 gallons) of hauled water carried a price tag of $US133, compared to $US2.73 for the same quantity of water delivered directly to homes via water infrastructure in nearby Flagstaff. The high cost of water is a contributing factor to the reservation's poverty rate—more than 40%—which is among the highest in the country," according to a 2010 article in the *Navajo-Hopi Observer*, a tribal paper.

Despite the acknowledged ecosystem, archeological and cultural issues, and determined opposition from Native nations and conservation organizations, the 9th US Circuit Court of Appeals recently allowed the Arizona Snowbowl Recreation project to proceed. Flagstaff's treated sewer water will be trucked to Snowbowl until a 14.8-mile pipeline is constructed, and then some 180 million gallons a year of treated effluent from Flagstaff will be pumped up the sacred mountain to the ski area to make snow. The treated sewage has been shown to contain contaminants such as pharmaceuticals and hormones. Snowbowl hopes to attract ski-starved desert dwellers to its resort with clever marketing; it remains to be seen how enticing a mouthful of Snowbowl effluent will be.

The Snowbowl owners have already clear-felled some 74 acres of rare alpine forest for new ski runs. A 10-million gallon retention pond and another 12 miles of pipeline will be built to distribute reclaimed sewer water along the ski runs, all desecrations in the eyes of the Diné people. In the Summer of 2012 protests continued in defense of a sacred place and ultimately at some level in a questioning of priorities, and access to water for people and the land. Yet, the project went ahead, and was installed.

This is the difference between a worldview where one society, an industrial society, views a land as a rich ore body or a playground, and another that views it as a source of great spiritual and cultural wealth. This is the story of the time in which we find ourselves....

Return to Sacred Lifeways

Even in periods of great injustice there is always hope; for those of us who remain involved in our ceremonies, there is also faith. That faith is reaffirmed when small miracles of spirit occur and the world changes.

On the banks of the McLeod River in northern California, the Wintu gather, despite citations and legal opposition by the state and others, to hold their sacred coming of age ceremonies for their young women. This is how life continues.

And one day, not too far away, the salmon will return from Aotearoa and the *Nur* and the Wintu will celebrate.

In the north woods, the Anishinaabeg celebrate one round of opposing the Beast—the huge Gogebic Taconite, LLC (GTAC) mine proposed for the Penokee Mountains of Wisconsin, which wants to desecrate and pollute the headwaters of the Bad River. The Penokee Mountains and Bad River are at the heart of the Bad River tribal community of Anishinaabeg. In 2012 the proposal for that mine, like another four before it in Wisconsin, was rejected. That may be a temporary victory, but it provides breathing room for Mother Earth.

In 2012, it seemed that Pe'Sla would be protected from being turned into luxury ranchettes and might continue to be a place where a people pray and reaffirm their relationship to Creation. In 2013, the Pe'Sla site was purchased by a coordinated effort between the Lakota tribes, led by the Rosebud Tribe and the Indian Land Tenure Foundation. The land remains protected.

Then, too, a renaming or recovery of names is occurring. Several decades ago, Mount McKinley was renamed Mount Denali. On the other side of the world, Australia's Ayers Rock reverted to its original name, Uluru. Ayers Rock was the name the White man gave it who found what native people already knew was there. In 2010, in Canada, the Haida homeland was formally renamed Haida Gwaii, erasing Queen Charlotte Island, named for a queen who had never visited that land and probably did not understand Haida traditions. Further south, the Salish Sea is likely to be the name for what has been called Puget Sound. Other reaffirmations of place and history are reframing our understanding of the holy land which is here. These stories merge with stories of a people and their allies who have come to live on this land.[4]

On a larger scale, the New Zealand Courts, a judicial system which emerged from colonial and church authorities, recently affirmed the rights of a river to exist. The Whanganui River became a legal entity, and in 2012 was given the same status as a person under New Zealand law. In an agreement in parliament between the Crown and the Maori (represented by the Whanganui Iwi), the river was given its legal status with the name *Te Awa Tupua*. Two guardians, one from the Crown and one from the Whanganui River Iwi, were assigned to protect the river. Brendon Puetapu, the spokesman for the Whanganui Iwi, explained: "Today's agreement which recognizes the status of the river as Te Awa Tupua (an integrated, living whole) and the inextricable relationship of Iwi with the river is a major step towards the resolution of the historical grievances of Whanganui Iwi and is important nationally."

...

Sacred Places Renewed, Sacred Stories Retold, Sacred Lives Relived

In the time of Thunderbeings and Underwater Serpents, humans, animals, and plants conversed, carried on lives of mischief and wonder, and fulfilled everyday tasks. The prophets told of times ahead, explained the deluge of the past, and predicted two possible paths in the future—one scorched and one green—from which the Anishinaabeg would have to choose.

All of us have the same choice. Somewhere in this time, the potential exists to take the right path. Let us choose that path and help to change the course of our history and renew the wellbeing of Mother Earth as we walk toward a bright—solar bright—new future. The new yet old path will carry forward the hopes and dreams and lives of our ancestors.

Endnotes

1 An extensive discussion of the Doctrine of Discovery is found in Miller (2006) and [Steven T. Newcomb, *Pagans in the Promised Land: Decoding the Doctrine of Christian Discovery* (Fulcrum, 2008)].
2 This is elaborated in LaDuke (2005).
3 Osage scholar and spiritual leader George Tinker describes the distinction between Indian peoples' primarily *spatial* focus on place and Euro-Americans' primarily *temporal* focus on chronological time. See Tinker (2008, 7–9).
4 See LaDuke (2005).

References

LaDuke, Winona. 1999. *All Our Relations: Native Struggles for Land and Life*. London: Haymarket Press (2nd ed., 2015).
LaDuke, Winona. 2005. *Recovering the Sacred: The Power of Naming and Reclaiming.* London: Haymarket Press (2nd ed., 2016).
LaDuke, Winona. 2016. *LaDuke Chronicles*. Ponsford, MN: Spotted Horse Press.
Miller, Robert J. 2006. *Native America, Discovered and Conquered: Thomas Jefferson, Lewis and Clark, and Manifest Destiny*. Westport, CT: Praeger.
Tinker, George. 2008. *American Indian Liberation: A Theology of Sovereignty.* Maryknoll, NY: Orbis Books.

Suggestions for Critical Reflection

1. Why would it be confusing to quantify the term 'sacred' when speaking about sacred places?
2. Contrast the different approaches, Indigenous and non-Indigenous, with respect to nature.
3. After considering the stories of sacred places, do you think that there is a possibility for cooperation, for consensus, with respect to the use of sacred places? Why or why not?
4. There are examples of nonhumans being granted moral status. How does this connect with religion?
5. What is the role of relations and relationships with respect to sacred places?

Additional Resources

For additional resources relating to this reading and its themes, visit **sites.broadviewpress.com/waysofbeing/2-3**

PART III

Metaphysics

INTRODUCTION

The Nature of Reality: What Is Real?

Generally speaking, the content of philosophical study is divided into three areas: metaphysics, epistemology, and value theory. The first area, metaphysics, is the study of nature, being, and existence; in other words, metaphysics deals with the nature of reality. The Indigenous people of Turtle Island participate in metaphysical pursuits through their oral traditions, ceremonies, practices, protocols, and rituals. A shared concept in the ontology of the Indigenous people of Turtle Island is relations, or relationships. Relations are not merely between other human individuals; rather, relations may be held with nonhuman animals, land and land features, etc.

In the first reading from Viola Cordova, the reader is introduced to an Indigenous conception of reality. Cordova shows how metaphysics informs epistemology, illuminating how and what one can or should know. In addition, Cordova reveals a metaphysics that introduces the notion that the Universe is sacred and that humans are co-creators of it. As such, there is a responsibility inherent in the way Indigenous people live. The rituals of Indigenous communities are intimately connected with the sacred. Much like the LaDuke piece in the previous section, the reading from Cordova would be suitable in other sections of the book, such as epistemology or perhaps religion. This underlines how the three areas of philosophy are not as easily separated in Indigenous philosophy.

Robin Wall Kimmerer provides a creation story for the second reading in this chapter. Stories often provide the philosophical content of Indigenous philosophies. One can look within the story for metaphysics, epistemology, and values. At the center of the story is the notion of a relationship and it would be part of the community's ontology. Relationships motivate the need to know about our relations and the obligations we incur simply by being part of this world. In the story, humans are dependent upon others, which entails humility and being grateful for the gifts given to us by our relations. The story places a demand on us to fulfill our obligations and share our gifts.

The third selection is on a subject that occurs frequently in Native American/First Nations, Métis, Inuit, and Native Alaskan Philosophy: identity. Hilary N. Weaver's use of story and her developed insights shed light on the ways in which colonization has been internalized by Indigenous communities, affecting determinations of who is actually Indigenous or a member of a particular community. As a result, not only do individuals have to deal with external assessments of identity, but they also must often meet unspoken criteria imposed by members of their own community. Weaver's final caution is to encourage Indigenous communities to think carefully about identity and create criteria themselves, as an exercise in sovereignty.

Leanne Betasamosake Simpson discusses the power of language in the fourth reading of this chapter. Stereotypes, especially those connected with Indigeneity, figure into the motives of colonialism. The exercise described in the reading attests to the challenges Indigenous people encounter every day. The reading is not only a lesson in philosophy of language; it also speaks to Indigenous resistance and resurgence, as well as nation-building.

The final selection in this chapter is a distinctly Indigenous take on the features that make an individual a person. Kurtis Boyer contrasts the standard view provided by Western philosophers, such as Descartes and Locke, with an Indigenous notion of being an integrated whole. Boyer's account has ramifications for various philosophical areas, such as notions of identity, science, ethics, and human nature. The reading provides a starting point for many different discussions about metaphysics.

3.1
"Coda: Living in a Sacred Universe"*

Viola Cordova (Jicarilla Apache)

ABOUT THE AUTHOR

Viola Cordova (1937–2002) was one of the first Native Americans to earn a PhD in Philosophy. She completed her bachelor's degree at Idaho State University, and obtained her MA and PhD in philosophy from the University of New Mexico. She has taught at various institutions, such as the University of Alaska Fairbanks and Oregon State University. In 1996–97, Cordova was a Rockefeller Foundation Fellow in Thunder Bay, Ontario. It was there that she helped establish the first university program in Native American Philosophy. Later, Cordova taught philosophy and honours courses at Idaho State University. Cordova was an originating member of the American Indian Philosophy Association and with Dr. Anne Waters (Seminole) she co-edited the American Philosophical Association's *Newsletter on American Indians in Philosophy*, now *Studies in Native American and Indigenous Philosophy*. In addition to the posthumous work *How It Is*, Cordova's work can also be found in the first collection of articles published by an American Indian holding a PhD in Philosophy, Anne Waters's *American Indian Thought: Philosophical Essays.*

KEY TERMS

Universe, Sacred, Beliefs, Pueblo, Kachina, Spirits, Ritual, Relations, Humans, War, Beauty, Mundane, Energy, Memory, Interconnectedness

"It is difficult to explain," a friend of mine says. He is speaking of the idea that it is the Universe itself that many Native Americans hold as sacred. How does one go about explaining that there are no other dimensions in which sacredness dwells because we can know only one dimension?

The late Tewa anthropologist Alfonso Ortiz claimed that all religious concepts were embraced by Native Americans, on the grounds that "the more religion the better." The alien religious concepts are seen as additions to Native beliefs and not as explanations, nor even equivalents, of Native beliefs. The various beliefs are welcome so long as they offer avenues to celebration of what is seen as sacred.

* From Kathleen Dean Moore, Kurt Peters, Ted Jojola, and Amber Lacy, eds., *How It Is: The Native American Philosophy of V.F. Cordova* (Tucson: The University of Arizona Press, 2007), 229–32.

We must take note here that Ortiz is a "Pueblo" Indian, and that all Pueblos seem to have in common a concept of the *kachina*. Kachinas are personifications of the animating "something" that causes a "thing" to exist as itself. Jesus and his mother, Mary, can be incorporated, by those inclined to do so, into the realm of kachinas, which includes also personifications of butterflies, sun, wind, trees, and a multitude of other things. The personification, if one is familiar at least with the carved kachinas that make it into the tourist market, is a humanlike figure with an inhuman head. During "sacred" ceremonies, humans take on the guise of a kachina in celebration of and thanksgiving to the particular entity that they represent. The idea of representing the animating "spirit" of the various forms that contribute to the well-being of a people is widespread in the Southwest; the Apache and the Navajo also share this idea of representation, perhaps as an influence from their Pueblo neighbors. The complication in explanation that arises here is that the kachinas, even as "spirits," are not from another dimension. They are part of *this* world. They serve to remind us that this world is sacred; this world is worthy of our reverence, awe, attention, and care. They represent those things on which we depend for our continued survival. The butterfly is given a special consideration, for example, because it pollinates the corn that feeds the people. It is not more, but also not less, a sacred being than the corn itself.

I have heard, from those familiar with the concept, that Einstein's idea of matter and energy as interchangeable states might serve as an explanation for what is actually "in attention" during a celebration of the sacred. A Native American would use the term, however, not as describing two distinct states but rather as one singular state with two facets: *matterenergy* rather than matter *and* energy.

Our daily life requires focus on particular *aspects* of things—the *process* of growing corn, for example. Our ritual life, on the other hand, reminds us that an aspect is a part of a greater whole: the water that gives the corn life, the Earth that sustains the plant, the Sun that provides energy, the Universe because it is *as it is*. Everything *that is* becomes a part of a whole that we deem "sacred." We live, in other words, in a Sacred Universe. And it is this "form of life" that my friend states is "difficult to explain."

Where *does* the human being fit into the sacred universe, and how? We are all familiar with the statement credited to Native Americans, that we believe that "all things are related." We seldom hear about what that "relatedness" entails. I suppose one could use the analogy of a stone thrown into a pond. Each "thing"—stone, air molecule, plant, animal, or vegetable—causes a ripple to form in the pond. The singular, particular being is not merely itself tossed into the pond. It is also the ripple, the wave, that is formed by the action. Our "waves" overlap and extend beyond what we can foresee.

Wisdom is knowing the effects of those "overlaps." This is how "relatedness" enters the picture: a statement that "all things are related" reminds us that we are not separate from all other things and that our actions have far-reaching consequences.

This view, of a stone tossed into a pond, is very far removed from the notion of a human being as "a bit of cosmic dust" floating in "empty" space. Human beings may have the broadest range of connections to the Universe of any being that exists. We might believe that our skin closes us off from the rest of the world, but it is in actuality a very permeable surface. Aside from absorbing the world through skin and lungs, we also see and hear and taste. Our senses connect us to the world. We have a broad range of emotional reactions; these, too, connect us to the world. And we have memory. Our extensive memory may be that which distinguishes us from other animals. Just as the bear can be distinguished from the cougar through his characteristics, lifestyle, body type, geographical range, we have our tremendous capacity to remember. Knowledge, in a Native American sense, is derived from the connections we make between all of the facets of our sensate experience and the memory of the consequences attendant upon all of those experiences. And, of course, all of our actions have consequences. We are not "meaningless" beings, because all of our actions bear a "meaning" for something else.

Throughout North America, indigenous peoples have the notion that they are cocreators of their world. We can bring things into existence that did not exist before. There are various versions of a mythic tale told in the Southwest about the Monster-Slayer. He, or they, as they are often twin sons of the Sun and the Earth, come to the people to rescue them from monsters ranging the Earth. Some monsters are slain, but not all of them. Some give good arguments for why they should remain. Death, for example, is allowed to remain, for without dying, Death claims, there could be no new people born, for the Earth would soon become overpopulated. Hunger is allowed to exist, because it maintains the industriousness of the people. Lice are left behind because they force the people to keep themselves and their environs clean. One monster that *is* slain is Fear. For all else the people must accommodate themselves. Those monsters not so specifically named that happen to arise are the responsibility of the people themselves; no hero will assist in those circumstances. One example of a human-created monster is War. Humans alone are responsible for the creation and the ousting of this "monster."

What the story "tells" is that humans, because they are cocreators, can bring into existence all sorts of things. It is better, in this sense, to bring into the world only what is harmonious with the whole. 'Beauty' is the usual translation of the idea of a harmonious whole. As in many Navajo poems, one is encouraged to "walk in beauty," to bring "beauty" into being.

The greatest "duty," if it can be so called, of a human being is to cause no disruption to the greater, and "beautiful," whole of whatever it is that is. Humans, too, are responsible for dealing with the "monsters" that continue to plague mankind—war, hunger, poverty, disease—particularly if they have, themselves, brought them into being.

All of the "descriptions" I have mentioned, of the Universe, of the Sacred, of human beings, have relevance in our daily lives. The Native American is admonished to maintain the sacredness of the entire whole. It is difficult to explain that the mundane is actually the sacred. But it is even more difficult to explain how it is that Native Americans, despite the many and continuing attempts to eradicate their belief and value systems, persist in thinking, *knowing*, that their descriptions are the *right* ones—for *this* "world."

Suggestions for Critical Reflection

1. According to Cordova, what types of religious beliefs are typically embraced by Indigenous people on Turtle Island? What types are not typically embraced?
2. How is an animating spirit similar to the idea of a soul (be careful to consider the religious understanding of a soul and other accounts, like that from Plato)?
3. Connect the Indigenous approach to ontology (relations, spirits, universe) to the Indigenous approaches to epistemology (rituals) and responsibility (obligations), as expressed in this article.
4. Do you agree that what is harmonious is beautiful? Defend your position.
5. Do you agree that humans are responsible for the monsters that plague humankind—war, hunger, poverty, disease—even if they individually have not contributed to them?

Additional Resources

For additional resources relating to this reading and its themes, visit sites.broadviewpress.com/waysofbeing/3-1

3.2
"Skywoman Falling"*

Robin Wall Kimmerer (Citizen Potawatomi Nation)

ABOUT THE AUTHOR

Robin Wall Kimmerer attended the State University of New York College of Environmental Science and Forestry and earned a bachelor's degree (1975) in botany. She spent two years working for Bausch & Lomb as a microbiologist. Kimmerer later moved to Wisconsin and attended the University of Wisconsin–Madison, earning her master's degree (1979) in botany, and a PhD (1983) in plant ecology. While studying forest ecology as part of her degree program, she first learned about mosses, which became the scientific focus of her career. Kimmerer was invited to participate as a panelist at a United Nations (2015) plenary meeting to discuss how harmony with nature can help to conserve and sustainably use natural resources. She is the author of numerous scientific papers on plant ecology, bryophyte ecology, traditional knowledge, and restoration ecology.

KEY TERMS

Oral tradition, Gratitude, Sweetgrass, Medicines, Kindness, Relationships, Gifts, Reciprocity, Wisdom, Spirit, Relations

In winter, when the green earth lies resting beneath a blanket of snow, this is the time for storytelling. The storytellers begin by calling upon those who came before who passed the stories down to us, for we are only messengers.

In the beginning there was the Skyworld

She fell like a maple seed, pirouetting on an autumn breeze.[1] A column of light streamed from a hole in the Skyworld, marking her path where only darkness had been before. It took her a long time to fall. In fear, or maybe hope, she clutched a bundle tightly in her hand.

Hurtling downward, she saw only dark water below. But in that emptiness there were many eyes gazing up at the sudden shaft of light. They saw there a small object, a mere dust mote in the beam. As it grew closer, they could see

* From Robin Wall Kimmerer, *Braiding Sweetgrass* (Minneapolis: Milkweed Editions, 2015), 3–10.

that it was a woman, arms outstretched, long black hair billowing behind as she spiraled toward them.

The geese nodded at one another and rose together from the water in a wave of goose music. She felt the beat of their wings as they flew beneath to break her fall. Far from the only home she'd ever known, she caught her breath at the warm embrace of soft feathers as they gently carried her downward. And so it began.

The geese could not hold the woman above the water for much longer, so they called a council to decide what to do. Resting on their wings, she saw them all gather: loons, otters, swans, beavers, fish of all kinds. A great turtle floated in their midst and offered his back for her to rest upon. Gratefully, she stepped from the goose wings onto the dome of his shell. The others understood that she needed land for her home and discussed how they might serve her need. The deep divers among them had heard of mud at the bottom of the water and agreed to go find some.

Loon dove first, but the distance was too far and after a long while he surfaced with nothing to show for his efforts. One by one, the other animals offered to help—Otter, Beaver, Sturgeon—but the depth, the darkness, and the pressures were too great for even the strongest of swimmers. They returned gasping for air with their heads ringing. Some did not return at all. Soon only little Muskrat was left, the weakest diver of all. He volunteered to go while the others looked on doubtfully. His small legs flailed as he worked his way downward and he was gone a very long time.

They waited and waited for him to return, fearing the worst for their relative, and, before long, a stream of bubbles rose with the small, limp body of the muskrat. He had given his life to aid this helpless human. But then the others noticed that his paw was tightly clenched and, when they opened it, there was a small handful of mud. Turtle said, "Here, put it on my back and I will hold it."

Skywoman bent and spread the mud with her hands across the shell of the turtle. Moved by the extraordinary gifts of the animals, she sang in thanksgiving and then began to dance, her feet caressing the earth. The land grew and grew as she danced her thanks, from the dab of mud on Turtle's back until the whole earth was made. Not by Skywoman alone, but from the alchemy of all the animals' gifts coupled with her deep gratitude. Together they formed what we know today as Turtle Island, our home.

Like any good guest, Skywoman had not come empty-handed. The bundle was still clutched in her hand. When she toppled from the hole in the Skyworld she had reached out to grab onto the Tree of Life that grew there. In her grasp were branches—fruits and seeds of all kinds of plants. These she scattered onto the new ground and carefully tended each one until the world turned from brown to green. Sunlight streamed through the hole from the Skyworld, allowing the seeds to flourish. Wild grasses, flowers, trees, and medicines spread everywhere. And now that the animals, too, had plenty to eat, many came to live with her on Turtle Island.

Our stories say that of all the plants, *wiingaashk*, or sweetgrass, was the very first to grow on the earth, its fragrance a sweet memory of Skywoman's hand. Accordingly, it is honored as one of the four sacred plants of my people. Breathe in its scent and you start to remember things you didn't know you'd forgotten. Our elders say that ceremonies are the way we "remember to remember," and so sweetgrass is a powerful ceremonial plant cherished by many indigenous nations. It is also used to make beautiful baskets. Both medicine and a relative, its value is both material and spiritual.

There is such tenderness in braiding the hair of someone you love. Kindness and something more flow between the braider and the braided, the two connected by the cord of the plait. *Wiingaashk* waves in strands, long and shining like a woman's freshly washed hair. And so we say it is the flowing hair of Mother Earth. When we braid sweetgrass, we are braiding the hair of Mother Earth, showing her our loving attention, our care for her beauty and well-being, in gratitude for all she has given us. Children hearing the Skywoman story from birth know in their bones the responsibility that flows between humans and the earth.

The story of Skywoman's journey is so rich and glittering it feels to me like a deep bowl of celestial blue from which I could drink again and again. It holds our beliefs, our history, our relationships. Looking into that starry bowl, I see images swirling so fluidly that the past and the present become as one. Images of Skywoman speak not just of where we came from, but also of how we can go forward.

I have Bruce King's portrait of Skywoman, *Moment in Flight*, hanging in my lab. Floating to earth with her handful of seeds and flowers, she looks down on my microscopes and data loggers. It might seem an odd juxtaposition, but to me she belongs there. As a writer, a scientist, and a carrier of Skywoman's story, I sit at the feet of my elder teachers listening for their songs.

On Mondays, Wednesdays, and Fridays at 9:35 a.m., I am usually in a lecture hall at the university, expounding about botany and ecology—trying, in short, to explain to my students how Skywoman's gardens, known by some as "global ecosystems," function. One otherwise unremarkable morning I gave the students in my General Ecology class a survey. Among other things, they were asked to rate their understanding of the negative interactions between humans and the environment. Nearly every one of the two hundred students said confidently that humans and nature are a bad mix. These were third-year students who had selected a career in environmental protection, so the response was, in a way, not very surprising. They were well schooled in the mechanics of climate change, toxins in the land and water, and the crisis of habitat loss. Later in the survey, they were asked to rate their knowledge of positive interactions between people and land. The median response was "none."

I was stunned. How is it possible that in twenty years of education they cannot think of any beneficial relationships between people and the environment? Perhaps the negative examples they see every day—brownfields, factory farms, suburban sprawl—truncated their ability to see some good between humans and the earth. As the land becomes impoverished, so too does the scope of their vision. When we talked about this after class, I realized that they could not even imagine what beneficial relations between their species and others might look like. How can we begin to move toward ecological and cultural sustainability if we cannot even imagine what the path feels like? If we can't imagine the generosity of geese? These students were not raised on the story of Skywoman.

On one side of the world were people whose relationship with the living world was shaped by Skywoman, who created a garden for the well-being of all. On the other side was another woman with a garden and a tree. But for tasting its fruit, she was banished from the garden and the gates clanged shut behind her. That mother of men was made to wander in the wilderness and earn her bread by the sweat of her brow, not by filling her mouth with the sweet juicy fruits that bend the branches low. In order to eat, she was instructed to subdue the wilderness into which she was cast.

Same species, same earth, different stories. Like Creation stories everywhere, cosmologies are a source of identity and orientation to the world. They tell us who we are. We are inevitably shaped by them no matter how distant they may be from our consciousness. One story leads to the generous embrace of the living world, the other to banishment. One woman is our ancestral gardener, a cocreator of the good green world that would be the home of her descendants. The other was an exile, just passing through an alien world on a rough road to her real home in heaven.

And then they met—the offspring of Skywoman and the children of Eve—and the land around us bears the scars of that meeting, the echoes of our stories. They say that hell hath no fury like a woman scorned, and I can only imagine the conversation between Eve and Skywoman: "Sister, you got the short end of the stick ..."

The Skywoman story, shared by the original peoples throughout the Great Lakes, is a constant star in the constellation of teachings we call the Original Instructions. These are not "instructions" like commandments, though, or rules; rather, they are like a compass: they provide an orientation but not a map. The work of living is creating that map for yourself. How to follow the Original Instructions will be different for each of us and different for every era.

In their time, Skywoman's first people lived by their understanding of the Original Instructions, with ethical prescriptions for respectful hunting, family life, ceremonies that made sense for their world. Those measures for caring might not seem to fit in today's urban world, where "green" means an advertising slogan, not a meadow. The buffalo are gone and the world has moved on. I can't return salmon to the river, and my neighbors would raise the alarm if I set fire to my yard to produce pasture for elk.

The earth was new then, when it welcomed the first human. It's old now, and some suspect that we have worn out our welcome by casting the Original Instructions aside. From the very beginning of the world, the other species were a lifeboat for the people. Now, we must be theirs. But the stories that might guide us, if they are told at all, grow dim in the memory. What meaning would they have today? How can we translate from the stories at the world's beginning to this hour so much closer to its end? The landscape has changed, but the story remains. And as I turn it over again and again, Skywoman seems to look me in the eye and ask, in return for this gift of a world on Turtle's back, what will I give in return?

It is good to remember that the original woman was herself an immigrant. She fell a long way from her home in the Skyworld, leaving behind all who knew her and who held her dear. She could never go back. Since 1492, most here are immigrants as well, perhaps arriving on Ellis Island without even knowing that Turtle Island rested beneath their feet. Some of my ancestors are Skywoman's people, and I belong to them. Some of my ancestors were the newer kind of immigrants, too: a French fur trader, an Irish carpenter, a Welsh farmer. And here we all are, on Turtle Island, trying to make a home. Their stories, of arrivals with empty pockets and nothing but hope, resonate with Skywoman's. She came here with nothing but a handful of seeds and the slimmest of instructions to "use your gifts and dreams for good," the same instructions we all carry. She accepted the gifts from the other beings with open hands and used them honorably. She shared the gifts she brought from Skyworld as she set herself about the business of flourishing, of making a home.

Perhaps the Skywoman story endures because we too are always falling. Our lives, both personal and collective, share her trajectory. Whether we jump or are pushed, or the edge of the known world just crumbles at our feet, we fall, spinning into someplace new and unexpected. Despite our fears of falling, the gifts of the world stand by to catch us.

As we consider these instructions, it is also good to recall that, when Skywoman arrived here, she did not come alone. She was pregnant. Knowing her grandchildren would inherit the world she left behind, she did not work for flourishing in her time only. It was through her actions of reciprocity, the give and take with the land, that the original immigrant became indigenous. For all of us, becoming indigenous to a place means living as if your children's future mattered, to take care of the land as if our lives, both material and spiritual, depended on it.

In the public arena, I've heard the Skywoman story told as a bauble of colorful "folklore." But, even when it is misunderstood, there is power in the telling. Most of my students have never heard the origin story of this land where they were born, but when I tell them, something begins to kindle behind their eyes. Can they, can we all, understand the Skywoman story not as an artifact from the past but as instructions for the future? Can a nation of immigrants once again follow her example to become native, to make a home?

Look at the legacy of poor Eve's exile from Eden: the land shows the bruises of an abusive relationship. It's not just land that is broken, but more importantly, our relationship to land. As Gary Nabhan has written, we can't meaningfully proceed with healing, with restoration, without "re-story-ation." In other words, our relationship with land cannot heal until we hear its stories. But who will tell them?

In the Western tradition there is a recognized hierarchy of beings, with, of course, the human being on top—the pinnacle of evolution, the darling of Creation—and the plants at the bottom. But in Native ways of knowing, human people are often referred to as "the younger brothers of Creation." We say that humans have the least experience with how to live and thus the most to learn—we must look to our teachers among the other species for guidance. Their wisdom is apparent in the way that they live. They teach us by example. They've been on the earth far longer than we have been, and have had time to figure things out. They live both above and below ground, joining Skyworld to the earth. Plants know how to make food and medicine from light and water, and then they give it away.

I like to imagine that when Skywoman scattered her handful of seeds across Turtle Island, she was sowing sustenance for the body and also for the mind, emotion, and spirit: she was leaving us teachers. The plants can tell us her story; we need to learn to listen.

Endnote

1 Adapted from oral tradition and [Joanne Shenandoah and Douglas M. George, *Skywoman: Legends of the Iroquois* (1998, Clear Light, Santa Fe)].

Suggestions for Critical Reflection

1. What areas of philosophy (metaphysics, epistemology, and value theory) do you find in the story of Skywoman? Provide examples to support your view.
2. What sorts of relationships are involved in the story of Skywoman? What conclusions about relations does the story provide?
3. Does the concept of reciprocity apply to our world today? Would it require a complete change in worldview to achieve it at the same level as it is achieved in the story?
4. What would ethical obligations or responsibilities look like for a worldview that focuses on the sorts of connections and relationships discussed in this piece?

Additional Resources

For additional resources relating to this reading and its themes, visit **sites.broadviewpress.com/waysofbeing/3-2**

3.3
"Indigenous Identity: What Is It, and Who Really Has It?"*

Hilary N. Weaver (Lakota)

ABOUT THE AUTHOR

Hilary N. Weaver, DSW (Lakota) is a Professor and Associate Dean for Diversity, Equity and Inclusion in the School of Social Work, University at Buffalo (State University of New York). She earned a BS from Antioch College in social work (1984) and her MSW (1986) and DSW (1994) from Columbia University. Her teaching, research, and service focus on cultural issues in the helping process with an emphasis on Indigenous populations. Weaver received funding from the National Cancer Institute to develop and test a culturally grounded wellness curriculum for urban Native American youth: the *Healthy Living in Two Worlds* program. She was inducted as a National Association of Social Workers Foundation Social Work Pioneer in 2020 and was named the American Public Health Association's Public Health Social Worker of the Year in 2020. Weaver has presented her work regionally, nationally, and internationally, including at the Permanent Forum on Indigenous Issues at the United Nations.†

KEY TERMS

Identity, Self-Identification, Community Identification, External Identification, Autonomy, Culture, Language, Internalized Colonization, Racism, Recognition, Misrecognition

Indigenous identity is a truly complex and somewhat controversial topic. There is little agreement on precisely what constitutes an indigenous identity, how to measure it, and who truly has it. Indeed, there is not even a consensus on appropriate terms. Are we talking about Indians, American Indians, Natives, Native Americans, indigenous people, or First Nations people? Are we talking about Sioux or Lakota? Navajo or Dine? Chippewa, Ojibway, or Anishnabe? Once we get that sorted out, are we talking about race, ethnicity,

* Hilary N. Weaver, "Indigenous Identity: What Is It and Who Really Has It?" *The American Indian Quarterly* 25 (2001): 240–55, https://doi.org/10.1353/aiq.2001.0030.

† Information obtained from The International Federation of Social Workers, https://www.ifsw.org/wp-content/uploads/2021/12/Biography.pdf.

cultural identity, tribal identity, acculturation, enculturation, bicultural identity, multicultural identity, or some other form of identity?

The topic of indigenous identity opens a Pandora's box of possibilities, and to try to address them all would mean doing justice to none. This article provides background information on three facets of identity—self-identification, community identification, and external identification—followed by a brief overview of measurement issues and my reflections on how internalized oppression/colonization is related to identity. The terms *Native* and *indigenous* are used interchangeably to refer to the descendants of the original inhabitants of North America. These are not, per se, the "right" terms or the only terms that could have been used. They reflect my preferences.

Cultural identity, as reflected in the values, beliefs, and worldviews of indigenous people, is the focus of the article. Those who belong to the same culture share a broadly similar conceptual map and way of interpreting language.[1] People can identify themselves in many ways other than by their cultures.[2] In fact, identity may actually be a composite of many things such as race, class, education, region, religion, and gender.[3] The influence of these aspects of identity on who someone is as an indigenous person is likely to change over time. Identities are always fragmented, multiply constructed, and intersected in a constantly changing, sometimes conflicting array.[4] Although in reality the various facets of identity are inextricably linked, for the purposes of this essay I will focus on culture as a facet of identity.

While indigenous identity is a topic that I have done some research on, it is also a topic that I, as a Lakota woman, approach with subjectivity. Rather than solely a limitation, this subjectivity adds an important dimension to the work. Native people must begin to examine their own histories and issues rather than leaving these analyses to nonnatives.[5] My work is influenced by the facts that my mother's parents left Rosebud decades ago after attending boarding school and I live in an urban setting largely made up of Haudenosaunee people. Additionally, my professional affiliation as a social worker leads me to focus on aspects of cultural identity that tend to have practical implications for helping service providers understand their indigenous clients. As well as drawing on the literature, I draw on my own experiences and bring my personal perspectives to the topic.

My father came from an Appalachian background. He was the one who remembered and told the stories. Thus, I begin with a story about cultural identity. I do not know the original source, but the story rings with an important truth and is a poignant commentary on contemporary indigenous identity. My appreciation goes out to the original storytellers, whoever they may be. A brief summary of the story is warranted here.

"The Big Game"

The day had come for the championship game in the all-Native basketball tournament. Many teams had played valiantly, but on the last day the competition came down to the highly competitive Lakota and Navajo teams. The tension was high as all waited to see which would be the best team.

Prior to the game, some of the Lakota players went to watch the Navajos practice. They were awed and somewhat intimidated by the Navajos' impressive display of skills. One Lakota who was particularly anxious and insecure pointed out to his teammates that some of the Navajo players had facial hair. "Everyone knows that Indians don't have facial hair," he stated. Another Lakota added that some of the Navajos also had suspiciously dark skin. They concluded, disdainfully, that clearly these were not Native people and, in fact, were probably a "bunch of Mexicans." The so-called Navajos should be disqualified from the tournament, leaving the Lakota team the winner by default.

That same afternoon, some Navajo players went to watch the Lakota team practice. The Lakotas had a lot of skillful moves that made the Navajos worry. One Navajo observed, "That guy's skin sure looks awful light." Another added, "Yeah, and most of them have short hair." They concluded, disdainfully, that clearly these were not Native people and, in fact, were probably a "bunch of white guys." The so-called Lakotas should be disqualified from the tournament, leaving the Navajos the winners by default.

The captains from both teams brought their accusations to the referee just before game time. Both teams agreed that Native identity must be established before the game could be played and that whichever team could not establish Native identity to everyone's satisfaction must forfeit. The Lakota captain suggested that everyone show his tribal enrollment card as proof of identity. The Lakotas promptly displayed their "red cards," but some of the Navajos did not have enrollment cards. The Lakotas were ready to celebrate their victory when the Navajo captain protested that carrying an enrollment card was a product of colonization and not an indicator of true identity. He suggested that the real proof would be a display of indigenous language skills, and each Navajo proceeded to recite his clan affiliations in the traditional way of introducing himself in the Navajo language. Some of the Lakotas were able to speak their language, but others were not. The teams went back and forth proposing standards of proof of identity, but each proposed standard was self-serving and could not be met by the other team. As the sun began to set, the frustrated referees canceled the championship game. Because of the accusations and disagreements that could not be resolved there would be no champion in the indigenous tournament.

Facets of Cultural Identity

Overview

In recent years there has been a growing literature on identity, accompanied by many deconstructive critiques of this concept.[6] Generally, identification is based on recognition of a common origin or shared characteristics with another person, group, or ideal leading to solidarity and allegiance. Beyond this, the discursive approach sees identification as an ongoing process that is never complete.[7] Additionally, identities do not exist before they are constructed.[8]

Most theorists agree that identity exists, not solely within an individual or category of individuals but through difference in relationship with others.[9] Thus, there was no Native American identity prior to contact with Europeans.[10] Likewise, immigrants from various European nations had to learn to define themselves as white rather than according to their national origins or cultural groups.[11] Before contact, indigenous people identified themselves as distinct from other indigenous people and constructed their identities in this way. Indeed, this is still the case for many who see themselves as members of their own nations rather than members of a larger group represented by the umbrella term *Native American*.

The constructionist approach to representation states that meaning is constructed through language.[12] Thus, the words we choose to use such as *American Indian, Native American*, or *First Nations* not only reflect but shape identity. Likewise, using English translations for indigenous words shapes meanings. Today, Native people often learn about themselves and their culture in English and therefore adopt some stereotypes and distorted meanings.[13]

The label "Indian" has served to reinforce the image of indigenous people as linked to a romantic past. "Indians" are the images in old photographs, movies, and museum cases.[14] It is a label for people who are fundamentally unknown and misrecognized by nonindigenous people. Indeed, an "Indian" is constituted in the act of naming.[15] Those who are relatively powerless to represent themselves as complex human beings against the backdrop of degrading stereotypes become invisible and nameless.[16]

Identity is shaped, in part, by recognition, absence of recognition, or misrecognition by others: "A person or group of people can suffer real damage, real distortion, if the people or society around them mirror back to them a confining or demeaning or contemptible picture of themselves. Nonrecognition or misrecognition can inflict harm, can be a form of oppression, imprisoning someone in a false, distorted, and reduced mode of being."[17]

This misrecognition has oppressed indigenous people and has imprisoned them within a false "Indian" identity.[18]

How an indigenous cultural identity is defined by Natives and nonnatives has been complex in both contemporary and historical times.[19] It is misleading to assume that all indigenous people experience a Native cultural identity in the same way just because they were born into a Native community. This glosses over the multifaceted and evolving nature of identity as well as cultural differences among and within Native nations.[20]

Additionally, identity can be multilayered. For some, a subtribal identity such as clan affiliation is primary. For others, identification with a tribe or a region like the Northern Plains is most meaningful. Still others espouse a broader identity as Native or indigenous people. Different levels of identity are likely to be presented in different contexts: "Thus, an American Indian might be a 'mixed-blood' on the reservation, from 'Pine Ridge' when speaking to someone from another reservation, an 'Oglala Sioux' or 'Lakota' when asked about tribal affiliation, or an 'American Indian' when interacting with non-Indians."[21]

Identity is a combination of self-identification and the perceptions of others.[22] There are widespread disputes about who can assert a Native identity and who has the right to represent indigenous interests. Such conflicts occur when self-identification and the perceptions of others are at odds. Some people who assert indigenous identity do not appear phenotypically Native, are not enrolled, and were not born on reservations or in some other Native communities. Some of these individuals indeed have indigenous heritage, and others do not. Other people are enrolled or have Native heritage but know little about their cultures. This may be because they have no interest or no one to teach them or because of factors such as racism and stereotypes that inhibit their willingness to pursue an indigenous identity.[23] Some indigenous communities, such as the Mashpee, have experienced significant racial mixing. Marriage between Europeans and indigenous people was sanctioned and rewarded by U.S. government officials as a way to assimilate and acculturate Native people.[24] This raises the question, Did the Mashpee and similar indigenous communities absorb outsiders, or were they absorbed into the American melting pot?[25] These issues of authenticity permeate the story "The Big Game" as players try to exclude others from the competition. Indeed, identity is always based on power and exclusion. Someone must be excluded from a particular identity in order for it to be meaningful.[26]

Self-Identification

Self-perception is a key component of identity. For some, expression of a Native identity may be little more than a personal belief about heritage expressed on a census form.[27] Cultural identity is not static; rather, it progresses through developmental stages during which an individual has a changing sense of who he or she is, perhaps leading to a rediscovered sense of being Native.[28] There is some level of choice involved in accepting a Native identity, although the range of choices is limited by factors such as phenotypical appearances.[29] Choice may also be influenced by social, economic, and political factors.[30] For example, a climate filled with discrimination may lead an individual to reject a Native identity, whereas a climate in which a Native identity is seen as fashionable and perhaps financially profitable may lead an individual to assert an indigenous identity.

In some instances, asserting an indigenous cultural identity is related to resisting assimilation. Navajo and Ute youth who grow up off the reservation with limited connections to their cultural past or traditional ceremonies often define their indigenous identity and cultural pride through resistance to the domination of the white community. For example, attending and doing well in school are defined as important and good by the surrounding white community, yet these youth often drop out, not because they are "bad" or incapable of school success but as a way of defying the dominant society. Resistance of "goodness" as framed by whites and insistence on living their lives as indigenous people, in the many different ways in which they define it, are at the core of their actions.[31]

Developing a cultural identity consists of a lifelong learning process of cultural awareness and understanding.[32] Because the formation of identity takes place over time, a strong cultural identity may increase with age.[33] In addition to a growing cultural attachment as individuals get older, there seems to be a revitalization in indigenous cultures and communities across the country. Indeed, individual cultural renewal and collective cultural renewal are intertwined.[34]

In the story "The Big Game," all the players see themselves as indigenous people, yet the ways in which they define themselves are contested by others. A stalemate occurs when it becomes impossible to reach an agreement between self-definitions and external definitions of identity.

Community Identification

Indigenous identity is connected to a sense of peoplehood inseparably linked to sacred traditions, traditional homelands, and a shared history as indigenous people.[35] A person must be integrated into a society, not simply stand alone as an individual, in order to be fully human.[36] Additionally, identity can only be confirmed by others who share that identity.[37] The sense of membership in a community is so integrally linked to a sense of identity that Native people often identify themselves by their reservations or tribal communities. This stands in striking contrast to the practice of many members of the dominant society who commonly identify themselves by their professional affiliations. Tribal members have an enduring sense of their own unique indigenous identity.[38] The sense of a traditional homeland is so strong for many Navajos that when outside their traditional territory and away from sacred geography they sometimes experience an extreme imbalance that can only be corrected by returning to their home communities for ceremonies.[39]

Tribal communities, and thus their members, maintain their identities relative to the identities of neighboring communities. In the past, neighboring communities consisted of other indigenous groups; now they are groups from other cultures.[40] Sometimes identity boundaries are defined by policy and law as well as convention. Tribes have the right to determine criteria for membership. This regulation of membership, in some ways a form of regulating identity, has implications for political access and resource allocation.[41] Likewise, enrollment (or lack thereof) has implications for how a person perceives him or herself and is perceived by others, both within and outside of the Native community.

Cultural identity not only exists in contrast to surrounding communities; differences are also found among indigenous people within a community. Csordas describes how the types of healing used by various Navajo people indicate and reinforce their cultural identity.[42] Whether an individual participates in traditional, Native American Church, or Christian forms of healing reflects a sense of identity and self-worth as a Navajo.

For some indigenous people, a sense of community identity comes increasingly from intertribal or pan-Indian groups. Nagel points to activist developments such as the occupation of Alcatraz, the development of the Red Power movement, the occupation of Wounded Knee, fish-ins, and the Trail of Broken Treaties as turning points in the evolution of indigenous identity. Through these activist efforts, some indigenous people began to see Native heritage as a valuable part of personal identity and as a foundation for pan-Indian solidarity. Although a growing climate of activism led to increased cultural renewal, this should not obscure the social and cultural continuity that has been maintained in some communities.[43]

In the story "The Big Game," the players are members of teams. The teams validate and reinforce each member's identity as a basketball player, just as Native communities validate and reinforce the identities of their members. Being part of a larger group is critical to identity in both cases.

External Identification

Native identity has often been defined from a nonnative perspective. This raises critical questions about authenticity: Who decides who is an indigenous person, Natives or nonnatives?[44] The federal government has asserted a shaping force in indigenous identity by defining both Native nations and individuals.[45] Federal policy makers have increasingly imposed their own standards of who is considered a Native person in spite of the fact that this is in direct conflict with the rights of tribes/nations.[46]

The role of the federal government in shaping an indigenous identity can be pervasive but hard to define. The United States declared indigenous people to be members of domestic dependent nations, wards of the federal government, and even U.S. citizens. This raises interesting questions, such as, What is the influence of social and economic policies on identity? Can someone else's laws define who we are? Do we adopt an identity as farmers because that is what the Allotment Act intended? Deloria sets the stage for many such questions, yet the answers are complex and elusive.[47]

Some Native nations are not acknowledged to exist by the federal government. This lack of recognition has implications for how these tribes/nations are viewed by other people as well as how they view themselves. Issues of authenticity are increasingly debated in the courts as some Native groups seek federal recognition and a return of traditional lands. In the case of the Mashpee, who sued for a return of land, the primary issue was whether the group calling itself the Mashpee Tribe was in fact an Indian tribe and, if so, whether it was the same tribe that lost land through a series of contested legislative acts in the mid-nineteenth century.[48] A similar issue of authenticity exists for individuals who are not enrolled in their nations for whatever reason: "Although tribal status and Indian identity have long been vague and politically constituted, not just anyone with some native blood or claim to adoption or shared tradition can be an Indian, and not just any Native American group can decide to be a tribe and sue for lost lands."[49]

Stereotypes have a powerful influence on identity. Popular notions of Native identity are stereotypical and locked in the past.[50] In movies and writing, indigenous people seem permanently associated with notions of the old American frontier. Nonnative people may view indigenous people as having a harmonious relationship with nature and possessing an unspoiled spirituality. Sometimes indigenous people are viewed as tourist attractions, victims, and historical artifacts.[51] Vizenor asserts that indigenous identities have been censored.[52] Nonindigenous people do not want to see aspects of Native people that do not support their own ideas and beliefs, thus leading to a perpetuation of stereotypes. These external perceptions may influence how indigenous people view themselves.

Historically, indigenous people knew who they were, and today most continue to trace identity through descent, lineage, and clan, but the federal government's preoccupation with a formal definition has caused many problems. Indeed, there is considerable variation within branches of the federal government as to how Native people are defined, and these definitions are often at odds with state and tribal definitions.[53]

The way we choose to define ourselves is often not the way that others define us.[54] "The Big Game" is an example of how conflicting definitions of identity can lead to hostilities. When the members of one team identify themselves with enrollment cards, this is perceived as a threat to the self-defined identities of those without cards. Likewise, when the other team asserts that identity is grounded in the ability to speak an indigenous language, this threatens the self-perceptions of those who speak only English. Searching for the "right" criteria is both counterproductive and damaging.

Reflections on the Facets of Identity

The facets of identity interact with and sometimes reinforce or challenge each other. Given the strong emphasis on the collectivity in indigenous cultures, it is problematic to have an individual who self-identifies as indigenous yet has no community sanction or validation of that identity. Historical circumstances, however, led to thousands of Native people being taken from their communities and raised without community connections through mechanisms such as interracial adoption, foster care, and boarding schools. Indeed, there are many indigenous people with tenuous community connections at best, and some of them try to reassert an indigenous identity and find their way home to their cultures.

Establishing community connections is often an arduous task. Some indigenous people may offer support and guidance to those who try to find their way home to their tribal communities. This can be a positive experience of reintegration and cultural learning. In other instances, support is not forthcoming, and many roadblocks are raised by other indigenous people playing a gatekeeping function.

External, nonindigenous validation of Native identity, unlike community validation, is not grounded in a reasonable foundation. While it makes sense that a community should define its members, it does not make sense for an external entity to define indigenous people. It is not up to the federal government or any dominant society institution to pass judgment on the validity of any individual's claim to an indigenous identity. Likewise, it is not up to the Navajos in the story to define who the Lakotas are, nor should the Lakota attempt to define who is truly Navajo.

Measuring Identity

Although there is no consensus about what indigenous cultural identity and its various facets are, there is no shortage of attempts to measure this phenomenon. Identity is expressed as a measurable or quantifiable entity far more for indigenous people than for any other group. The federal government and most tribes use some form of blood quantum measurement.[55] Such measures are commonly used, although biological heritage is clearly not synonymous with any level of cultural connection. When the practice of defining Native identity by blood quantum is combined with the highest rate of intermarriage of any group (75 percent), Native people seem to be on a course of irreversible absorption into the larger U.S. society.[56] Scholars such as Jaimes and Rose suggest that the federal government has an interest in the statistical extermination of indigenous people, thereby leading to an end to treaty and trust responsibilities.[57]

Because race is not an adequate indicator of culture, identity is something that should be assessed rather than assumed.[58] Various scales have been developed to assess indigenous people's cultural identity along a continuum from traditional, to integrated/bicultural, to assimilated. See, for example, the scales developed recently by Young, Lujan, and Dixon and Garrett and Pichette.[59] Such scales are often modeled on scales developed for other cultural groups such as Latinos and tend to have questions that focus on language, ethnic origin of friends and associates, music and food preferences, and place of birth.

Many measures of cultural identity are actually measures of acculturation (into the dominant society). Additionally, some measures, such as the one developed by Zimmerman, Ramirez-Valles, Washienko, Walter, and Dyer, have been developed to assess enculturation, the lifelong learning process of cultural awareness and understanding.[60] Both acculturation and enculturation scales tend to use linear continua. The utility of a linear model in representing such a complex concept has been challenged by scholars such as Oetting and Beauvais, who propose an orthogonal model of cultural identification in which attachment to one culture does not necessarily detract from attachment to another and multiple cultural identifications are not only possible but potentially healthy.[61] Likewise, Deyhle has found that linear and hierarchical models of biculturalism are limited and neglect the context of racism.[62] Theorists and researchers who use linear models often speak of cultural conflict and individuals being caught between two worlds, a circumstance that leads to a variety of social difficulties, but Deyhle believes that this perspective does not accurately depict the realities of Native youth. Rather than determining where someone fits on a continuum between two cultural identities or worlds, it may be more accurate to say that indigenous people live in one complex, conflictual world.

In the end, although it is clearly inappropriate to make assumptions about an individual's cultural identity based on appearance or blood quantum, most attempts to measure identity are of questionable adequacy and accuracy: "Indianness means different things to different people. And, of course, at the most elementary level, Indianness is something only experienced by people who are Indians. It is how Indians think about themselves and is internal, intangible, and metaphysical. From this perspective, studying Indianness is like trying to study the innermost mysteries of the human mind itself."[63] The conflict in the story "The Big Game" illustrates the difficulty inherent in measuring identity by any one standard.

Internalized Oppression/Colonization

Perhaps the harshest arbiters of Native identity are Native people themselves. Federal policies that treated Native people of mixed heritage differently than those without mixed heritage effectively attacked unity within Native communities, thereby turning indigenous people against each other.[64] Some Native people fight others fiercely to prevent them from claiming a Native identity. Sometimes Native people, as well as the federal government, find a financial incentive to prevent others from declaring themselves to be indigenous. In 1979, the Samish and Snohomish of Puget Sound were declared "legally extinct" by the federal government in part because other Native groups such as the Tulalips did not view them as genuine. Likewise, the Lumbees of North Carolina, one of the largest tribes in the 1990 census, had difficulty gaining social and federal acceptance as constituting legitimate indigenous communities because of intertribal disputes over timber resources. After a long fight they received only limited federal acknowledgment with the proviso that they receive no federal services.[65]

Internalized oppression, a by-product of colonization, has become common among indigenous people. We fight among ourselves and often accuse each other of not being "Indian enough" based on differences in politics, religion, or phenotype: "Mixed-heritage members may see traditionals as uncivilized and backwards. Traditionalists may believe that progressives are 'less Indian' because of cultural naivete and that multi-heritage people only claim tribal membership for land and annuity purposes."[66] Such fighting among ourselves only serves to divide communities. In some regions of the country it is common to see the bumper sticker "FBI: Full Blooded Indian." What message does this communicate to people of mixed heritage? Does this mean that they are somehow lesser human beings and cannot have strong cultural connections?

Skin color and phenotype lead to assumptions about identity, suspicion, and lack of acceptance.[67] A survey of indigenous helping professionals has found that one of the most prominent challenges of indigenous people in higher education is struggling with the stereotypes that others hold about them.[68] Sometimes these stereotypes are held by people of other cultural groups, but often they are held by other Native people who make assumptions about cultural identity based solely on physical appearance. These assumptions have led to painful experiences such as ostracism from other indigenous people and people having their identities contradicted and denied.

Some of the propensity toward exclusivity and denying the cultural identities of mixed-blood people comes from the exploitation experienced by Native people and communities for centuries. There is well-founded suspicion of people who claim a Native heritage but have no apparent connections to an indigenous community. In today's climate, in which New Age spirituality has become popular and so much cultural appropriation has happened, there is a fear of the ultimate cultural appropriation: the usurpation of Native cultural identity. When people with minimal Native heritage, no cultural knowledge, and no kinship ties attempt to assert an indigenous identity, it is often hotly contested among indigenous people, yet this does not appear to be much of an issue for others who are not indigenous.[69] It is fairly common for the nonnatives I encounter to have difficulty seeing any reason for concern when a person claims to be Native but has no cultural knowledge, community connections, or verifiable ancestry.

Suspicion about the identity of some Native people has been fueled by the recent growth of the indigenous population according to U.S. census counts. Some people believe that others are inappropriately self-identifying as indigenous because it may be "fashionable" at this time. Another possible explanation is that now it is safer for people of mixed heritage to publicly proclaim cultural pride in an indigenous identity. A renaissance in Native cultures has been paralleling dramatic population growth since the 1960s. Political revitalization, linguistic revival, membership growth, and cultural revitalization have all taken place in recent decades. The proliferation of indigenous organizations and activism has served as a catalyst for the resurgence of individual Native identity as reflected in the census and the renewal of tribal and urban community life.[70]

Although I stated earlier that there is no "correct" terminology for indigenous people, semantics is certainly an issue that evokes strong feelings. Many people express clear preferences for certain terms (e.g., *Native American* rather than *American Indian* or *First Nations people* rather than more commonly used terms). Indigenous people who attempt to dictate to other indigenous people what they should call themselves replicate the oppression that has been imposed on them. In recent years many Native nations have begun to return to their traditional names rather than use those imposed by external forces. While many people, myself included, view this as a positive step toward cultural revitalization and pride, it would be inappropriate to impose this requirement on others. As a child I was raised referring to myself as Sioux. As I grew older and the political climate changed, I took pride in calling myself Lakota. It is not unusual, however, for some to continue using the term *Sioux*. This is their right and reflects aspects of their identity. Although the names that indigenous groups were given by others often have a derogatory origin, we only make this worse when indigenous people who consider themselves decolonized mock others who continue to use such terms.

While we as indigenous people were busy guarding against cultural appropriation, we may have missed a much bigger threat to indigenous continuity. Indeed, there are some nonnatives who pose as Natives and some Natives who sell traditions and spirituality for a profit, but the self-appointed "identity police," those who divide communities and accuse others of not being "Indian" enough because they practice the wrong religion, have the wrong politics, use the wrong label for themselves, or do not have the right skin color, should also be an issue of concern. Some indigenous people ask, "Are you Indian, or are you Christian?" as if these are mutually exclusive categories. I have seen caring indigenous people driven to tears at their jobs at a Native community center when they were berated for having some white ancestry. People have been publicly humiliated because someone decided that their tribal affiliations were inappropriate. This harassment and badgering is conducted by indigenous people, against indigenous people. The roots for this type of behavior probably lie deep in the accusers' own insecurities about identity and racism learned as part of the colonization process.

Many indigenous traditions speak of people returning who have been alienated from their communities. I know of no indigenous people who are not well aware of the generations of Native people that grew up outside their traditions. Although there is no doubt of the existence of these people, there is often suspicion when an unknown individual seeks information on possible community connections. This is one of the factors that mobilizes the "identity police." While, indeed, there probably are some people pretending to have indigenous heritage along with those who really do, pretenders will ultimately get what they deserve without any intervention from the "identity police."

Through internalized oppression/colonization, we have become our own worst enemy. The hateful accusations that are hurled at some serve to hurt our communities. "The Big Game" illustrates this point. It is a story of the pain we inflict on each other as a result of internalized colonization. Indigenous identity is a complex and multifaceted topic. I have discussed some of these facets here along with my own reflections on internalized oppression/colonization. Although a variety of literature is cited from people currently writing in this area, the perspective that comes across is a reflection of my own beliefs, sense of self, and identity as a Lakota woman living in a particular time and place. While my views may differ from those of some indigenous people, others may find something in my words that resonates with their own perspectives.

Sometimes we are our own worst enemies. Our divisions should be reconcilable, but internalized colonization and oppression just lead to deeper divisions. Features of internalized oppression and colonization can be found in many oppressed communities in addition to the indigenous communities discussed here. Actions and reactions born of internalized oppression and colonization are themselves acts of colonization that mirror the oppressors' acts. Until we are able to put aside our own insecurities that lead us to accuse others, there will be no winners among indigenous people.

Endnotes

1 S. Hall, "The Work of Representation," in *Representation: Cultural Representations and Signifying Practices*, ed. S. Hall (London: Sage Publications, 1997), 13–74.

2 B. Sayyid and L. Zac, "Political Analysis in a World without Foundations," in *Research Strategies in the Social Sciences: A Guide to New Approaches*, ed. E. Scarbrough and E. Tanenbaum (Oxford: Oxford University Press, 1998), 249–67.

3 On race, class, education, region, and religion, see N.C. Peroff, "Indian Identity," *The Social Science Journal* 34, no. 4 (1997): 485–94. On gender, see R.L. Dukes and R.O. Martinez, "The Effects of Ethnic Identity, Ethnicity, and Gender on Adolescent Well-Being," *Journal of Youth and Adolescence* 26, no. 5 (1997): 503–16; and G.H. Grandbois and D. Schadt, "Indian Identification and Alienation in an Urban Community," *Psychological Reports* 74 (1994): 211–16.

4 S. Hall, "Introduction: Who Needs 'Identity'?" In *Questions of Cultural Identity*, ed. S. Hall and P. DuGay (London: Sage Publications, 1996), 1–17.

5 L. Rose, "Iyeska Win: Intermarriage and Ethnicity among the Lakota in the Nineteenth and Twentieth Centuries," M.A. thesis, Northern Arizona University, 1994.

6 Hall, "Introduction."

7 Hall, "Introduction."

8 Sayyid and Zac, "Political Analysis in a World without Foundations."

9 Hall, "Introduction"; Sayyid and Zac, "Political Analysis in a World without Foundations"; C. Taylor, "The Politics of Recognition," in *Multiculturalism: A Critical Reader*, ed. D.T. Goldberg (Oxford: Blackwell Publishers, 1994), 75–106.

10 J. Durham, *A Certain Lack of Coherence: Writings on Art and Cultural Politics* (London: Kala Press, 1993).

11 C. West, "The New Politics of Cultural Difference," in *Out There: Marginalization and Contemporary Cultures*, ed. R. Ferguson, M. Gever, T.T. Minh-ha, and C. West (Cambridge: MIT Press, 1990), 19–36.

12 Hall, "The Work of Representation."

13 Durham, *A Certain Lack of Coherence.*

14 G. Vizenor, *Fugitive Poses: Native American Indian Scenes of Absence and Presence* (Lincoln: University of Nebraska Press, 1998).

15 Durham, *A Certain Lack of Coherence.*

16 West, "The New Politics of Cultural Difference."

17 Taylor, "The Politics of Recognition," 75.

18 Vizenor, *Fugitive Poses.*

19 D.A. Mihesuah, "American Indian Identities: Issues of Individual Choices and Development," *American Indian Culture and Research Journal* 22, no. 2 (1998): 193–226.

20 Y.K. Young, P. Lujan, and L.D. Dixon, "I Can Walk Both Ways," *Human Communication Research* 25, no. 2 (1998): 252–75.
21 J. Nagel, *American Indian Ethnic Renewal: Red Power and the Resurgence of Identity and Culture* (New York: Oxford University Press, 1996), 21.
22 Hall, "Introduction"; Nagel, *American Indian Ethnic Renewal.*
23 Mihesuah, "American Indian Identities."
24 Rose, "Iyeska Win."
25 J. Clifford, *The Predicament of Culture: Twentieth Century Ethnography, Literature, and Art* (Cambridge MA: Harvard University Press, 1988).
26 Hall, "Introduction."
27 Peroff, "Indian Identity."
28 Dukes and Martinez, "The Effects of Ethnic Identity, Ethnicity, and Gender on Adolescent Well-Being"; Mihesuah, "American Indian Identities."
29 Nagel, *American Indian Ethnic Renewal.*
30 Mihesuah, "American Indian Identities."
31 D. Deyhle, "From Break Dancing to Heavy Metal," *Youth and Society* 30, no. 1 (1998): 3–26.
32 M.A. Zimmerman, J. Ramirez-Valles, K.M. Washienko, B. Walter, and S. Dyer, "The Development of a Measure of Enculturation for Native American Youth," *American Journal of Community Psychology* 24, no. 2 (1996): 295–310.
33 Dukes and Martinez, "The Effects of Ethnic Identity, Ethnicity, and Gender on Adolescent Well-Being."
34 Nagel, *American Indian Ethnic Renewal.*
35 Peroff, "Indian Identity."
36 Durham, *A Certain Lack of Coherence.*
37 Rose, "Iyeska Win."
38 Peroff, "Indian Identity."
39 T. Griffin-Pierce, "When I Am Lonely the Mountains Call Me: The Impact of Sacred Geography on Navajo Psychological Well-Being," *American Indian and Alaska Native Mental Health Research Journal* 7, no. 3 (1997): 1–10.
40 Peroff, "Indian Identity."
41 Nagel, *American Indian Ethnic Renewal.*
42 T.J. Csordas, "Ritual Healing and the Politics of Identity in Contemporary Navajo Society," *American Ethnologist* 26, no. 1 (1999): 3–23.
43 Nagel, *American Indian Ethnic Renewal.*
44 Durham, *A Certain Lack of Coherence.*
45 Nagel, *American Indian Ethnic Renewal.*
46 M.A. Jaimes, "Federal Indian Identification Policy: A Usurpation of Indigenous Sovereignty in North America," in *The State of Native America: Genocide, Colonization, and Resistance*, ed. M.A. Jaimes (Boston: South End Press, 1992).
47 V. Deloria Jr., ed., *American Indian Policy in the Twentieth Century* (Norman: University of Oklahoma Press, 1985).
48 Clifford, *The Predicament of Culture.*
49 Clifford, *The Predicament of Culture*, 289.
50 Peroff, "Indian Identity"; Taylor, "The Politics of Recognition"; Vizenor, *Fugitive Poses.*
51 Peroff, "Indian Identity."
52 Vizenor, *Fugitive Poses.*
53 J. Chaudhuri, "American Indian Policy: An Overview," in *American Indian Policy in the Twentieth Century*, ed. V. Deloria Jr. (Norman: University of Oklahoma Press, 1985), 15–33.
54 A. Bowd and P. Brady, "Note on Preferred Use of Ethnic Identity Labels by Aboriginal and Non-aboriginal Canadians," *Psychological Reports* 82 (1998): 1153–54; Vizenor, *Fugitive Poses.*
55 Peroff, "Indian Identity."
56 Peroff, "Indian Identity."
57 Jaimes, "Federal Indian Identification Policy"; Rose, "Iyeska Win."
58 M.T. Garrett and E.F. Pichette, "Red as an Apple: Native American Acculturation and Counseling with or without Reservation," *Journal of Counseling and Development* 78 (2000): 3–13; Zimmerman et al., "The Development of a Measure of Enculturation for Native American Youth."
59 Young, Lujan, and Dixon, "I Can Walk Both Ways"; Garrett and Pichette, "Red as an Apple."
60 Zimmerman et al., "The Development of a Measure of Enculturation for Native American Youth."
61 E.R. Oetting and F. Beauvais, "Orthogonal Cultural Identification Theory: The Cultural Identification of Minority Adolescents," *The International Journal of the Addictions* 25, nos. 5A–6A (1991): 655–85.
62 Deyhle, "From Break Dancing to Heavy Metal."

63 Peroff, "Indian Identity," 487.
64 Rose, "Iyeska Win."
65 Nagel, *American Indian Ethnic Renewal.*
66 Mihesuah, "American Indian Identities," 211.
67 Mihesuah, "American Indian Identities."
68 H.N. Weaver, "Balancing Culture and Professional Education: American Indians/Alaska Natives and the Helping Professions," *Journal of American Indian Education* 39, no. 3 (2000): 1–18.
69 Mihesuah, "American Indian Identities."
70 Nagel, *American Indian Ethnic Renewal.*

Suggestions for Critical Reflection

1. What groups/organizations/people have historically assumed the right to grant Indigenous identity to individuals and communities? Were the criteria they used justifiable?
2. What is the argument that supports the claim that "identity exists, not solely within an individual or category of individuals but through difference in relationship with others"?
3. Which form of oppression do you find more harmful: nonrecognition or misrecognition. Why?
4. How has colonization impacted determinations of identity for Indigenous people on Turtle Island?
5. Is identity something that can be measured? If so, what do you think is the best method of measuring identity (qualitative, quantitative, etc.)?

Additional Resources

For additional resources relating to this reading and its themes, visit **sites.broadviewpress.com/waysofbeing/3-3**

3.4
"Endlessly Creating Our Indigenous Selves"*

Leanne Betasamosake Simpson (Michi Saagiig Nishnaabeg)

ABOUT THE AUTHOR

Leanne Betasamosake Simpson (Michi Saagiig Nishnaabeg) is a renowned scholar, writer, and artist. She is the author of several books that engage with Indigenous thought and practices in Canada. Simpson is also known for her work with the 2012 Idle No More protests. Simpson completed a BSc in biology from the University of Guelph and a MSc in biology from Mount Allison University. She earned her PhD (1999) in Interdisciplinary Studies from the University of Manitoba. Simpson is currently a faculty member at the Dechinta Centre for Research and Learning in Yellowknife, Northwest Territories.

KEY TERMS

Gender, Stereotypes, Colonialism, Sexuality, Patriarchy, Internalized Beliefs, Bias, Power, Binary, Masculinity, Sexism, Allyship, Autonomy, Heteropatriarchy

For the past few years, when I talk about gender in Indigenous postsecondary classrooms, primarily classes on self-determination, resurgence, and governance, I lead the students through a simple exercise to begin. As a group, I ask them to list all the stereotypes they have been the target of or have heard about Indigenous women. There is a moment of pause after I outline the exercise, and I always make sure I look into the eyes of Indigenous women, because I know they are wondering if this is a safe thing for them to participate in, and they are wondering why I'm asking them to go to such a horribly painful place inside themselves. Often, I will start by writing the word *slut* on the flip chart or chalkboard and explain that for as long as I remember, going way back into my history as a girl of five or six, people have associated me and my body with this word. I explain that this term is used by colonialism to regulate and control my body and sexual behavior, and I explain that I have sovereignty over my body, my sexuality, and my relationships.[1] I explain that many women and 2SQ people have reclaimed this word as a mechanism for enacting their own self-determination, values, and ethics over their bodies. There are always nods, and eyes drop to the ground. The class adds to the

* From Leanne Betasamosake Simpson, *As We Have Always Done: Indigenous Freedom through Radical Resistance* (Minneapolis: University of Minnesota Press, 2017), 83–94.

list: dirty, squaw, bad mothers, lazy, promiscuous, irresponsible, addicts, criminals, prostitutes, easy, bad with money, bad wives, dumb, stupid, hysterical, angry, wild in bed, useless, drunks, worthless, without feeling, violent, weak, partiers, alcoholics. After the first three or four stereotypes are on the list, they come faster, and the energy starts to shift from shame and hurt to an expulsion of those same things. Heads are held up high, as we name and then cast off and cast out the internalized racism and patriarchy of the colonizer.

Then I ask the group to list all of their truths about Indigenous women: intelligent, strong, brave, courageous, sexy, committed, hardworking, good mothers, partners, wives, loving, caring, honest, brilliant, spectacular, empathetic, compassionate, beautiful, smart, kind, gentle, good lovers, organized. We do the same for Indigenous men and for the queer community. Groups come up with between thirty to fifty gendered stereotypes specific to each gender and gender/sexual orientation. They come up with beautiful lists of truths, and in essence all three lists are the same. In one class, at the land-based Dechinta Centre for Research and Learning, the women of the group came up with the list of racist stereotypes for Indigenous women.[2] As the instructor, I often have to start the process because it is too painful for young Indigenous women to even speak. With this group, when it came time to list the truths, they were silent, and then something really profound and transformative happened. The Dene men in the group made a beautiful list that left nearly everyone in the room in tears (smart, intelligent, beautiful, sexy, good mothers, good partners, strong, connected, spiritual, good hunters, good fishers, good providers, excellent sisters, aunties, and grandmothers, powerful). When we got to the part of the exercise where we listed the positive things about men, the women did the same, and then the group came together and generated a similar list for 2SQ people.

During our discussion of 2SQ people, we talk about sex, gender, sexual orientation, and relationship orientation. We talk about terminology and pronouns. We talk about transphobia and how all bodies are real bodies. We talk about how groups with the highest rates of suicide in our communities are 2SQ people and trans youth. We talk about how learning on the land can be a safe space, or it can be a nightmare for trans youth.

This particular time I did the exercise was special. It was moving for everyone involved. As the men listed off positive attribute after positive attribute, the women, myself included, were emotional because we have been told over and over again, through pop culture, the mainstream media, our experiences with the church and Indian Affairs, by teachers and parents that we are all of the things on the negative list. This was perhaps the first time in our lives we had been told directly that we are not any of those things, and to have it come from our Dene male colleagues was extremely meaningful. It felt like they had our backs.

This is one of the most powerful learning experiences that I've had in a classroom in my teaching career. The exercise is simple enough in itself. The act of naming stereotypes is a commanding space because it brings my attention to the very personalized violence of colonialism on my internal thoughts and beliefs about myself. When I write the word *slut* on the chart, I am thinking and feeling every time that word has been used to push me down, control me, and limit my potential. When I write *dumb* on the chart, I can't help but to reflect on how that internalized belief is so implanted in me by settler colonialism that I have to remind myself every time I speak or sit down to write or walk into the classroom that I'm not actually dumb. Each time I participate in this exercise, it reveals to me the degree to which I have unconsciously internalized these lies, and that we as communities of people have unconsciously internalized these lies, and it provides a chance to speak back.

The next layer is a collective realization that we all to varying degrees carry around these unconscious colonial beliefs about ourselves, despite the fact that some of us have obtained measures of success in Indigenous worlds, settler colonial society, or both. This begins to shift the power dynamics between the students and me and how the class sees me as an Indigenous women instructor. I am no longer "better" than them because I have a PhD or because of these false successes. I have not been removed from the violences of settler colonial life. I carry the same damage as they do, and I am not ashamed of that damage, because the shame does not rest within Indigenous peoples but with settler colonial Canada.

As the group moves through the exercise, the energy of the class moves from shame and humiliation, to celebration and joy, to happiness. We talk about how *good it feels* to recognize when our own people recognize our positive attributes and see us through Dene or Nishnaabeg eyes rather than through the eyes of settler colonialism. We talk about how good that feels in ourselves, and we pause and feel it. We link our personal feelings and experiences with the other subjects of the course—the Indian Act, residential schools, the public education system, self-government policy, the criminalization of Indigeneity, environmental destruction, gender violence—and students begin to realize that the negative beliefs they carry within themselves were planted in them and the generations that came before them for a very specific reason: dispossession of their lands. We talk about how shame prevents us from connecting to our loved ones, learning our languages, and being on the land. We are honest about the stereotypes of other genders and sexual orientations that we carry and amplify in our own lives.

People bring up stories of grandmothers chopping wood, hunting, trapping, and fishing, and of grandfathers cooking, sewing, and doing childcare. We talk about binaries and fluidity around gender and how in Indigenous contexts it is often important that we all have a baseline of skill and knowledge about how to live. Oftentimes someone will bring up a relative who didn't fit so easily into the colonial gender binary, and we talk about how the community, the church, and the state responded and responds to this. We talk about how we gender the land in English and if this is the same in their languages.

We talk about Indigenous men and how all genders have experienced and do experience gender violence, although it affects individuals in asymmetric ways because of the hierarchy it instills. We talk about how Indigenous peoples are in a difficult position: simultaneously being targeted by gender violence and therefore carrying trauma, benefiting to varying degrees from hierarchy, and oftentimes knowingly or unknowingly perpetuating gender discrimination, violence, and anti-queerness. We talk about how difficult it can be to hear that an action or a phrase is hurting Indigenous women or 2SQ people. We talk more about shame.

Inevitably someone will ask if some of the stereotypes are true, often referring to the epidemic of gender violence in our communities, and if the students themselves don't bring that up, I do, because I know someone is thinking about that. We talk about the nature of stereotypes. We talk about how we are not the sum of the list of stereotypes. We talk about how stereotypes are not just "backwards thinking" but a system of social control. We talk about consent, accountability, self-determination, responsibility. We acknowledge how all genders, including Indigenous men, have been the target for sexualized and gender violence. We talk about how that is not an excuse for perpetuating it. We account for things. I ask them to pick one of the stereotypes from the negative list. I use my own nation as an example and draw a rough trajectory that cuts through four centuries of heteropatriarchy as a tool of dispossession:

- Nishnaabeg people have self-determination over their bodies and sexuality. Sex is not shameful within Nishnaabewin. All genders and ages hold political power and influence. There is a diversity of genders, sexual orientations, and relationship orientations and respect for body sovereignty.[3]
- Colonizers want land, but Indigenous bodies forming nations are in the way because they have a strong attachment to land and because they replicate Indigeneity. All Indigenous genders as political orders also replicate Indigenous nationhood, but the colonizers are looking through the eyes of heteropatriarchy, so they see Indigenous women's and girl's

bodies as the bodies that reproduce nations, and they see 2SQ bodies as the biggest threat to their assimilation and dispossession project.[4]

- Colonizers notice that women, children, and 2SQ people hold power and influence in Indigenous governance. They notice this is not the same in European nations. Hierarchy is key to their system of control.[5]
- During times of violent conflict, sexual and gender-based violence is widely recognized as a tactic of both war and genocide because it is frequently used as "a military tactic to harm, humiliate and shame" and because violence and war weaken systems of "protection, security and justice."[6] Sexual violence is an effective colonial tool in genocide and dispossession because the damage it causes to families is so overwhelming that it makes it very difficult to have the emotional capital to continue to resist.
- Indigenous nations are attacked physically and symbolically through things like the Indian Act, policy, colonial laws, and fraudulent and unfair treaty negotiations at the same time as they are coping with violence, land loss, loss of an economic base, and disease.
- Indigenous nations lose political power and can no longer hold settlers accountable in their lands. There are fewer Indigenous bodies on Indigenous lands. We are confined to reserves. We are "governed" by the heteropatriarchy and settler colonialism of the Indian Act. Our children are in residential or day schools. We are rewarded with recognition when we assimilate.
- The gender binary is introduced and reinforced through residential schools, the church, and the Indian Act. 2SQ people are disappeared. Indigenous women are domesticated into the role of Victorian housewives. Native men are domesticated into the wage economy and taught their only power is to ally with white men in the oppression of Indigenous women through church, school, law, and policy.[7]
- Christian beliefs about heterosexual, monogamous, churched relationships and sexuality are infused into the community through missions and residential schools and reinforced by Indian agents.[8]
- Propagation of negative stereotypes of Indigenous women, men, and 2SQ people is widespread in popular culture, as evidenced in the first newspaper reporting on Indigenous peoples in Canada.[9]
- Canadian society through the media, books, and oral culture continues to justify the strangulation of Indigenous women's body sovereignty and to justify the violence against Indigenous women, which has led to the epidemic of murdered and missing Indigenous women and girls.[10]
- Indigenous women are blamed by the state for causing the violence by making poor lifestyle choices, and Indigenous men are named as the perpetrators of this violence.[11]

- Canadian citizens born into heteropatriarchy and normalized gender and sexualized violence against Indigenous peoples replicate this violence in their personal lives with structural support of the state's legal, education, and political systems.
- Disconnected from land and our knowledge systems, and the targets of four centuries of state violence, we replicate the violence we've experienced in our communities.
- We as a class can list in less than thirty minutes nearly a hundred stereotypes of Indigenous peoples, and many of us hold particular ones inside us that make us feel not good enough.

At first, they are surprised the Nishnaabeg prof from the south with degrees and the privilege credentials gives me still sometimes believes the worst about myself because colonialism has conditioned me to do so. This reframing, though, illuminates the deliberate nature of this on the part of the colonizer to get land, and that when we repeat it and live it, we are helping the colonizers.[12] This critical reframing, drawing on issues already discussed in class, then offers students a new orientation to themselves and their communities, one in which the interrogation of colonialism, the historical context, and the resistance of Indigenous peoples figure prominently. It is the approach Mohawk scholar Audra Simpson takes in her fantastic book *Mohawk Interruptus*: that there are signposts in our nations, communities, and bodies of colonialism's ongoing existence and simultaneous failure. She writes,

> Colonialism survives in a settler form. In this form, it fails at what it is supposed to do: eliminate Indigenous people; take all their land; absorb them into a white, property-owning body politic. Kahnawa:ke's *debates over membership* index colonialism's life as well its failure and their own life through their grip on this failure.[13]

This is a subtle and elegant shift in our analysis of Indigenous politics because it provides the proper and truthful context within which our analysis can take place. This approach also nests and confounds polarity: colonialism is violent and evil, and Indigenous peoples agree on that, and we have a range of *responses* to that horrific and ongoing violence that is ultimately rooted in a fog of love, anger, fear, shame, pride, and humiliation. For Simpson, the issue of membership is not about whether we should kick white people off the reserve; the fundamental question her people are grappling with is how do we continue to exist as *Kanien'kehá:ka* people in the face of settler colonialism elimination?

Simpson emphasizes "debates over membership" because this could be any issue in Indigenous political life. You can replace that phrase with "debates over land protection," "debates over governance," "debates over gender violence" because her intervention is that we need to shift our lens of analysis from one that plays into the limits of Western thought to one that is holy and diversely Indigenous at its core, both in experience and in intellectual thought, but that brings with it the most robust critical analysis of our times.

Following Simpson's intervention on framing, I want to use the pain and anger that heteropatriarchy strikes to reject the replication of settler colonial gender violence within our bodies, communities, and nations. We need all genders to do this, and we all need to think critically about how we replicate this in our communities and in our daily lives. Placing the interrogation of heteropatriarchy at the center of our nation-building movements ensures that our nation building counters the impact the settler colonial political economy has on Indigenous bodies, intimacies, sexualities, and gender. It counters the continual violent attack on bodies, intimacies, sexualities, and gender as a dispossessing force. We have a choice. We can choose to uphold white, heterosexual, masculine control over Indigenous bodies, or we can choose to collectively engage in the dismantling of heteropatriarchy as a nation-building project. Nation building in Indigenous contexts is a collective effort, and in critically undoing the gender hierarchy, what happens to Indigenous women, children, and 2SQ bodies is the measure of our success as nations.

Stereotypes are not attitudes that can be changed by using a different terminology. They are windows into the pervasive logics of white supremacy and heteropatriarchy and how they operate through time and space in Canada on my body and mind as an Indigenous woman. These terms are part of a much more omnipresent and ubiquitous system of control that has stolen not only my land from me but also my body and the way I think about my body. I am not murdered, and I am not missing, but parts of me have been disappeared, and I remain a target because I was born a Native women, and I live as kwe.

Students at Dechinta have already heard me talk about consent and individual self-determination within the context of Indigenous politics, and so we then talk about creating these alternative systems of accountability. I use the example of the Community Holistic Circle Healing project in Hollow Water First Nation, an Nishnaabeg community on the east side of Lake Winnipeg, in Manitoba. We talk about how this group found that 80 percent of their residents had experience with sexual abuse, and how they used Nishnaabeg processes of accountability to create a community-based alternative to the Canadian criminal justice systems for cases of sexual violence.[14] We talk about how this system requires the admission of guilt on the part of the perpetrator to proceed. There is a truth telling as the first step. The circle of healing involves support for all of the individuals and families involved. It involves the perpetrator witnessing the full impacts of his actions. It involves the larger community witnessing the full impacts of sexualized violence and an accounting for how we contribute to the epidemic levels of violence in our communities. It involves ceremony and Nishnaabeg practices of regeneration. It involves regenerating relationships.

Students often share their frustrations with the criminal justice system and with our communities in terms of how we handle these issues. They often have a wealth of ideas for visioning systems of accountability in their own lives.

Thinking back to the bush classroom at Dechinta and Denendeh, I learned something else important that day. I learned that I *want*, but don't necessarily need, Indigenous men to have my back. I don't want to be continually seeking out the solidarity, the recognition of white women because I want the solidarity of straight cisgendered Indigenous men. I want them to stop exploiting, abusing, and degrading women and children. I want them to stop engaging in systemic, structural and casual sexism and patriarchy. I want them to hold each other accountable when there are no women around, and casual and not-so-casual sexism in the form of the objectification, ongoing criticism, and other forms of white patriarchy enter their social, personal, and professional lives. I want them to hold each other accountable when casual and not-so-casual homophobia, transphobia, heterosexism and all forms of anti-queerness appear. I want them to support and assist and to be critically engaged in, but not lead, the dismantling of heteropatriarchy as the crucial nation-building exercise of our time. I want them to see that they have been targeted by white men working strategically and persistently to make allies out of Indigenous men, with clear rewards for those who come into white masculinity imbued with heteropatriarchy and violence, in order to infiltrate our communities and nations with heteropatriarchy and then to replicate it through the generations, with the purpose of destroying our nations and gaining easy access to our land.

White supremacy, rape culture (although Sarah Hunt recently reminded me that when rape happens to us, it is rarely named as "rape"), and the attack on gender, sexual identity, agency, and consent are very powerful tools of colonialism, settler colonialism, and capitalism primarily because they work very efficiently to remove Indigenous peoples from our territories and to prevent reclamation of those territories through mobilization.

These forces have the intergenerational staying power to destroy generations of families, as they work to prevent us from intimately connecting to each other. They work to prevent mobilization because communities coping with epidemics of gender violence don't have the physical or emotional capital to organize. They destroy the base of our nations and our political systems because they destroy our relationships to the land and to each other by fostering epidemic levels of anxiety, hopelessness, apathy, distrust, and suicide. They work to destroy the fabric of Indigenous nationhoods by attempting to destroy our relationality by making it difficult to form sustainable, strong relationships with each other.

Dismantling heteropatriarchy and generating modes of scholarship, organizing, mobilizing, and living that no longer replicate it must be a core project of radical resurgence. Centering the voices of children, women, and 2SQ people within the Radical Resurgence Project is a mechanism through which to counter the gendered nature of heteropatriarchy and build systems of consent, accountability, and agency so that all Indigenous political orders are valued, cherished, and celebrated as a crucial part of our communities and nations, and fully engaged in the regeneration of alternative Indigenous worlds. Indigenous freedom means that my sovereignty over my body, mind, spirit, and land is affirmed and respected in all of my relationships.

Endnotes

1 I often use Nishnaabe feminist Dory Nason's "We Hold Our Hands Up" as a reading to follow up this discussion; see "We Hold Our Hands Up: On Indigenous Women's Love and Resistance," *Decolonization: Indigeneity, Education and Society* (blog), February 12, 2013, https://decolonization.wordpress.com/2013/02/12/we-hold-our hands-up-on-indigenous-womens-love-and-resistance/.

2 I have used this exercise a number of times at Dechinta; this particular event took place in the fall of 2014.

3 This is explained fully in the next chapter of [*As We Have Always Done*].

4 Audra Simpson, *Mohawk Interruptus: Political Life across the Borders of Settler States* (Durham, N.C.: Duke University Press, 2014), 156; Jaskiran K. Dhillon, "Indigenous Girls and the Violence of Settler Colonial Policing," *Decolonization: Indigeneity, Education and Society* 4, no. 2 (2015): 1–31.

5 Shari M. Huhdorf and Cheryl Suzack, "Indigenous Feminism Theorizing the Issues," in *Indigenous Women and Feminism: Politics, Activism, Culture*, ed. Cheryl Suzack, Shari M. Huhndorf, Jeanne Perreault, and Jean Barman (Vancouver: UBC Press), 21–29.

6 "Sexual and Gender Based Violence in Crisis Situations," United Nations Development Programme, http://www.undp.org/content/undp/en/home/ourwork/crisispreventionandrecovery/focus_areas/gender_equality_andwomensempowerment/sexual-violence-in-conflict.html.

7 This is well documented by several feminist historians studying Indigenous women and coloniality working in different time spans and regions in Canada. In my own community, the work of Robin Jarvis Brownlie and Joan Sangster does this, as evidenced in [chapter 7 of *As We Have Always Done*].

8 Robin Jarvis Brownlie's archival work on the Indian Act and the regulation of Indigenous women's sexuality is critically important here; see Robin Jarvis Brownlie, "Intimate Surveillance: Indian Affairs, Colonization, and the Regulation of Aboriginal Women's Sexuality," in *Contact Zones: Aboriginal and Settler Women in Canada's Colonial Past*, ed. Katie Pickles and Myra Rutherdale (Vancouver: UBC Press, 2005), 160–78; as is Karen Stote's recent work on sterilization and genocide in Indigenous women in Canada; see Karen Stote, *An Act of Genocide: Colonialism and the Sterilization of Aboriginal Women* (Halifax: Fernwood, 2015); Sarah Carter, *The Importance of Being Monogamous: Marriage and Nation Building in Western Canada to 1915* (Edmonton: University of Alberta Press, 2008); and Lesley Erickson, *Westward Bound: Sex, Violence, the Law and the Making of a Settler Society* (Vancouver: UBC Press, 2011).

9 For a particularly detailed treatment of this, see Sarah Carter, *Capturing Women: The Manipulation of Cultural Imagery in Canada's Prairie West* (Kingston, ON: McGill-Queen's, 1997).

10 There are literally countless Indigenous women and organizations that I could cite here, but I will point readers in the direction of Bev Jacob and the Amnesty International report she wrote in 2004 called *Stolen Sisters: Discrimination and Violence against Native Women in Canada* (Ottawa: Amnesty International Canada, 2004); and the 2009 report *No More Stolen Sisters: The Need for a Comprehensive Response to Discrimination and Violence against Women in Canada* (Ottawa: Amnesty International Canada, 2009).

11 Gloria Galloway, "70 Per Cent of Murdered Aboriginal Women Killed by Indigenous Men: RCMP," *The Globe and Mail*, April 9, 2015, https://www.theglobeandmail.com/news/politics/70-per-cent-of-murdered-aboriginal-women-killed-by-indigenous-men-rcmp-confirms/article23868927/.

12 The evidence that sexualized and gender violence was a deliberate tool of genocide, assimilation, and settler colonialism is overwhelming. However, it in no way matters that it was deliberate or whether this occurred consciously and strategically or unconsciously. It in no way matters, because it is sheer violence, and within Indigenous legal systems, the magnitude of the damage caused to our nations can in no way be mitigated by a defense of unintention or the context of "not knowing."

13 A. Simpson, *Mohawk Interruptus*, 7–8.

14 I worked with Hollow Water First Nation in the late 1990s and had the opportunity to participate in and observe the Community Holistic Circle Healing project in action. See Berma Bushie, "Community Holistic Circle Healing," August 7, 1999, International Institute for Restorative Practices, http://www.iirp.edu/article_detail.php?article_id=NDco.

Suggestions for Critical Reflection

1. Simpson opens her essay by describing the exercise of listing the stereotypes that participants have encountered in their lives. How are these stereotypes connected with colonialism?
2. If you were part of the class, would you try the naming stereotypes exercise in terms of identities you share? Why or why not?
3. Why is allyship not necessarily needed to achieve accountability regarding colonialism and the control of Indigenous bodies via stereotypes?
4. How does nation-building address the impacts of colonialism?
5. How are internal debates over identity and membership in Indigenous groups detrimental to nation-building?

Additional Resources

For additional resources relating to this reading and its themes, visit sites.broadviewpress.com/waysofbeing/3-4

3.5
"Where Does Agency Come From? Exploring Indigenous Models of Mind"

Kurtis Boyer (Métis)

ABOUT THE AUTHOR

Kurtis Boyer is a citizen of the Métis Nation–Saskatchewan and a political scientist working in the areas of Indigenous governance and political psychology. Originally from Southern Saskatchewan, Boyer earned a BA (2007) with a minor in Indigenous Studies from the University of Saskatchewan. He completed an MA (2011) in Political Science from the University of Northern British Columbia and his PhD (2018) in Political Science from the University of Lund in Sweden. Boyer has worked extensively on issues related to Indigenous politics, self-governance, and law—with a focus on topics such as Inuit self-determination via living resource management, Métis governance, and drivers for collaborative economic development between municipal and band administrations. He has professional experience working with Indigenous organizations and governments, including the Métis Nation–Saskatchewan, where he has worked as an advisor on governance and constitutional reform. In 2021 Kurtis was appointed a member of the UNESCO Inclusive Policy Lab.

KEY TERMS

Identity, Experience, Reason, Cognition, Self, Rationality, Agency, Autonomy, Integration, Neuroscience

Introduction

What is it that makes us persons? Defining what it is to be human has, for much of Western thought, depended on a story we have consistently told ourselves. At its core, this is a story of separation. We have separated "man" from nature, man from woman, civilized from uncivilized and so on. However, at the core of all of these claims is a more foundational claim that Western philosophers have, for a very long time, advanced: that the knowing mind comes from a consciousness that is anatomically separated from the "outside" world. Yet this is not the only story that explains what makes us persons. Other stories exist, which speak to an existence characterized by connection, co-determination, and communion with all our relations. Interestingly, and as described in this chapter, the more Western science learns about the brain and the nature of human experience, the more this alternative story—one reflected in the teachings of Indigenous thought—is being supported.

What Are We?

To be human was to have reason. René Descartes' declaration, "Je pense, donc je suis," ("I think, therefore I am") resulted from a project that separated that which determines our thoughts from that which determines the outside material world. In this separation, our thinking mind became able to know the material or non-rational, from a position of separation. Because of this idea, we could come to know ourselves. This idea of a cognition that is separate from the laws of the natural/instinctual world is a prerequisite for what has become the conventional way of defining human autonomy as we know it today—as "the capacity to be one's own person, to live one's life according to reasons and motives that are taken as one's own and not the product of manipulative or distorting external forces."[1] In Europe, and with Renaissance humanism, the source of virtue and moral development, and consequently thoughts about how power should be legitimately distributed, became situated not through divine transmissions via the soul (and by extension the divine right of kings), but by the autonomy of the individual and the freedom to express and develop from it. This internalist ontological turn has been entrenched in the early development of the concept of free will, which had fundamental status in much of the early Western political and moral philosophy.[2]

Much of the liberal tradition, and perhaps political theory more generally, is built on this assumption that the mind exists anatomically separate from the outside world. Because of this, our thoughts and actions are not predetermined but are transposed unto the world by an autonomous will. Persons, John Locke informs us, are in "a State of perfect Freedom to order their Actions ... as they think fit ... without asking leave, or depending on the Will of any other Man."[3] This belief in a basic autonomy is vital for political theory as it precedes any discussion of what sort of political order best represents that freedom, or under what conditions is a restriction of that freedom justified. Because it is assumed we exist *a priori* in a state of freedom, a need to justify restrictions to liberty is then created. The onus is not on individuals to justify their ability to be free to act in ways that represent their interests, but rather the onus is on those wishing to restrict our freedom to establish justifiable grounds for doing so.[4] John Stuart Mill himself argued that "the burden of proof is supposed to be with those who are against liberty; who contend for any restriction or prohibition.... The a priori assumption is in favor of freedom...."[5] Mill's original assertion that the onus is on those who seek to restrict our (naturally occurring) freedom has predominated liberal theory up to this day.[6]

It is clear that what we believe about human agency has huge implications for how we order society. In describing what sort of qualities this lived experience entails, Ward notes, "persons can build upon their experiences, forming an experience unique in shape and pattern, contributing distinctive personal actions to the world which manifest their nature and what they have made of it by their relatively free decisions."[7] It is these sets of qualities that denote personhood. Being human means being the source of one's agency and personal development. To some extent the definition of the human demands that there are instances of a negative case. In that sense, knowing what we are—a self and a thinking mind—depends in part on maintaining the story that nonhumans, animals for example, do not have the same capacity to know what they know, to know what their motivations are, to be able to relate to them from a place of clarity. Within "this cultural caricature, to be human is to be wholly rational, and to view the world via emotions is a fault, a frailty, that requires weeding out."[8] This need for a negative case between the rational and the irrational laid the ground for a cultural heritage that includes a double dualism—where there is a separation between reason and things like emotion (or instinct), and (by implication) between humans who have reason and those who are placed in a social category that do not. Western philosophers justified colonial endeavours by the way they conceptualized the origins of the mind. Yet, the lived experience of slaves, Indigenous Peoples, women, animals and others placed in the social category of being sub/nonhuman, had an essence that in being close to, or within nature, did not preclude our relatability towards it. On the contrary, when the 'civilized person' encountered such a creature, this meant inferring a lived experience that was in some way relatable, but only to the extent it represented a degraded/deprived form of their own experience.

Today we are seeing more and more evidence that this model of mind does not reflect reality. From the denial of climate change to the rise of social extremism, there has been a growing awareness of the need to account for the role of "non-rational" forces in molding behavior. Advances from within cognitive neuroscience have begun to reveal the extent to which our thoughts are formed by unconscious and embodied reactions to the environment. While this idea that a person's actions are relationally constituted may be new to Western science, this notion has long been reflected in the relational metaphysics, ethical systems, and cultural protocols that still pervade many Indigenous cultures today.

The medicine wheel is used by many nations on Turtle Island for a variety of different teachings. The wheel speaks to seemingly four separate qualities that make up a person: spiritual, mental, emotional, and the physical. However, these "separate" qualities or parts of the body do not exist independently of each other. They are in consistent interaction and co-determination. Relaying the views of Nêhiyaw Elder Louis Sunchild, Kathy Walker states that "internally, one domain of the self (e.g., cognitive) not only has an effect or resonance in another domain (e.g., physical)—it 'exists' in that other domain as well and a similar extrinsic connection exists among all living entities with the capacity for resonance."[9] So, our experience as persons does not come from a little person within our heads, separate from other parts of our body, or the rest of the world. For generations and generations, our experience, Indigenous thought has reminded us, comes from the integration of our "parts." It was only recently that Western science came to begin to understand just how our experience is relationally determined. For example, in 1954, EEG studies began showing that our conscious experience unfolds due to an integrated process. These studies found that the parts of our brain that were active when we performed certain bodily motions also became active when we simply saw another doing the same action.[10] So not only are we, our experiences, relationally constituted through the integration of the physical to mental and so on, but our internal faculties are expressed through their integration with the "outside" world. In fact, this concept of the human self exists not through its apparent distinction from the outside world, but through its integration with it. "We are part of the whole. We are the whole."[11]

Further findings from neuroscience are supporting the idea that "we are the whole," or that our experience is dependent on how our bodies are integrated with those "outside" of our bodies, in the environment. For example, special kinds of vision-motor neurons called "mirror neurons" are now believed to be activated both when we perform specific goal-directed hand (and mouth) movements ourselves, and when we observe or hear about the same actions.[12] Since mirror neurons respond to both conditions, it has been argued that the mirror system functions as a kind of action representation, since it links "action" and "action-perception." When it comes to being emotionally "moved" by another, the "innateness" of this process is corroborated through a sub-field of neuroscience that links neural processes to social behavior.[13] The non-conscious, automatic process of "mirroring" is what many have claimed as providing a theory of the brain's ability to manifest representations of sensations experienced by other people.[14] Iacoboni explains the theory as follows:

> Mirror neuron areas help us understand the emotions of other people by some form of inner imitation. According to this mirror neuron hypothesis of empathy, our mirror neurons fire when we see others expressing their emotions, as if we were making those facial expressions ourselves. By means of this firing, the neurons also send signals to emotional brain centers in the limbic system to make us feel what other people feel.[15]

For a long time, our ability to empathize—something often presumed to distinguish us from animals—was thought as something achieved by our minds by imaginatively "putting ourselves in the shoes" of another. Because there would have to be someone or something that decides to engage in this process of perspective taking, this idea of empathy recreates the notion that there is a little person, or source of consciousness, that is isolated and separate from all our relations. Nêhiyaw Tâpisinowin or Plains Cree worldview relays the understanding that "... there is no clear separation between the realities of self, society, environment, or the cosmos."[16] When modern studies show that another's physical pain is relatable because our bodies automatically reconstitute, in a non-inferential manner, the psycho-physiological sensations of others,[17] we begin to see just how much we as persons have experiences not because we are separated, but because we are connected.

Conclusion

Any attempt to qualify "what humans are" has always been pursued through a kind of story about what the non/subhuman world lacks. What we have and what they don't is what separates us from the natural and nonhuman world. This story persists: that there is something fundamentally different about how humans experience the world—and in particular the depths of, as well as what drives the generation of, the content of our conscious experience. Being human means being a "person"—to have a conscious experience that is not pre-determined (for example by our mammalian instincts), but instead (as the story goes) generating thoughts from a thinking mind that is separate from and not determined by our physical, emotional, and spiritual existence in the world. Liberal social orders seemingly depend on this story that a person, and the source of their agency, exist in separation. It is becoming increasingly clear, however, that our traditional views of the person and personal autonomy is ill-fitted for integrating a scientific understanding of human nature. Moreover, and as we have discussed, these scientific revelations resonate less with what Liberal theorists like Mill thought of human nature, than they do with non-Western Indigenous views of human autonomy.

Endnotes

1 See John Christman, "Autonomy in Moral and Political Philosophy."
2 See Immanuel Kant, *Groundwork for the Metaphysic of Morals* (1785), as well as J.S. Mill, *On Liberty* (1859).
3 John Locke, *Two Treatises of Government* (1689).
4 See G.F. Gaus, *Justificatory Liberalism*, 162–66.
5 *Collected Works of John Stuart Mill*, vol. 21, 262.
6 See S.I. Benn, *A Theory of Freedom*, P. Pettit, *A Theory of Freedom*, and J. Rawls, *A Theory of Justice*.
7 Keith Ward, "Persons, Kinds and Capacities," 83.
8 E. Aaltola, "Politico-Moral Apathy and Omnivore's Akrasia."
9 Walter Lightning, "Compassionate Mind."
10 See H. Gastaut, "On the significance of 'wicket rhythmus,'" and H. Gastaut and J. Bert, "EEG changes during cinematographic presentation."
11 Paiute Medicine Man, as quoted in C. Ahenakew, "Sacred Pain in Indigenous Metaphysics."
12 See V. Gallese, "Embodied simulation," V. Gallese and A. Goldman, "Mirror Neurons," and G. Rizzolatti et al., "From mirror neurons to imitation."
13 See J. Decety and G.J. Norman, "Empathy: A Social Neuroscience Perspective," and P.L. Jackson et al., "How do we perceive the pain of others?"
14 See M. Iacoboni, "Imitation, Empathy, and Mirror Neurons," and M. Iacoboni, *Mirroring People*.
15 M. Iacoboni, *Mirroring People*, 199.
16 Katherine Walker, "Okâwîmâwaskiy: Regenerating a Wholistic Ethics," 108.
17 D.A. Effron et al., "Embodied temporal perception of emotion."

References

Aaltola, E. "Politico-Moral Apathy and Omnivore's Akrasia: Views from the Rationalist Tradition." *Politics and Animals* 1, no. 1 (2015): 35–49.

Ahenakew, C. "Sacred Pain in Indigenous Metaphysics: Dancing towards Cosmological Reconciliations." *Canadian Journal of Native Education* 32, no. 2 (2022): 176–88.

Benn, S.I. *A Theory of Freedom*. Cambridge: Cambridge University Press, 1988.

Christman, J. "Autonomy in Moral and Political Philosophy." In *The Stanford Encyclopedia of Philosophy*, edited by E.N. Zalta. Stanford, CA: Metaphysics Research Lab, Stanford University, 2018.

Decety, J., and G.J. Norman. "Empathy: A Social Neuroscience Perspective." In *International Encyclopedia of the Social & Behavioral Sciences*, ed. J.D. Wright, 541–48. Amsterdam: Elsevier, 2015.

Effron, D.A., P.M. Niedenthal, S. Gil, and S. Droit-Volet. "Embodied Temporal Perception of Emotion." *Emotion* 6, no. 1 (2006): 1–9.

Gallese, V. "Embodied Simulation: From Neurons to Phenomenal Experience." *Phenomenology and the Cognitive Sciences* 4, no. 1 (2005): 23–48.

Gallese, V., and A. Goldman. "Mirror Neurons and the Simulation Theory of Mind-Reading." *Trends in Cognitive Sciences* 2, no. 12 (1998): 493–501.

Gastaut, H. "On the Significance of 'wicket rhythmus' in Psychosomatic Medicine." *Electroencephalography and Clinical Neurophysiology* 6 (1954): 687.

Gastaut, H., and J. Bert. "EEG Changes during Cinematographic Presentation (Moving Picture Activation of the EEG)." *Electroencephalography and Clinical Neurophysiology* 6 (1954): 433–44.

Gaus, G.F. *Justificatory Liberalism*. Oxford: Oxford University Press, 1996.

Iacoboni, M. "Imitation, Empathy, and Mirror Neurons." *Annual Review of Psychology* 60, no. 1 (2009): 653–70.

Iacoboni, M. *Mirroring People: The New Science of How We Connect with Others*. New York: Farrar, Straus and Giroux, 2009.

Jackson, P.L., A.N. Meltzoff, and J. Decety. "How Do We Perceive the Pain of Others? A Window into the Neural Processes Involved in Empathy." *NeuroImage* 24, no. 3 (2005): 771–79.

Kant, I. *Groundwork for the Metaphysic of Morals*, 1785.

Kant, I. "Lectures on Pedagogy." In *Anthropology, History, and Education*, edited by Günter Zöller and Robert B. Louden. Cambridge: Cambridge University Press, 2007.

Lightning, Walter. "Compassionate Mind: Implications of a Text Written by Elder Louis Sunchild." *Canadian Journal of Native Education* 19, no. 2 (1992): 206–19.

Locke, J. *A Letter Concerning Toleration*, 1689.

Locke, J. *Two Treatises of Government*, 1689.

Mill, J.S. *On Liberty*. London: Longman, Roberts & Green, 1859.

Mill, J.S. *Collected Works of John Stuart Mill*. Edited by J.M. Robson. Vol. 21. Toronto: University of Toronto Press, 1963.

Pettit, P. *A Theory of Freedom: From the Psychology to the Politics of Agency*. London: John Wiley and Sons, 2013.

Rawls, J. *A Theory of Justice*. Cambridge: Harvard University Press, 2009.

Rizzolatti, G., L. Fadiga, L. Fogassi, and V. Gallese. "From Mirror Neurons to Imitation: Facts and Speculations." In *The Imitative Mind: Development, Evolution, and Brain Bases*, edited by A.N. Meltzoff and W. Prinz, 247–66. Cambridge: Cambridge University Press, 2002.

Ward, Keith. "Persons, Kinds and Capacities." In *Rights and Wrongs in Medicine: King's College Studies 1985–86*, edited by Peter Byrne. Oxford: Oxford University Press, 1986.

Walker, Katherine. "Okâwîmâwaskiy: Regenerating a Wholistic Ethics." PhD diss., University of British Columbia, 2021. https://open.library.ubc.ca/soa/cIRcle/collections/ubctheses/24/items/1.0398723.

Suggestions for Critical Reflection

1. Contrast the Western conception of a liberal free will with the Indigenous conception of a spirit born into a network of relations.

2. What are the implications (both positive and negative) of delineating what it means to be human? How do these implications change depending on the assumptions of separation and connection which respectively ground the non-Indigenous and Indigenous views of identity?
3. What are some things that are justified under the Western conception of the origins of the mind but not justified under Indigenous conceptions?
4. Is a separation between that which determines our thoughts and that which determines the outside material world necessary, in order to have autonomy?
5. Describe the Indigenous conception of the person that is expressed in the statement "we are the whole."

Additional Resources

For additional resources relating to this reading and its themes, visit **sites.broadviewpress.com/waysofbeing/3-5**

PART IV

Epistemology

INTRODUCTION

The Nature of Knowledge: Relations, Land, and the Right Path

Epistemology is the philosophical examination into the nature of knowledge. More specifically, it deals with the origins, methods, and standards of knowledge. Recent investigations into the social dynamics of knowledge generation examine conceptions of trust, justice, and ignorance. Yet, despite the inclusion of a communal account of knowledge, Western epistemology and Indigenous epistemologies vary greatly, especially as regards what can or should be known, the aspirations of knowledge accumulation, and the ways in which knowledge is collected and conveyed.

The first reading in this chapter by Kyle Powys Whyte (Citizen Potawatomi Nation) introduces the many definitions ascribed to Traditional Ecological Knowledge (TEK). Although written for a broader scope—one that includes global Indigenous nations and communities—his view is particularly applicable to the nations and communities on Turtle Island. Whyte notes that "there is no such thing as a knowledge system that is more neutral than any other."* The many ways of defining TEK result in different power dynamics. Non-Indigenous governments and agencies should not attempt to apply a definition of TEK in all cases, but should instead consider the different conceptions of TEK as an invitation to collaborate and become familiar with the communities with whom they enter projects.

The second reading explores dreams and visions—often discredited in Western epistemology—as sources of knowledge. The author, Joel Alvarez (Puerto Rican, Ecuadorian), draws from different Indigenous communities to demonstrate the various ways in which dreams and visions serve in diverse epistemologies. Not normally considered a reliable source of facts, dreams and visions may provide insight and guidance for individuals and communities.

In the last reading of this chapter, Paul Simard Smith (Métis) employs a model of deep disagreement to cast light on the tension between the evidence contained in Indigenous oral histories and narratives and the Western understanding of

* Kyle Powys Whyte, "On the Role of Traditional Ecological Knowledge as a Collaborative Concept: A Philosophical Study," *Ecological Processes* 2, no. 1 (2013), https://doi.org/10.1186/2192-1709-2-7.

testimonial evidence in legal cases. Given that the fundamental principles present in different epistemologies are at odds with one another, the author suggests it may be an example of a case of deep disagreement. Deep disagreement occurs when participants in rational discourse cannot appeal to fundamental epistemic source principles to resolve that disagreement. This poses a problem when Western and Indigenous epistemologies conflict. The author considers three solutions to the problem of deep disagreement and notes what should be taken into consideration for each.

4.1
"On the Role of Traditional Ecological Knowledge as a Collaborative Concept: A Philosophical Study"*

Kyle Powys Whyte (Citizen Potawatomi Nation)

ABOUT THE AUTHOR

Kyle Whyte (Citizen Potawatomi Nation) is the George Willis Pack Professor at the University of Michigan School for Environment and Sustainability. He is also the founding Faculty Director of the Tishman Center for Social Justice and the Environment, the Principal Investigator of the Energy Equity Project, and a faculty affiliate in the Native American Studies and Philosophy departments at Michigan State University. Whyte's research addresses environmental justice, focusing on moral and political issues concerning climate policy and Indigenous peoples, the ethics of cooperative relationships between Indigenous peoples and science organizations, and problems of Indigenous justice in public and academic discussions of food sovereignty, environmental justice, and the Anthropocene.† He graduated from Babson College (2001) with a degree in business administration and earned an MA (2004) from the University of Memphis and a PhD (2009) from Stony Brook University. He currently serves on the White House Environmental Justice Advisory Council and the National Academies' Resilient America Roundtable.

KEY TERMS

Traditional Ecological Knowledge (TEK), Indigenous Knowledge, Native Science, Relations, Collaborations, Stewardship, Colonialism, Imperialism, Resource Management, Archives, Flourishing, Well-Being, Moral Character, Value-ladenness

Introduction

The concept of traditional ecological knowledge (TEK) comes up frequently in certain segments of environmental and natural resources science and

* Kyle Powys Whyte, "On the Role of Traditional Ecological Knowledge as a Collaborative Concept: A Philosophical Study," *Ecological Processes* 2, no. 1 (2013), https://doi.org/10.1186/2192-1709-2-7.

† Biographical information from University of Michigan School for Environment and Sustainability, "Kyle White," https://seas.umich.edu/research/faculty/kyle-whyte.

policy literatures (Houde 2007). For some people, the term has come to refer to indigenous peoples'[1] legitimate systems of knowledge production. Such systems have empirically tested (and testable) understandings of the relationships among living things and their environments, though there may be notable differences with scientific approaches characteristic of disciplines like ecology or biology. The English language articulation of TEK—along with synonymous or closely related terms like indigenous knowledge (Brokensha et al. 1980) and native science (Cajete 1999)—originates in literatures on international development (Agrawal 1995; Warren et al. 1995) and adaptive management (Berkes 1999). It continues to show up regularly in science conferences, like the 97th Annual Meeting of the Ecological Society of America in 2012, which featured approximately 13 papers on TEK. It is also found increasingly in the plans and policies of government agencies, such as the Northwest Forest Plan (Harris 2011) and the Natural Resources Conservation Service (Leonetti 2010) in the U.S., and international regimes such as the United Nations Environmental Programme (UNEP 1998).

Examples of TEK in scientific and policy literatures are diverse. They range from historical practices like the creation of forest islands for the production of fruit and attraction of game (Gadgil et al. 1993), to currently practiced skill-based traditions like deer cleaning techniques embodying community value systems (Reo and Whyte 2012), to practical applications for natural resource management and climate change like burning practices (Kimmerer and Lake 2001) and observations of changes in water levels, sea ice, lake processes, and the movements of animal populations (Voggesser 2010; Wildcat 2009; Nakashima et al. 2012; Eisner et al. 2009).

Yet TEK is often invoked in ways that are controversial. There are three plausible reasons why this may be the case. (1) TEK often refers to knowledge production systems whose value has been overlooked or disapproved of by scientists and policy makers. Ignorance and disapproval are often tied to colonial, imperial, and other discriminatory attitudes and institutions of science toward "non-Western" knowledge systems (Harding 1998, 2011; Salmon 1996). (2) Definitions of TEK are often formulated by scholars or professionals who are not community members and hence have tendencies to privilege their own agendas for environmental and natural resources stewardship and management (McGregor 2008; Ellen 2000; Nadasdy 1999; Huntington 2000). (3) TEK is perceived as being a competing authority with science, creating divisions between indigenous expert authorities and scientific expert authorities (Kofinas 2005; McGregor 2008).

A good portion of this controversy revolves around a tendency to want to determine one definition for TEK that can satisfy every stakeholder in every context. Yet a scan of environmental science and policy literatures reveals there to be sufficiently large differences in definitions of TEK that may obstruct the possibility of moving toward a consensus on the best definition. These differences suggest an alternative direction for philosophical reflection on TEK. Perhaps what is important is not only defining TEK; rather, what should be additionally explored is the role that the concept of TEK plays in facilitating or discouraging cross-cultural and cross-situational collaboration between indigenous and non-indigenous institutions such as tribal natural resources departments, federal agencies working with tribes, and co-management boards.

I argue that the concept of TEK should be understood as a collaborative concept. It serves to invite diverse populations to continually learn from one another about how each approaches the very question of "knowledge" in the first place, and how these different approaches can work together to better steward and manage the environment and natural resources. Therefore, any understanding of the meaning of TEK is acceptable only so long as it plays the role of bringing different people working for different institutions closer to a degree of mutual respect for one another's sources of knowledge. The implication is that environmental scientists and policy professionals, indigenous and non-indigenous, should focus more on creating long-term processes that allow for the implications of different approaches to knowledge in relation to stewardship and management priorities to be responsibly thought through.

The paper starts in the Methods section with a description of the philosophical method used to make the argument just mentioned. In the Results and Discussion section, I cover some of the different assumptions that make it hard for consensus to form on what TEK means. The subsection "TEK and knowledge mobilization" describes assumptions about knowledge mobilization; the subsection "The relation between TEK and science" describes assumptions about the relation between TEK and disciplines like ecology or biology. The subsection "The role of TEK as a collaborative concept" shows why TEK should be considered as a collaborative concept that bridges cross-cultural and cross-situational divides. The "Conclusions" section ends the paper with thoughts on the implications for cooperative environmental and natural resources stewardship and management. From now on, I will refer to environmental and natural resource stewardship and management as simply environmental governance.

Methods

This is a philosophical paper (written by an environmental philosopher) that explores how the concept of TEK is defined in science and policy literatures and what purpose it serves for improving cooperative environmental and natural resources stewardship and management between indigenous and non-indigenous institutions. The philosophical method applied here is one that outlines numerous possible meanings of a concept (TEK, in this paper) and the implications of each meaning for science and policy. The argument about TEK as a collaborative concept intends to spur greater reflective discussion among the relevant audiences on the meaning of a concept that may be controversial or simply taken for granted....

Results and Discussion

In science and policy literatures, there are different definitions of TEK. Controversy can brew over TEK when people hold definitions that are based on different assumptions. There are two kinds of assumptions about the meaning of TEK. The first kind refers to assumptions about the mobilization of TEK, or what I call knowledge mobilization. Knowledge mobilization refers to assumptions about what different types of knowledge can be used for and their adaptability to suit different contexts. The second kind involves assumptions about how to understand the relationship between TEK and disciplines like ecology or biology, or, in other words, the relation between TEK and science. The two kinds of assumptions (knowledge mobilization; TEK and science) can generate controversy because they imply differences about "whose" definition of TEK gets privileged, who is counted as having expert authority over environmental governance issues, and how TEK should be factored into policy processes that already have a role for disciplines like forestry or toxicology in them. The section "TEK and knowledge mobilization" begins to discuss these assumptions, starting with knowledge mobilization. The section "The relation between TEK and science" begins the discussion on the second kind of assumption (the relation between TEK and science).

TEK and Knowledge Mobilization

Some definitions see TEK as a basic body of knowledge. According to Nakashima, TEK is "the knowledge of Native people about their natural environment" (Nakashima 1993, 99). This basic body of knowledge is usually defined as having been gathered across generations: "Indigenous or traditional knowledge refers to the knowledge and know-how accumulated across generations, and renewed by each new generation, which guide human societies in their innumerable interactions with their surrounding environment" (Nakashima et al. 2012, 8). Definitions like this emphasize TEK as a substantive body of knowledge that is created and stored by human societies to aid in their flourishing in the face of environmental and natural resources challenges. The time scale of this knowledge is many generations. In this sense, TEK is taken as archival in nature. It is a store of knowledge of the relationships between living things and their environment.

A key assumption about knowledge mobilization in this definition is that TEK is a supply of knowledge ready to hand to be used by people in different contexts. In the policy document, *Weathering Uncertainty: Traditional Knowledge for Climate Change Assessment and Adaptation* (United Nations), Nakashima et al. write that such "community-based and local knowledge may offer valuable insights into environmental change due to climate change, and complement broader-scale scientific research with local precision and nuance" (2012, 6). They go on to state, as an example, that "Indigenous observations and interpretations of meteorological phenomena have guided seasonal and inter-annual activities of local communities for millennia. This knowledge contributes to climate science by offering observations and interpretations at a much finer spatial scale with considerable temporal depth and by highlighting elements that may not be considered by climate scientists" (8). In this example, TEK is a body of knowledge, or archive, waiting to be picked up by climate science. TEK is conceived as an archive that is continually updated or an archive of a society that no longer exists, yet biologists or ecologists can nonetheless find the knowledge and incorporate it into their research.

The assumption that TEK is a basic body of knowledge is often accompanied by the idea that elements of a society's worldview are an intimate dimension of its TEK system. Berkes, for example, defines TEK as "a cumulative body of knowledge, practice and belief, evolving by adaptive processes and handed down through generations by cultural transmission, about the relationship of living things (including humans) with one another and with their environment" (Berkes 1999, 8; see also Gadgil et al. 1993, 151). This definition situates TEK as a body of "knowledge, practice and belief" inspired by a particular worldview and bioregion. It is interwoven with a society's cultural fabric. Here, TEK is not just an archive, but a part of what members of a particular culture think, believe and do. It is situated knowledge.

The definition of TEK as a situated body of knowledge is found in policy documents. For example, the Natural Resources Conservation Service (NRCS) published *Indigenous Stewardship Methods and NRCS*, which aims to guide NRCS staff to work better with tribes. TEK is seen as bound up with "indigenous stewardship method," which is defined as the "ecologically sustainable use of natural resources within their capacity to sustain natural processes." Indigenous stewardship method (ISM) is possibly a

> ... subset of Traditional Ecological Knowledge (TEK), in which indigenous peoples acquired the knowledge base over hundreds of years through direct experience and contact with the environment. ISM is the physical, spiritual, mental, emotional, and intuitive relationship of indigenous peoples with all aspects and elements of their environment.
>
> These relationships include, but are not limited to, a combination of knowledge, experience, tradition, places, locality, all living and nonliving things, skills, practices, theories, social strategies, moments, spirituality, history, heritage, and more; and may not be fully embraced by people who fail to understand all those dimensions (Leonetti 2010, 13).

In this definition, TEK is considered a knowledge "base," or body of knowledge, though one embedded within multiple relationships among living beings, non-living things, and the environment. The passage above also raises a question concerning the degree that outsiders will be able to respect or comprehend a TEK system. But the purpose of the NRCS guide is to advance a set of best practices and principles so that NRCS staff can begin to work with communities for whom TEK forms a significant dimension of their lifeways.

An implication of definitions based on the assumption that TEK is a body of knowledge is that TEK can be picked up and used by scientists or agency staff. Each of the policy documents just cited involves the idea that TEK can be gleaned from the communities who have it, either through historical research or working with actual communities, and can then be incorporated into the environmental governance of non-indigenous institutions like those of the United Nations or U.S. Department of Agriculture. So the assumption about knowledge mobilization is that TEK, no matter what the society, is "something" that can be seen as archival. With some effort, it can be interpreted for use in different contexts, especially science policy contexts, that is, contexts where there is a given role for scientific information in environmental governance.

Some indigenous scientists, in particular, have offered definitions of TEK that resist the assumption that it is mainly a body of knowledge. McGregor, for example, argues that TEK involves the relationships between "knowledge, people, and all Creation (the 'natural' world as well as the spiritual) ... TEK is viewed as the process of participating (a verb) fully and responsibly in such relationships, rather than specifically as the knowledge gained from such experiences. For Aboriginal people, TEK is not just about understanding relationships, it is the relationship with Creation. TEK is something one does" (McGregor 2004a,b, 2008, 145). For McGregor, TEK refers to the activities that people in indigenous societies are doing as part of their stewardship. It is not archival or body-like. To speak of a society's TEK is to speak of ongoing activities expressive of responsibilities.

The ideas of "fully" and "responsibly" suggest what in the field of philosophy is often called moral character or just character. Character refers to the idea that acting responsibly (and hence ethically) is a matter of possessing embodied traits like courage or respect that enable one to know the right thing to do in particular situations and to act in ways that maintain relations of balance within one's society. People who possess the character traits also possess the internal motivation to do what is right. Within a society's system of responsibilities, character refers to the particular traits that people acquire over many years (since childhood) in order to express responsibilities and balanced relationships in all that they do. Definitions like McGregor's see TEK systems as systems of responsibilities that cannot be detached from the character traits required to fulfill the moral demands of these systems.

Other native scholars have also emphasized the responsibilities and character dimensions of TEK. Pierotti and Wildcat see TEK as

> ... based in the knowledge that native societies existed under conditions of constant pressure on the resources upon which they depended, and that a means had to be found to convince communities and families to economize with regard to their use of natural Resources ... The connections that are a crucial aspect of TEK are based on a mixture of extraction, e.g., animals are taken as prey, combined with recognition of the inherent value and good of non-human lives. Traditional knowledge is based on the premise that humans should not view themselves as responsible for nature, i.e., we are not stewards of the nature world, but instead that we are a part of that world, no greater than any other part. In this way TEK deals largely with motivating humans to show respect for nonhumans (Pierotti and Wildcat 2000, 1336).

Pierotti and Wildcat see motivation, an important aspect of character, as a key component of TEK. They even suggest that terms like stewardship are not sufficient for describing the actual intimacies involved in relationships among living beings and non-living things on which TEK systems are based. As with McGregor, TEK is a doing, a full participation in a system of responsibilities needed for a society's flourishing. For both Pierotti and Wildcat and McGregor, great emphasis is placed on the idea that TEK is not knowledge about relationships but is the complete participation in the responsibilities. Similar definitions are found in the work of other indigenous scholars (Reo and Whyte 2012; Cajete 1999).

TEK systems, then, are systems of responsibilities that arise from particular cosmological beliefs about the relationships between living beings and non-living things or humans and the natural world. There is an important implication for knowledge mobilization. TEK cannot be readily transferred to different contexts unless the people in the new context also learn the systems of responsibilities and character traits. Such learning entails complete cultural immersion. Thus, it could be problematic, on the system of responsibility assumption, to see TEK as something that could be incorporated by, for example, climate science. For climate science may not be used in a policy context that seeks to integrate the system of responsibilities of a particular indigenous people into its strategies for environmental governance.

The body of knowledge assumption and the system of responsibility assumption are different in important ways to the degree that they underlie various definitions of TEK. In terms of the former, TEK can be extracted from its society and fit into policy-relevant science. The gist goes something like this: climate science, for example, already fits within a particular policy context. This fit is not determined by indigenous peoples. That is, indigenous peoples are not active participants in the majority of decisions of governments, universities, and organizations about what funding programs to create for climate science and for selecting who should be on review panels. Moreover, TEK is not taken to be tied, in any important ways, to particular stewardship or management strategies. Insofar as climate science, in sticking with the last example, fits into a particular kind of understanding of management or adaptation, TEK is seen to contribute to that by being plugged into structures of scientific inquiry. But definitions based on the assumption that TEK is a system of responsibilities suggest that for TEK to be genuinely included, the people who participate fully in it must be at the table equally with non-indigenous scientists and policy makers. TEK is not a piece broken off of one of these strategies and applied to another. TEK just is the living environmental governance of indigenous peoples stemming directly from their cosmologies in relation to the environmental challenges they have faced over many generations.

The difference between the two assumptions can engender some difficulties in forming a consensus on the definition of TEK in terms of knowledge mobilization. One assumption seeks to fit TEK within established science policy decision-making frameworks, whereas the other seeks to change this framework in favor of greater participation by indigenous peoples.

The Relation between TEK and Science

TEK is also defined in ways that are based on assumptions about its relation to disciplines like forestry or climatology. The kind of assumption active in these definitions involves how TEK can be compared or contrasted to scientific disciplines (i.e., science). There are three assumptions covered in this subsection: (1) TEK and science should be seen as separate knowledge production systems. This distinction should never be collapsed. (2) TEK and science should be seen as twins, or two knowledge-bearing perspectives on the world that complement each other. (3) There is no basis for distinguishing TEK, or Indigenous knowledge, from science, and the term TEK or its synonyms should not be used. In all three of these views, there is a lot riding on how TEK and science are seen as related to each other because there are implications for what sorts of empirical authorities are deemed relevant for environmental governance.

The first version of this kind of assumption is that TEK and science are sufficiently different to warrant maintaining separate definitions. Proponents of this view believe that there are definite differences in the values and aspirations of science and those of TEK systems. El-Hani and Souza de Ferreira Bandeira exemplify this view. They use the term "indigenous knowledge" instead of TEK, though their use of this term is synonymous with TEK because they are talking about indigenous peoples' knowledge of the natural world and the relationships between living things and the environment.[2] They see Western modern science as "the most powerful way of producing naturalistic explanations of natural phenomena." Yet it is also the case that "there are plenty of different accounts of the world [i.e., indigenous knowledge] which are also powerful in their own ways" (2008, 756). They see indigenous knowledge as part of this latter grouping: these other accounts "are producing explanations about supernatural (or, maybe non-natural is a better term) beings and phenomena that are useful to several human cultures. And, in the face of natural phenomena, they are producing explanations that appeal to spiritual domains, going beyond naturalistic chains or networks of events" (2008, 756). The key to this difference, then, is that indigenous knowledge usually involves some account of non-natural beings whereas science always excludes these non-natural beings. This reflects some of the ideas of the previous section, where TEK is tied to spirituality.

To call something science, then, for El-Hani and Souza de Ferreira Bandeira, certain standards must be met. For example, science embodies values and skills such as "technical precision, control, creative genius, and explanatory power ..." Quoting Siegel, they argue that science and indigenous knowledge could only be the same thing "if it could be cogently argued that some particular 'ethnic' science ... offered compelling theories/predictions/explanations of natural phenomena. Could an animistic ethnic theory of volcanic activity and lava flow ... provide the sort of explanation, prediction, grasp of relations among unobservables and between observables and unobservables, and depth of scientific understanding provided by

Western science?" (El-Hani et al. 2008, 757; Siegel 1997, 100). According to this understanding, there are definite values and knowledge-bearing capabilities of science that cannot be attributed to indigenous knowledge of the environment.

Indigenous knowledge, while it may produce important knowledge, does not do so in the ways that scientific disciplines do. This is, according to the authors, not a form of discrimination: "Notice that we are not saying that the way this community builds knowledge, the knowledge built, or the criteria employed to appraise cognitive statements are epistemically superior to any other body of approaches, ideas, statements, criteria. We are just saying that they are different, and should be kept different, for the sake of clarity about the nature of knowledge and the nature of science" (El-Hani and Souza de Ferreira Bandeira 2008, 758). In this assumption about indigenous knowledge (or TEK) and science, there are definite criteria, values, skills, and so on that science and TEK have, but there is not a lot of crossover. So TEK's supernatural and social aspects, respectfully so, exclude the possibility of the kind of rationality associated with science. Moreover, societies without computing capacities built into their TEK systems cannot value quantitative research in the same way that it is valued in natural sciences disciplines, nor can they engage in the same kind of research.

This first assumption, that TEK and science are fundamentally different, differs from the second assumption, which sees the former and the latter as two complementary perspectives on the environment that stem from complementary views on the world. The views are complementary because there is both crossover as well as gap filling. Kimmerer argues that

> Traditional ecological knowledge refers to the knowledge, practice, and belief concerning the relationships of living beings to one another and to the physical environment, which is held by peoples in relatively nontechnical societies with a direct dependence upon local resources ... It is born of long intimacy and attentiveness to a homeland and can arise wherever people are materially and spiritually integrated within their landscape. TEK is rational and reliable knowledge that has been developed through generations of intimate contact by native peoples with their lands (Kimmerer 2002, 431).

TEK and science, for Kimmerer, can be seen as having a complementary relation to each other. Indeed, TEK can be seen as the "intellectual twin to science," a term she borrows from Deloria (433). Kimmerer claims that TEK exists "in parallel to Western science" (433). She claims that "Both knowledge systems yield detailed empirical information of natural phenomena and relationships among ecosystem components." This can include "predictive power," overlapping biological information, "detailed empirical knowledge of population biology, resource assessment and monitoring, successional dynamics, patterns of fluctuation in climate and resources, species interactions, ethnotaxonomy, sustainable harvesting, and adaptive management and manipulation of disturbance regimes ..." (Kimmerer 2002, 433). Yet TEK differs from science for Kimmerer in important ways:

> TEK observations tend to be qualitative, and they create a diachronic database, that is, a record of observations from a single locale over a long time period. The National Science Foundation, in its support of the Long-Term Ecological Research program, has validated the importance of such continuous data. In TEK, the observers tend to be the resource users themselves, for example, hunters, fishers, and gatherers whose harvesting success is inextricably linked to the quality and reliability of their ecological observations. In contrast, scientific observations made by a small group of professionals tend to be quantitative and often represent synchronic data or simultaneous observations from a wide range of sites, which frequently lack the long-term perspective of TEK ... Western science is conducted in academic culture in which nature is viewed strictly objectively ... TEK is woven into and is inseparable from the social and spiritual contexts of the culture ... TEK may also extend its explanatory power beyond the strictly empirical, where science cannot go ... In indigenous science, nature is subject, not object ... Embraced as an equal partner to the power of Western science, TEK offers not only important biological insights but a cultural framework for environmental problem solving that incorporates human values (Kimmerer 2002, 433–34).

Here, then, for Kimmerer, TEK and science are two parallel, complementary perspectives on the environment and natural resources. They go hand in hand. Different from the first assumption, Kimmerer has no problem using concepts like "prediction" or "rational" with respect to TEK, nor stating straightforwardly that techniques in TEK systems fit well with and are valued by science. She also shows that the influence of culture in TEK systems could be considered beneficial to science. Though she admits differences, they are not the stark differences that are maintained in the first assumption. For Kimmerer, then, knowledge production that fails to incorporate both TEK systems and the relevant sciences would be missing key perspectives on the world. Instead of saying that they are valuable in their own ways (as in the first assumption), Kimmerer is saying that they are valuable together. Both knowledge production systems can learn a great deal from each other.

A third assumption diverges, in general, from the first two by desiring to dispense altogether with the pursuit of defining differences and complementarities between TEK systems and science. That is, in this assumption, there is really no use in even talking theoretically about a distinction between TEK and science because at the end of the day they are faces of the same phenomena: the pursuit of usable knowledge by human societies. Agrawal, for example, argues that

> The attempt to create distinctions in terms of indigenous and western is potentially ridiculous. It makes much more sense ... to talk about multiple domains and types of knowledges, with differing logics and epistemologies. Somewhat contradictorily, but inescapably so, the same knowledge can be classified one way or the other depending on the interests it serves, the purposes for which it is harnessed, or the manner in which it is generated ... [A]nchored unavoidably in institutional origins and moorings, knowledge can only be useful. But it is useful to particular peoples. Specific strategies for protecting, systematizing and disseminating knowledge will differentially benefit different social groups and individuals. The recognition of this simple truism is obscured by the confounding labels of indigenous and western. It is only when we move away from the sterile dichotomy between indigenous and western, when we begin to recognize intra-group differentiation; and when we seek out bridges across the constructed chasm between the traditional and the scientific, that we will initiate a productive dialogue to safeguard the interests of those who are disadvantaged (Agrawal 1995, 433).

This third view, then, suggests that to use terms like indigenous knowledge or TEK or Western science obscures several important points. First, TEK and science are all value-laden knowledge systems. The literature in social studies of science shows multiple ways in which science is guided by particular values and even associated with spirituality (Biagioli 1999; Turnbull 2000). Second, there is no reason why the criteria and values attributed to various sciences cannot also be those of various TEK systems. Moreover, by "intra-group" differentiation, Agrawal points out that there are few indigenous people who rely on a single, homogenous TEK system; rather their knowledge system has changed and they likely also rely on different scientific disciplines as well. Examples of this abound, like Gupta's 1998 study of how rural farmers in India engage in hybrid agricultural practices that mix Western scientific and traditional knowledge systems (Gupta 1998). Or Watson-Verran and Turnbull discuss how Western science is composed of heterogeneous elements (Watson-Verran and Turnbull 1995).

Agrawal's position is based on the idea that every society has some sort of knowledge system, which may be a patchwork of systems with multiple origins (e.g., European, indigenous). There is no such thing as a knowledge system that is not guided by people's interpretations of the challenges that they face. And interpretations are influenced by worldviews. There is no such thing as a knowledge system that is more neutral than any other. In the case of scientific disciplines, values of objectivity are based on cosmological assumptions about there being subjects and objects in the world and which beings, entities, and phenomena fall under one or the other. A science based on such assumptions may be of limited use to a society that does not carve up reality in this way. But on the other hand, such a society may have great use for this kind of information. Context is key. Agrawal's assumption speaks to the situation that many indigenous peoples encounter in the world. They need reliable information for the environmental governance challenges they face. And they are likely in the position to draw from many sources of knowledge. What knowledge they can use depends on how suitable different forms of knowledge are for their purposes. Whether forms of knowledge are indigenous or not does not really matter in the end. Some indigenous peoples may be served perfectly well by disciplines like biology as the basis of their environmental governance strategies. So the implication is that terms like TEK or indigenous knowledge are not very useful and may even waste our time. We should focus more on figuring out what knowledge systems best serve the needs of particular communities and how to realize them in practice.

As with knowledge mobilization, the distinction between TEK and science does not generate many easy options for consensus on how to define the two in relation to each other. First, the view that TEK and science must be labeled as such, and kept distinct, misses the realities of indigenous environmental governance today. There is no reason why any so-called TEK system cannot embrace similar empirical values that are found commonly in various scientific disciplines. One who adopts this assumption would perhaps have to consider dropping it were one to concede that certain values and criteria are not exclusive to science. So it would be tricky for one to accept certain parts of both the first and second assumptions. Moreover, contemporary tribal environmental governance involves examples of institutions that are guided by TEK but that use technologies and methods that originate from non-tribal scientific disciplines (Woodard 2005). Even examples of practices like hunting show that TEK systems are adaptive in their adoption of technologies (Reo and Whyte 2012). In these cases, it is hard to imagine a rigid separation between TEK and science and technology because TEK systems can incorporate scientific techniques. Advocates of the third assumption, of course, would find it fairly difficult to accept the first two assumptions because they invoke a distinction between TEK and science too readily. Agrawal's conclusion is that the term TEK must be dispensed with altogether, as must particularly loaded conceptions of science. So the first assumption seeks to maintain a rigid separation in definitions; the second assumption seeks a definition that reveals complementarity; the third assumption can be seen as desiring to dispense with the business of the first two assumptions altogether.

It is somewhat hard to see people who hold any of these three assumptions coming to a consensus definition. Combined with differences regarding knowledge mobilization, it is even harder to see there ever being a single definition acceptable to all stakeholders. But I want to offer another, fruitful approach to coming to an understanding of TEK that can advance environmental governance even as we discuss and disagree on the assumptions underlying various definitions. My approach is different from Agrawal's insofar as I do not see the need to dispense with the term TEK. While Agrawal comes close to my understanding of the difficulties in defining TEK, he does not draw the only possible conclusion from accepting the reality of these difficulties. The fact that a term is defined in ways that are problematic and subject to deep differences does not entail that it has no use. Rather, this fact motivates us to consider whether the term, given all its potential definitions and confusing dimensions, has a proper role to play in advancing collaborative environmental governance. I turn to this topic in the next subsection.

The Role of TEK as a Collaborative Concept

This subsection shows why TEK should be considered as a collaborative concept that bridges cross-cultural and cross-situational divides. To make this case, the initial pages of this section focus on the environmental governance situations in which many tribes are embedded, and I use the term co-management as an example of this. I then move on to define what a collaborative concept is and how this relates to the discussion of TEK I have been building so far in this paper. In this sense, the initial pages of this section take a slight detour before returning to the concept of TEK.

Regardless of how TEK can be defined, what is the role of the concept of TEK, in the first place, in the world of environmental governance? The world of environmental governance, here, involves relations between environmental governance institutions associated with and responsible to indigenous peoples, like tribal natural resources departments and those regulating indigenous hunting practices, and governance institutions associated with states and subnational units like the U.S. Forest Service and Environment Canada. All of these institutions have evolved ways of doing things out of histories in which the very idea of indigenous environmental governance was overtly and subtly marginalized. Times are changing, and greater respect is accorded to indigenous peoples through international, federal, and local law and policy. These changes create opportunities for indigenous peoples to work collaboratively with non-indigenous peoples, instead of against them or in secrecy from them (covertly). Indigenous peoples can begin to build institutions of environmental governance that are integrated with non-indigenous institutions in ways that benefit indigenous communities and respect the stewardship goals of their worldviews.

But institution building of this kind is always a work in progress because of cross-cultural and cross-situational divides. Cross-cultural divides are simply the differences in worldview, language, lifestyle, and so on that obtain between indigenous and non-indigenous populations. For example, an indigenous people may see the goal of restoring a native fish species as rekindling the relationship between that species and humans living in the region, whereas a non-indigenous population may see restoration of the same species as a matter of achieving certain population numbers conducive to a recreational outcome like increasing tourism in the region. Cross-cultural divides can also have an intra-group dimension to them, as there may be differences in beliefs about building relationships with a species in an indigenous community and territory, for example. Cross-situational divides are differences in capacities for environmental governance. For example, an indigenous people may have access to fewer financial resources than the neighboring state or province, have limited political control over the entire region where its members live, and have less representation in national decision-making than representatives of the neighboring state or province. Cross-cultural and cross-situational divides make collaboration challenging. It may be hard for federal institutions to incorporate indigenous people's goals within their policy frameworks. It may be frustrating to work across institutions with different bureaucratic capabilities.

Since the possibility of meaningful collaboration is a relatively recent turn of events, there is yet to be perfect guidance about how collaboration that bridges cross-cultural and cross-situational divides ought to be done. There are cases of success and cases of failure. And there is still a lot to be learned regarding whether the lessons from cases of success can simply be transferred over to other contexts. Caught in this predicament, there are a host of concepts that are being debated as concepts that facilitate or discourage genuine collaboration. For example, the concept of co-management has been used to suggest a possible route to cooperative environmental and natural resources governance (Goetze 2005).[3] Co-management invokes the idea of joint political relationships between indigenous and non-indigenous institutions that work together according to standards of fairness to govern particular areas and resources. Standards of fairness include norms like equal representation and voting rights. The concept of co-management is the basis of actual co-management boards and committees that are composed of indigenous and non-indigenous participants and that are responsible for managing a fishery or forested area, or particular species, like a caribou population. Indigenous and non-indigenous institutions often rely on the term co-management as part of a shared language for bridging cross-cultural and cross-situation divides. However, there is also dialogue on how the concept of co-management can be taken the wrong way and provide insufficient guidance for collaboration. It is often argued that the concept co-management implies that the nation-state's (e.g., Canada, U.S.) vision for environmental governance is used to evaluate the collaborative efforts between indigenous and non-indigenous institutions. This is because the term "management" can connote a non-indigenous view of the appropriate relationship among humans, other living beings, and the environment. This term can slant the meaning of co-management so that non-indigenous participants in a co-management board, for example, come in with expectations that their assumptions about "management" should be prioritized and may not listen to their indigenous colleagues. The term, then, can have the effect of silencing genuine negotiation of cross-cultural and cross-situational differences.

Instead, the concept of co-existence is offered (McGregor 2004b), which suggests the importance of balancing indigenous and non-indigenous aspirations of governance into the evaluation of collaboration. In this case, one might be inclined to think cynically that it is all about *labels*. But there is much more going on than preferences about labels. We need to consider the role played by concepts like co-management and co-existence in facilitating or discouraging collaboration. People who reject the concept of co-management based on the contexts they are familiar with see in it problematic assumptions about how indigenous and non-indigenous institutions should work together. Non-indigenous people may not see how the concept of co-management might encourage these assumptions, even though, perhaps, co-management is the preferred concept in some contexts. Those who reject the concept of co-management and wish to replace it with the concept of co-existence are inviting non-indigenous people to learn more about cross-cultural and cross-situational divides. This is the role that concepts like co-management and co-existence play. The concept of co-existence does not in itself contain enough meaning for non-indigenous persons to suggest in advance exactly how a collaborative process should play out. What proponents of co-existence are saying is that there is much learning to do. The concept of co-existence suggests a very different possibility for collaboration than what non-indigenous peoples may be used to. Work on co-existence expresses an invitation to learn about cross-cultural and cross-situational divides so as to achieve better collaborations in particular contexts.

There are two important points here regarding the role of these concepts. First, co-management and co-existence are invoked, for better or worse, by many different institutions in contexts where they are trying to collaborate across cross-cultural and cross-situational divides. Second, the example of co-existence I gave is an example of how some people seek to use concepts to improve collaboration by inviting people to consider alternatives that may not have been on their conceptual radar before. The concept of TEK and its synonyms plays a somewhat analogous role to the term co-existence. As in the first point, various definitions of TEK are used in collaborative contexts, for better or worse. As in the second point, those who bring new definitions of TEK into dialogue are inviting others to consider new possibilities for thinking about the function of knowledge systems in environmental governance.

However, we need to be precise about what this means—because I am not arguing that there is a single definition of TEK that can count for all. This is impossible. TEK, no matter how it is defined, is not adequate for any indigenous community. The English articulation, TEK, is not an indigenous word or concept, and it is likely not used within very many communities unto themselves. The terms traditional and ecological are awkward. *Traditional* can have the effect of putting knowledge in the past, whereas TEK is often supposed to mean contemporary knowledge. *Ecological* aligns TEK with a particular discipline, whereas TEK refers to knowledge that does not stem from that discipline. Terms like indigenous knowledge and native science are similarly awkward when we unpack what associations and dissociations they may imply. Moreover, there may be many contexts where an indigenous people *does* see the concept as referring to accumulated observations, for example, or contexts where TEK is viewed as a *Western* construct irrelevant to environmental governance. There are likely other contexts where TEK needs to refer to systems of responsibilities. There are multiple possible scenarios. The concept of TEK cannot possibly do justice to the knowledge systems and articulations of knowledge systems belonging to the thousands of indigenous peoples. TEK is also not a concept that was an integral part of the education of most ecologists or foresters, nor is it a concept that has existed for a long time in the federal policies of a nation-state. This does not mean, though, that the concept should be dispensed with. Non-indigenous peoples may be equally uncomfortable with referring to something they are not familiar with as *science* or linked with a particular scientific discipline. It may be no easier for them to change out terms like TEK with even more general terms like Agrawal's "usable knowledge."[4]

Thus, whenever the concept of TEK is invoked, the role that it plays is to suggest that indigenous communities may approach the very question of the nature of knowledge and how it relates to environmental and natural resource governance rather differently than disciplines like ecology or biology and the policy contexts in which they are used. By "rather differently" I do not mean in some sense that applies to all communities. For example, there may be some indigenous communities that invoke TEK to mean a radically different cultural paradigm, one in which it is not appropriate to speak of *knowledge* as distinct from practice or belief. But other indigenous communities who live in different regions because of historical removal may invoke TEK to stand for the values that they believe disciplines like ecology should serve, even if they lack intimate experiences with the environment they currently inhabit. Yet other communities might use TEK to suggest different ways in which multiple empirical techniques for gathering knowledge, from hunters' observations to scientific field methods, can be used in harmony. TEK could also refer to ideas about how elders should be involved in the design and peer review of research in tribal environmental departments that collect their own data about the environment and the condition of natural resources. There are many more scenarios, of course. These scenarios indicate the diversity of how people, at a philosophical level, think about the meaning of knowledge in relation to their lives. And their thinking arises from multiple cultural, historical, global, social, and personal sources.

The significance of this point is that when the concept of TEK is used, it really points to the possibility that there are cross-cultural and cross-situational divides that make it so that non-indigenous parties cannot expect their own assumptions to apply to indigenous contexts. The concept of TEK should be invoked to invite non-indigenous parties to learn more about how particular indigenous communities approach fundamental questions of the nature of knowledge and how it fits into their visions of environmental governance. This invitation is not one that promises easy answers. Rather, it is an invitation to become a part of a long-term process whereby cross-cultural and cross-situation divides are better bridged through mutual respect and learning, and relationships among collaborators are given the opportunity to mature. Examples of long-term processes include "the way of peace" used among indigenous and non-indigenous participants in the Ontario Model Forest (Holmes et al. 2002; Story and Lickers 1997). There are many other examples. We need not only be concerned with striking the right definition of TEK. Rather, we need to cultivate attitudes of awareness that the concept of TEK plays a role as a collaborative concept, which is what I call a concept that invites people to engage in a process of respectful learning about significant differences.[5]

Conclusions

TEK and its synonyms indigenous knowledge and native science have been defined mainly based on two kinds of assumptions: how knowledge is to be mobilized and what TEK's relation to science is. The different assumptions make it tricky to come to a consensus definition that satisfies all stakeholders. This makes us interrogate what the role of TEK is in a world of relationships among different institutions of environmental governance for whom TEK is an issue. TEK must play the role of inviting cross-cultural and cross-situational learning for indigenous and non-indigenous policy makers, natural resource managers, scientists, activists, elders, and youth.

An important implication of this is that science and policy literatures that invoke TEK should discuss it as a collaborative concept. That is, care must be taken to show that the concept invites participation to a long term process of mutually respectful learning. And more effort needs to be taken to understand what these processes should look like. Already, of course, there is work that exemplifies this interpretation of TEK (Barnhardt 2005; Ross et al. 2010). Yet the point has not been brought out that TEK is playing the role of a collaborative concept in this work. This point should figure more in natural resources and policy literatures. Differences over the meaning of TEK should be seen as invitations to learn more in circumstances where the possibility of genuine collaboration is a relatively recent development.

Endnotes

1 Indigenous peoples refer to the pre-invasion inhabitants of lands now dominated by others, examples being the Maori in New Zealand or the Anishinaabe in the United States and Canada (Anaya 2004).

2 I will use the term indigenous knowledge specifically when I refer to the work of these authors and shift back to the term TEK for my own analysis. My analysis of Agrawal, later on in the same section, will also use indigenous knowledge when referring specifically to his work and TEK when referring to my own analysis.

3 Other collaborative literature includes Fortmann 2008 and Colwell-Chanthaphonh and Ferguson 2008.

4 Agrawal too has considered the role of the concept of TEK in cross-cultural and cross-situational collaboration. He argues that

> ... it is possibly the case that advocates of indigenous knowledge find in the term a particularly potent way to summarize and invoke many of their concerns and hopes about peoples, livelihoods, life styles, and resource systems they view as disappearing. The phrase evokes embattled ways of living-in-the-world that real economic, social and political pressures are nudging and frog-marching toward further marginalization and oblivion. Because the indigenous/scientific division of knowledge effectively represents durable underlying social confrontations, the study and defense of indigenous knowledge continues to attract attention. Indeed, even as one questions the need to contrast indigenous and scientific knowledges, one underscores this contrast—in the very use of the contrasting adjectives. Indigenous knowledge is here to stay, even if what it represents is forever and always disappearing (Agrawal 2009, 158).

I hope to articulate in this paper that there are far more reasons why people invoke concepts like TEK or indigenous knowledge than what Agrawal states.

5 Collaborative concepts also differ from boundary objects (Star and Griesemer 1989). Boundary objects are commonly shared by diverse stakeholders and serve to coordinate their actions despite different interests. Collaborative concepts are invitations to learn more, which suggest the need for a long-term process of mutually respectful learning.

Acknowledgments

I wish to thank Kristie Dotson, Michael O'Rourke, Nicholas Reo, and the anonymous reviewers for their insightful comments on this paper.

References

Agrawal A (1995) Dismantling the divide between indigenous and scientific knowledge. Dev Change 26(3):413–439

Agrawal A (2009) Why "indigenous" knowledge? J R Soc N Z 39(4):157–158

Anaya SJ (2004) Indigenous peoples in international law, 2nd edition. Oxford University Press, New York

Barnhardt R (2005) Indigenous knowledge systems and Alaska Native ways of knowing. Anthropol Ed Q 36(1):8–23

Berkes F (1999) Sacred ecology: traditional ecological knowledge and resource management. Taylor & Francis, Philadelphia

Biagioli M (1999) The science studies reader. Routledge, New York

Brokensha DW, Warren DM, Werner O (1980) Indigenous knowledge systems and development. University Press of America, Washington DC

Cajete G (1999) Native science: natural laws of interdependence. Clear Light Books, Santa Fe, NM

Colwell-Chanthaphonh JS, Ferguson TJ (2008) Collaboration in archaeological practice: engaging descendant communities. AltaMira, Lanham, MD

Eisner WR, Cuomo CJ, Hinkel KM, Jones BM, Brower S, Ronald H (2009) Advancing Landscape Change Research through the Incorporation of Iñupiaq Knowledge. Arctic 62(4):429–442

El-Hani C, de Ferreira S, Bandeira F (2008) Valuing indigenous knowledge: to call it "science" will not help. Cult Stud Sci Educ 3(3):751–779. doi:10.1007/s11422-008-9129-6

Ellen R (2000) Indigenous environmental knowledge and its transformations: critical anthropological perspectives, vol 5. Routledge, New York

Fortmann L (2008) Participatory research in conservation and rural livelihoods: Doing science together, vol 3. Wiley-Blackwell, Hoboken

Gadgil M, Berkes F, Folke C (1993) Indigenous knowledge for biodiversity conservation. Ambio 22(2/3):151–156

Goetze TC (2005) Empowered co-management: towards power-sharing and indigenous rights in Clayoquot Sound, BC. Anthropologica 47(2):247–265

Gupta A (1998) Postcolonial developments: agriculture in the making of modern India. Duke University Press, Durham, NC

Harding S (1998) Is science multicultural?: postcolonialisms, feminisms, and epistemologies. Indiana University Press, Bloomington

Harding S (2011) The postcolonial science and technology studies reader. Duke University Press, Durham, NC

Harris G (ed) (2011) Northwest Forest Plan—the first 15 years [1994–2008]: effectiveness of the federal-tribal relationship. Tech. Paper R6-RPM-TP-01-2011. U.S. Department of Agriculture, Forest Service, Pacific Northwest Region, Portland

Holmes E, Lickers H, Barkley B (2002) A critical assessment of ten years of on-the-ground sustainable forestry in eastern Ontario's settled landscape. For Chron 78(5):643–647

Houde N (2007) The six faces of traditional ecological knowledge: challenges and opportunities for Canadian co-management arrangements. Ecol Soc 12(2):34

Huntington H (2000) Using traditional ecological knowledge in science: methods and applications. Ecol Appl 10(5):1270–1274

Kimmerer R (2002) Weaving traditional ecological knowledge into biological education:7 a call to action. Bioscience 52(5):432–438. doi:10.1641/0006-3568(2002)052[0432:WTEKIB]2.0.CO;2

Kimmerer R, Lake F (2001) The role of indigenous burning in land management. J For 99(11):36–41

Kofinas GP (2005) Caribou hunters and researchers at the co-management interface: emergent dilemmas and the dynamics of legitimacy in power sharing. Anthropologica 47(2):179–196

Leonetti C (2010) Indigenous stewardship methods and NRCS conservation practices. United States Department of Agriculture. Natural Resources Conservation Service, Anchorage

McGregor D (2004a) Coming full circle: indigenous knowledge, environment, and our future. Am Indian Q 28(3&4):385–410

McGregor D (2004b) Traditional ecological knowledge and sustainable development: towards coexistence. In: Blaser M, Feit HA, McRae G (ed) In the way of development: indigenous peoples, life projects and globalization. Zed/IDRC, Ottawa

McGregor D (2008) Linking traditional ecological knowledge and western science: aboriginal perspectives from the 2000 State of the Lakes Ecosystem Conference. Can J Nativ Stud XXVIII(1):139–158

Nadasdy P (1999) The politics of TEK: power and the "integration" of knowledge. Arct Anthropol 36(1–2):1–18

Nakashima DJ (1993) Astute observers on the sea ice edge: Inuit knowledge as a basis for arctic co-management. In: Inglis J (ed) Traditional ecological knowledge: concepts and cases. International Program on Traditional Ecological Knowledge and International Development Research Centre, Ottawa, pp 99–110

Nakashima DJ, Galloway McLean K, Thulstrup HD, Ramos Castillo Á, Rubis JT (2012) Weathering uncertainty: traditional knowledge for climate change assessment and adaptation. UNESCO and Darwin, UNU, Paris

Pierotti R, Wildcat D (2000) Traditional ecological knowledge: the third alternative. Ecol Appl 10(5):1333–1340

Reo N, Whyte K (2012) Hunting and morality as elements of traditional ecological knowledge. Hum Ecol 40(1):15–27. doi:10.1007/s10745-011-9448-1

Ross A, Sherman R, Snodgrass JG, Delcore HD (2010) Indigenous peoples and the collaborative stewardship of nature: knowledge binds and institutional conflicts. Left Coast Press, Walnut Creek, CA

Salmon E (1996) Decolonizing our voices. Winds Change 11(3):70–72

Siegel H (1997) Science education: multicultural and universal. Interchange 28 (2):97–108

Star SL, Griesemer JR (1989) Institutional ecology, 'Translations' and boundary objects: amateurs and professionals in Berkeley's museum of vertebrate zoology, 1907–39. Soc Stud Sci 19(3):387–420

Story P, Lickers F (1997) Partnership building for sustainable development: a First Nations perspective from Ontario. J Sustain For 4(3–4):149–162

Turnbull D (2000) Masons, tricksters and cartographers: comparative studies in the sociology of scientific and indigenous knowledge. Taylor & Francis, Philadelphia

UNEP (1998) Report of the fourth meeting of the parties to the convention on biodiversity. UNEP/CBD/COP/, Nairobi, Kenya

Voggesser G (2010) The tribal path forward: confronting climate change and conserving nature. Wildlife Prof 4(4):24–30

Warren DM, Slikkerveer LJ, Brokensha D (1995) The cultural dimension of development: indigenous knowledge systems. Intermediate Technology Publications, London

Watson-Verran H, Turnbull D (1995) Science and other indigenous knowledge systems. In: Jasanoff S, Markle G, Petersen J, Pinch T (ed) Handbook of science and technology studies. Sage, London, pp 115–139

Wildcat DR (2009) Red alert! Saving the planet with indigenous knowledge (Speaker's corner). Fulcrum, Golden, CO

Woodard S (2005) Blending science and tradition in the Arctic. Indian Country Today, 590 Madison Avenue, New York. 10022

Suggestions for Critical Reflection

1. How might a definition of TEK limit the relations between Indigenous and non-Indigenous scientists and communities?
2. What are the underlying assumptions of TEK being a collaborative concept and how does that address colonialism?
3. What are the dangers of thinking of TEK as an archive of knowledge? How might these negatively impact Indigenous communities?
4. Why should we not do away with the concept of TEK? What purpose might it serve between Indigenous and non-Indigenous communities?
5. Explain the rationale behind the belief that any type of knowledge production that does not include TEK and Western science "misses key perspectives on the world."

Additional Resources

For additional resources relating to this reading and its themes, visit sites.broadviewpress.com/waysofbeing/4-1

4.2
"Native American Epistemology through Dreams"

Joel Alvarez (Puerto Rican, Ecuadorian)

ABOUT THE AUTHOR

Joel Alvarez (Puerto Rican and Ecuadorian) earned an undergraduate degree in Philosophy (2019) with a minor in history and Latino studies from Brooklyn College. Currently, he is pursuing a PhD in Philosophy at the University of South Florida. His paper, "Christian Materialism, Logic & The Spiritual Realm," won third prize in the 2022 Tyndale House Cambridge for Philosophers of Religion. He also has a forthcoming publication titled "Spinozism & Native Americans on Pantheism & Panentheism" (Springer). His particular interest in philosophy is topics on religion/theology, identity, metaphysics, and topics that pertain to the problem of evil, free will, and God's Omniscience. His other interest in research is archaeology and science and their relation to philosophy and theology.

KEY TERMS

Knowledge, Dreams, Guidance, Identity, Epistemology, Truth, Objectivity, Subjectivity

Introduction

In *Meditations on First Philosophy*, René Descartes argues that one cannot trust one's senses since they are not a reliable source of obtaining knowledge of the world. One of Descartes's main contentions to support such an argument is from his explanation of dreams, where one can feel one is awake but instead one is dreaming. Native Americans, however, may argue that the experiences one has in dreams are real and are a source of knowledge of the real world.[1] Although Descartes uses dreams to support his argument, some Native Americans have a different take on dreams. Dreams for Native Americans are a source of knowledge as well as a source for obtaining one's identity. Gregory Cajete, in *American Indian Thought*, notes that "Dreams and Visions are a natural means for accessing knowledge and establishing relationship to the world. They are encouraged and facilitated."[2] In other words, it is through dreams that individuals are guided, destined, and informed.

Therefore, dreams as understood by some Native Americans are an extension of reality that anticipate events that will happen or can happen. The focus of this paper is an exploration of the philosophical and religious epistemology pertaining to Native Americans as described in their accounts of dreams.

§1 Native American Dream-Vision and Legends

For some Native Americans, phenomena or experiences in dreams (or visions) are real, and the knowledge someone obtains in dreams can assist them when they are awake. For example, the value of dreams is apparent in what some Native American traditions call the vision quest.[3] A vision quest is a cultural practice that many Native Americans follow and, when successful, the individual gains power, guidance, protection, understanding, and knowledge from a spirit. For example, according to Shay Welch, in *Dance as Native Performative Knowledge*,

> The vision quest is its own mechanism through which to gain insight into intuitive knowledge through bodily practices; but it is also a bodily practice through which access to blood memory, more specifically, might be gained. Most times, vision quests are an individual journey towards deeper meaning and knowledge of the world and oneself through an extended testing of the body in exposed natural conditions. In some instances, these quests can be taken on in the confines of a sweat lodge alone, in community, and/or in the presence of a medicine person. But in all cases, the embodied practice is to deprive the body of nourishment and expose it to extreme conditions in order to turn in towards the inscape to tap into the knowledge that lives there.[4]

The quest is extremely important for many Native American tribes since the vision provides individual enlightenment and guidance. Visions or dreams are "a way of closing the gap between our internal connection to the energy of the universe and our more explicit knowing and understanding of the world."[5] But more importantly, visions or dreams are, for many Native Americans, "a primary source of revealed knowledge" where the individual obtains knowledge of what they should do in the real world.[6]

§1.1 The Dunne-za and Ojibwa Tribe and Their Vision Quest Culture

David Martinez cites a couple of examples of the vision quest, notably from the Dunne-za and Ojibwa tribes. In these cases, the visions and dreams guide the individual in their life journey. From a young age, children are instructed to fast so they can experience dreams and visions. For instance, the Dunne-za believe that when a child reaches a certain age, they are ready to begin their vision quest journey.[7] In particular, what the child pursues in their vision quest is a song that is given by an animal spirit. Martinez describes the practice:

> What the Dunne-za boy will be seeking in particular during his vision quests is a *m a yine*, which is an animal's song, itself modeled 'after the songs that are the cries of giant prototypical animals represented in myth.' In order to acquire this song, the boy will have to travel away from camp into the bush.... Going into the bush, then, on a vision quest means joining the world of animals.... If the boy can fend off his apprehensions and maintain the fast that's part of his quest, the boy will enter a 'transformation when he is "just like drunk" or in a dreamlike state.' At this point the meeting between an animal and the vision seeker will be one in which the boy will understand the animal's speech. During this time, which may seem to be 'for days or even weeks,' the animal who visits a vision seeker will impart its song....[8]

During the quest, the child seeks the song because it is believed that it provides them with information about their identity. In other words, the song from the spirit gives the person "an understanding of his own humanity."[9] Therefore, the aim of the vision quest for the Dunne-za tribe is to receive knowledge of their identity, which is only given by the animal spirit that visits the vision seeker.

In a similar fashion to the Dunne-za, the Ojibwa take the vision quest journey when they are young. Like the Dunne-za, the Ojibwa seek a spirit that would provide them with important knowledge and guidance. As Sam D. Gill, a scholar of religious studies, states in *Native American Religions*,

> In the Great Lakes area Ojibwa culture, it was the practice to begin early in a child's life to prepare him or her for a vision fast. The parents implored their children to engage in short fasts to prepare them for receiving the power of a *manido*, or spiritual being. By age eight, a child might fast two meals every other day.... While religious awareness through the visionary experience was certainly momentous, it was not attained without much training and preparation. During the years of scheduled fasting, the child was made to think constantly about the power and guidance that he or she would receive in a vision.[10]

Gill mentions that Ojibwa children would take this journey of fasting to obtain a vision. The importance of this vision or dream was for the child to know which *manido* (spiritual being) would assist them in their journey through life, during which the *manido* would provide the individual with the necessary knowledge, protection, and advice they should take.[11] However, one's vision does not only provide what *manido* the individual will have, but the vision also shows what power the individual gained. In other words, such a vision or dream would provide them with important existential information such as how to live, what directions to follow, and what powers they have gained. For the Ojibwa, therefore, visions or dreams are extremely important since they provide the individual with the reality and knowledge of their identity in the world.

§1.2 Tribal Legends on Dreams

Since dreams are an essential component in everyday Native American life, communities have shared and passed down legends that show the effectiveness of dreams. One example of a legend about dreams is from the Pawnee tribe, which insists that dreams provide the individual with knowledge and guidance. The Pawnee legend, *The Medicine Grizzly Bear*, illustrates an individual receiving strength and power from a bear and obtaining guidance from a Bear spirit through a dream.[12] The specific guidance that the bear spirit gave was not to marry the Chief's daughter since this would cause the individual to lose the power that was given to him. The information given to the individual was an instruction regarding what they should do about a problem they wished to avoid.

The Seneca tribe also has a similar perspective on dreams. According to the Seneca legend *The Woman Who Fell from the Sky*, a Chief receives guidance regarding his very sick daughter. Every remedy or medicine had been given to her, but none made her well. A friend of the Chief had a dream in which he was instructed to tell the Chief to place his daughter beside a tree so she could be cured.[13] The Chief followed the guidance of his friend's dream. These Pawnee and Seneca legends demonstrate that it is through dreams that spirits communicate to individuals, directing and giving them information that instructs them in how they should act when confronted with a particular problem.

Gregory Cajete provides a legend shared by many Native American communities that illustrates why dreams or visions are essential. The legend maintains that humans had at one time the ability to speak to animals, but communication between them was terminated due to human malevolence towards the animals. Despite this loss, however, humans and animals can still communicate with each other through dreams or visions. Cajete describes it this way:

> In the beginning of time, Native myth contends that humans and animals could communicate with each other. Animals cared for humans, helping them find food, water, and shelter. They even sacrificed themselves when needed to help humans survive. They would assist humans in knowing when to prepare for the change of seasons or the coming of storms. This intimacy with animals came to an end when humans began to be disrespectful to their animal relations. Humans, it is mythically related, began to abuse animals, kill them without need, steal the food they had stored for winter, and arrogantly mistreat them in various ways. In some Native myths, such as those of the Southeastern tribes, it is said that the animals had a grand council meeting in which it was decided to punish humans by leaving them to fend for themselves and by refusing to communicate with them through language. This early direct connection to animals thereafter became submerged and could only be evoked through ritual, dream, and visioning.[14]

Although this passage claims one can only communicate with animals through dreams or visions, the legend also mentions that animals used to provide humans with a great deal of assistance. Thus, this passage notes that prior to the malice of humans, the animals protected and directed them by informing them. In other words, they helped humans by giving them information on how to obtain food, where they should go, or what they should do. But unfortunately, as all this information is now difficult to obtain because we no longer have such communication with animals, one needs to dream or have visions in order to receive direction or protection from animals.

§1.3 Other Native American Tribes on Dream-Visions

Along with the Dunne-za, Ojibwa, Pawnee, and Seneca, other tribes also hold dreams to be important. The Zuni assert that dreams provide information about real events,[15] while the Huron believe that dreams have the same value of existence as experiences while awake.[16] In other words, dreams for the Huron tribe are an extension of the world, with a reality comparable to that of the world where people are awake. This perspective is similar to that of the Dunne-za, who believe that "waking and dreaming are both part of the same life story."[17] The Menomini, on the other hand, take dreams even further and believe that dreams are not only real but also provide prophecy and warnings:

> For the Menomini of the Great Lakes region, all dreams had significance, and the prophecies or warnings that dreams might contain were to be

> observed scrupulously. For example, if a man dreamed of drowning, he would make a small canoe as a talisman and carry it about with him at all times. If the meaning of a dream was unclear, a person sought the interpretation of an elder, who, being nearer the end of his life or her life, was believed to be closer to the world of the spirits.[18]

As every dream for the Menomini has significance and meaning in the real world, one should take precautions as a consequence of the warning received in one's dream. In a similar fashion, the Nozinho believe dreams are symbolic and can indicate danger or good fortune.[19] For example, in the Nozinho tradition, dreaming about hawks, elks, or thunder would symbolize good luck or good fortune.[20] This interpretation of the symbolism in dreams is similar to that of the Cherokee. One Cherokee legend, for example, illustrates that someone dreaming of an eagle or its feathers symbolizes that one should perform an Eagle Dance.[21] In addition, the Mohave,[22] Cocopah,[23] and Maricopa[24] incorporate dreams to speak to their ancestors so they can receive direction from them. Overall, therefore, many Native American tribes depend on the information they receive in dreams because such information directs them in decision-making.[25]

Although many dreams have a certain reality for Native Americans and provide them with important information, some dreams can be false. The next section discusses how Native Americans still trust dreams even though some dreams provide false information.

§2. *Verifying If Dream Information Is True or False*

The Cree have a legend called *Mudjikiwis*, which tells the story of a father-in-law who thought his dream was true but then realized that it was indeed false:

> So he told all the people to go and get fish and eat them freely. On the following day, the young man, according to his mother-in-law's wish, took his wife to fish. They took many fish, and carried them home. The father-in-law knew, before they returned, that they had caught many. The old man had a dream. When he saw how the youth prepared the spear which his daughter had given him, he said, referring to his dream, 'My dream was wrong, I thought the youngest of the ten liked me the best. I made the spear in the way I saw it, not as this one has shown me. It is due to my dream that it is wrong.'[26]

Thus the father-in-law had a dream that gave him false information, and such information did not have its truth in the real world. For a dream to be considered true, it must be consistent with other facts in the world of reality. The father-in-law's case dream was not true since, in reality, the youngest of ten did not like him the best, and he made the wrong spear. Therefore, although dreams are important, some can be false.

Although dreams have the potential to mislead, there are ways to test a dream's veracity. One example can be found in the Huron tradition, where dreams are confirmed by events in the real world. Larry J. Zimmerman, an anthropologist and a scholar of Native American culture, writes this about the Huron tribe:

> ... the Huron paid particular attention to any dreams that occurred just before they went hunting, fishing, trading, or to war. So much did they rely on dreams for guidance in everyday life that the first Jesuit priests to contact the Huron described dreams as the tribespeople's main god. Sometimes advice received in dreams followed in preference to advice given by the tribal chiefs. However, not all dreams were assumed to be reliable—public confidence in an individual's dream varied according to his or her social status and how many of that person's earlier dream predictions had come true.[27]

As Zimmerman notes, the Huron, like all other Native American tribes, is dream-driven, but dreams are counted as true when they reveal themselves as true in the real world. In other words, although dreams are essential for Indigenous people, dreams must show their veracity in reality. The more one's dreams are verified in the real world, the more one will be respected among the community.

§3 Conclusion

For Native Americans, dreams are a source of knowledge and a way of obtaining one's identity. For this reason, Native Americans would take their dreams or visions seriously since they could provide important information. Such information received through dreams or visions can provide the individual with a power that a spirit has bestowed on them or with the direction one should take in life. Additionally, dreams can mean misfortune, prophecy, luck, or have a symbolic meaning. However, sometimes the information in dreams can be false, but in order to verify its veracity, the dream must be confirmed in reality. This stands in contrast to Descartes's claim that our sensed experience in dreams is not a reliable source of knowledge. Generally speaking, then, Native Americans learn and know things about the real world thanks to the information gathered in the world of dreams. Dreams are therefore an essential component of everyday Native American life.

Endnotes

1 The Native American tribes discussed here are the Ojibwa, Zuni, Seneca, Pawnee, Cree, Cherokee, Mohave, Nozinho, Cocopah, Maricopa, Dunne-za, Huron, and Menomini.
2 Gregory Cajete, "Philosophy of Native Science," in *American Indian Thought*, ed. Anne Waters (Oxford: Blackwell, 2004), 54.
3 Gregory Cajete, in *American Indian Thought*, mentions other forms of quests that the Native Americans would undergo: "Paths: Predetermined systematic activities of learning are viewed as ways to search for and find knowledge. All of nature has these inherent patterns of trajectories, 'rights paths,' which reflect the unfolding of natural pathways through which it may be understood. The 'Good Red Road', 'Dream-time Path', 'Earth Walk', and 'Pipe Way' are some of the ways Native peoples have referred to the directed path in the quest for knowledge, meaning, and understanding" (54).
4 Shay Welch, "Dance as Native Performative Knowledge," *Native American and Indigenous Philosophy Newsletter* 18, no. 1 (Fall 2018): 28. See also Richard Erdoes and Alfonso Ortiz, *American Indian Myths and Legends* (New York: Pantheon Books, 1984), 69.
5 Shay Welch, "Dance as Native Performative Knowledge," 27. See also McPherson and Rabb, *Indian from the Inside: Native American Philosophy and Cultural Renewal* (Jefferson, NC: McFarland & Company, 2011), 63.
6 Shay Welch, "Dance as Native Performative Knowledge," 27.
7 David Martinez, "The Hidden Path from Dream to Reality: Myth, Character, and the Dunne-za," *Newsletters on American Indians in Philosophy* 1, no. 1 (Fall 2001): 6.
8 Ibid., 6.
9 Ibid., 7.
10 Sam D. Gill, *Native American Religions: An Introduction* (Belmont, CA: Wadsworth, 2005), 71.
11 Ibid., 72.
12 "That night the Bear came to the boy in his sleep and spoke to him. He said: 'My son, tomorrow the chief of the tribe is going to ask you to take his daughter for your wife, but you must not do this yet. I wish you to wait until you have done certain things. If you take a wife before that time, your power will go from you'.... In the night, before he slept, he filled the pipe and smoked as the Bear had told him to do, and then he went to bed. In dreams the Bear said to him: 'My son, you have done what I wished you to do. Now the power will remain with you as long as you shall live. Now you can marry, if you will.'" George Bird Grinnell, "The Medicine Grizzly Bear," *Harper's New Monthly Magazine* 102 (1901): 741.
13 "A long time ago human beings lived high up in what is now called heaven. They had a great and illustrious chief. It so happened that this chief's daughter was taken very ill with a strange affliction. All the people were very anxious as to the outcome of her illness. Every known remedy was tried in an attempt to cure her, but none had any effect. Near the lodge of this chief stood a great tree, which every year bore corn used for food. One of the friends of the chief had a dream, in which he was advised to tell the chief that in order to cure his daughter he must lay her beside this tree, and that he must have the tree dug up. This advice was carried out to the letter." Frank de Caro, ed., *An Anthology of American Folktales and Legends* (Abingdon, UK: Taylor & Francis, 2014), 42.
14 Gregory Cajete, *Native Science: Natural Laws of Interdependence* (Santa Fe: Clear Light, 2000), 151–52.
15 Larry J. Zimmerman, *The Sacred Wisdom of the American Indians* (London: Watkins, 2011), 142.
16 Ibid.
17 David Martinez, "The Hidden Path from Dream to Reality," 8.
18 Larry J. Zimmerman, *The Sacred Wisdom of the American Indians*, 210.
19 Ibid., 224.
20 Ibid.
21 James Mooney, *Myths of the Cherokee* (Outlook Verlag, 2020), 283.
22 Bertha P. Dutton, *Indians of The American Southwest* (Hoboken, NJ: Prentice Hall, 1975), 171.
23 Ibid., 177.
24 Ibid., 233.

25 A Dunne-za tribal leader is obligated to use dreams or visions to make tribal decisions; e.g., whether they should go to war. David Martinez, "The Hidden Path from Dream to Reality," 15.
26 Alanson Skinner, "European Tales from the Plains Ojibwa," *The Journal of American Folklore* 29, no. 113 (July–Sept. 1916), 341–67.
27 Larry J. Zimmerman, *The Sacred Wisdom of the American Indians*, 142.

References

Cajete, Gregory. "Philosophy of Native Science." *American Indian Thought*, edited by Anne Waters. Oxford: Blackwell, 2004.

Cajete, Gregory. *Native Science: Natural Laws of Interdependence.* Santa Fe: Clear Light, 2000.

De Caro, Frank, ed. *An Anthology of American Folktales and Legends.* Abingdon, UK: Taylor & Francis, 2014.

Dutton, Bertha P. *Indians of the American Southwest.* Hoboken, NJ: Prentice Hall, 1975.

Erdoes, Richard, and Alfonso Ortiz. *American Indian Myths and Legends.* New York: Pantheon Books, 1984.

Gill, Sam D. *Native American Religions: An Introduction.* Belmont, CA: Wadsworth, 2005.

Grinnell, George Bird. "The Medicine Grizzly Bear." *Harper's New Monthly Magazine* 102 (1901): 736–44.

Martinez, David. "The Hidden Path from Dream to Reality: Myth, Character, and the Dunneza." *Newsletters on American Indians in Philosophy* 1, no. 1 (Fall 2001): 5–10.

Mooney, James. *Myths of the Cherokee.* Outlook Verlag, 2020.

Skinner, Alanson. "European Tales from the Plains Ojibwa." *The Journal of American Folklore* 29, no. 113 (July–Sept. 1916).

Welch, Shay. "Dance as Native Performative Knowledge." *Native American and Indigenous Philosophy Newsletter* 18, no. 1 (Fall 2018): 23–35.

Zimmerman, Larry J. *The Sacred Wisdom of the American Indians.* London: Watkins, 2011.

Suggestions for Critical Reflection

1. In what ways do Native Americans learn through dreams?
2. How do Native Americans verify if a dream is true? Do you think a dream can be verified to be true? Why or why not?
3. Why are dreams and visions important for Native Americans?

4. What knowledge does one obtain when going on a vision quest or when one has a dream?
5. Do you think dreams can provide someone with important information? Why or why not?

Additional Resources

For additional resources relating to this reading and its themes, visit sites.broadviewpress.com/waysofbeing/4-2

4.3
"The Epistemology of Deep Disagreement and Indigenous Oral Histories"

Paul Simard Smith (Métis)

ABOUT THE AUTHOR

Paul Simard Smith is a citizen of the Métis Nation–Saskatchewan. He was born and raised in Regina, Saskatchewan, in Treaty Four Territory and the Homeland of the Métis Nation. His Métis family is from Meadow Lake, Saskatchewan, with roots in the Qu'Appelle Valley of Saskatchewan and in the White Horse Plains of Red River. He earned a BA (2005) in Philosophy from the University of Regina, an MA (2007) in Philosophy from the University of Windsor, and a PhD (2013) from the University of Waterloo. Simard Smith is currently Assistant Professor of Philosophy at the University of Regina. His research ranges across a variety of theoretical and applied issues in epistemology and metaphysics, philosophy of language, and social and political philosophy.

KEY TERMS

Law, Culture, Oral Histories, Epistemic Principles, Elders, Aboriginal Title, Rational Argument, Recognition, Reconciliation, Consent, Justification

§1 Introduction

Broadly construed, the purpose of this paper is to explore some of the dialectical tensions that emerge at the intersections of North American Indigenous epistemologies and juridical epistemologies employed within settler legal traditions.

Since the notion of "epistemology," or of "an epistemology," plays an important role in this discussion, I want to begin by making some clarifying comments on how I use those terms here. In their book *Indigenous Statistics: A Quantitative Research Methodology*, Chris Anderson and Maggie Walter characterize epistemology as follows:

> Epistemology explores theories of knowledge or, more pragmatically, ways of knowing.... Yet, while traditional Western philosophy saw epistemology as outside of, or prior to, culture, what we regard as 'knowledge' is in

> fact encapsulated within a social and culture framework. Epistemological theory concerns itself with understanding how the (mostly unwritten) rules about what is counted as knowledge are set—what is defined as knowledge, who can and cannot be 'knowledgeable,' which 'knowledges' are valued and, by extension, which are marginalized.[1]

Thus, epistemology involves a philosophical study of knowing and knowledge, as well as several related concepts, such as justification, belief, evidence, and certainty. Western epistemology, as characterized by Walter and Andersen, sets aside issues of which culture, society, or field in pursuing its study of knowledge. This approach seeks a neutral conception of knowledge that is valid for all times, places, and cultures. In posing the question "What is knowledge," one does so, on this conception, by setting aside their ethnic, social, economic, racial, and gender backgrounds and seeks an answer that is uninfluenced by these varying socio-cultural positionalities and valid for any combination of them. However, contrasting with this picture of epistemology, Walter and Andersen focus on "ways of knowing." On this view, all forms of knowledge, including that of traditional Western philosophy, are enmeshed in a "social and cultural framework." Rather than posing the question "What is knowledge" from outside of a socio-cultural positionality, one cannot step outside such a framework in posing this question. On this view, attributing knowledge to a person, or truth to a claim, is entangled in complex socio-cultural practices pertaining to who has authority to teach; what kinds of skills are valued; what protocols are in place for one to acquire knowledge, respect, and credibility; and what sorts of claims are commonly treated as knowledge. In this way, varying ethnic, social, economic, gender, and racial positionalities can be associated with different "knowledges" or "ways of knowing."

The tension between settler juridical epistemologies and the variety of Indigenous epistemologies from Turtle Island that I home in on here turns on conflicting perspectives on the evidentiary role and value of Indigenous oral histories. My contention is that the notion of deep disagreement, as articulated within recent social epistemic and argumentation theoretic literature, can, while falling short of offering a perfect model, help one understand *some* of the tensions that arise among these distinctive epistemic traditions.

In section two, I briefly discuss the notion of deep disagreement. In section three, I consider the possibility that some disagreements over the evidentiary role of Indigenous oral histories constitute deep disagreements in the sense characterized. In section four I consider three different approaches to resolving the disagreement.

§2 Deep Disagreement

Deep disagreement consists of a conflict, or dispute of some kind, over *fundamental epistemic principles*.[2] Michael Lynch characterizes an *epistemic principle* as a principle that tells us "what is or isn't justified, and thus constitute our general standard of justification."[3] Among the set of epistemic principles is that subset which holds that some source of evidence is reliable.

For example, an *epistemic source principle* (ESP) may hold that a thermometer reliably indicates the temperature of a fowl baking in an oven, or that a track with such and such characteristics reliably indicates that a certain species of animal passed through this spot. When disagreement turns on the application of different ESPs, the discussion commonly shifts to a consideration of the contested principle rather than focusing on the contested proposition. These sorts of disagreements are often easily resolved.

For example, consider two hunters who have different points of view about some animal tracks they have come across. One hunter claims the tracks were left by an elk, while the other contends they were left by a moose. Perhaps they discover that their disagreement is not at base about what animal left these tracks, but about how to interpret the significance of certain characteristics of the tracks themselves. One hunter takes the characteristic to mean it is an elk track, while the other takes the characteristic to, in fact, be indicative of a moose track. Both hunters, however, regard a respected elder hunter as knowledgeable on such matters. So, to resolve their disagreement, they consult the elder's opinion. In this case, the disagreement over the ESP—whether the relevant characteristics signify elk or moose tracks—is resolved through the application of a more fundamental ESP that both hunters agree with, *viz.*, that the elder hunter is authoritative on such matters.

However, sometimes disagreements arise that revolve around a *fundamental epistemic source principle* (FESP). A FESP does not only endorse a certain source of evidence as reliable. According to Lynch, a FESP "is a principle such that it can't be shown to be true without employing the source that the relevant principle endorses as reliable."[4] Unlike the dispute over the tracks just discussed, disagreements involving FESPs "cannot be resolved by appealing to a more fundamental epistemic principle."[5]

Lynch calls disagreements that turn on FESPs *deep disagreements*. It is unclear how to proceed to resolve such disagreements. Why? Because "the FESP that one person accepts the other doesn't."[6] FESPs can only be justified by arguments that require endorsing the source of evidence the FESP itself regards as reliable. Thus, someone who rejected the FESP will not regard its source of evidence as reliable and will not be rationally persuaded by any argument in its support.[7] A common example of this kind of disagreement in Western philosophy is disputes surrounding a principle of induction. At one pole, some variant of a Humean skeptic might hold that one cannot establish an inductive method as reliable without employing induction in such a method's justification. Thus someone skeptical of induction would not be persuaded by any justification for induction.[8]

§3 A Case of Deep Disagreement?

Some recent episodes in the legal history of Canada provide a possible case study of deep disagreement, or at least a deeply entrenched disagreement that is difficult to rationally resolve. Specifically, I am thinking of disagreements over the evidentiary role of Indigenous oral history in support of Indigenous legal arguments involving the legal concept of "aboriginal title."

On my understanding, the legal notion of *aboriginal title* refers to a unique collective right to the use and jurisdiction of an Indigenous group's traditional territory.[9] One well-known case involving the use of oral histories to establish claims to aboriginal title occurred in the *Delgamuukw v British Columbia* case. In this case, the Gitxsan and the Wet'suwet'en nations in British Columbia asserted "ownership" and "jurisdiction" of over tens of thousands of square kilometers in Northwestern BC. These nations provided oral histories as evidence of their ownership and jurisdiction of these territories. However, according to the ruling of Chief Justice Allan McEachern of the BC Court of Appeal, "the broad concepts embodied in oral tradition did not conform to juridical definitions of truth," and thus he claimed that "I am unable to accept ... oral traditions as reliable bases for detailed history, but they could confirm findings based on other admissible evidence." Presumably, Justice McEachern is asserting that he deems unreliable the principle—deemed reliable by the Gitxsan and Wet'suwet'en—that oral traditions, independent of any archeological or written testimony, provide sufficient evidence for their ownership and jurisdiction of their traditional territories.[10]

So where is the deep disagreement? Presumably one component of the disagreement turns on whether oral histories are independently sufficient evidence of an Indigenous nation's ownership of and jurisdiction on its traditional territories. However, to characterize the disagreement a bit more carefully, I float the following formulation of what might be characterized as an oral history principle (OHP). Indigenous oral histories are sufficient for acquiring knowledge of the cultural, legal, and political conventions of Indigenous nations; about the philosophical, scientific, and moral knowledge of Indigenous nations; and about the history and traditional territories of Indigenous nations.

Broadly speaking, one pole of the dispute over OHP is embodied in an epistemology that regards reasoning in accordance with OHP as a reliable source of knowledge about the relevant subject matters. The other pole is embodied in an epistemology that would require written, archeological, or other forms of physical evidence. This latter pole holds that, when these forms of evidence are unavailable, one cannot rationally form judgments based on oral traditions.

§4 Three Approaches to Resolving the Disagreement

How could such disagreements be resolved? In this section, I'll consider three different approaches. The first holds that the appearance of a deep disagreement is illusory and there are truth-conducive features of OHP that provide grounds for its adoption. The second and third approaches would understand this disagreement as genuinely deep.

§4.1 Some Truth-Conducive Features of Oral History

A variety of reasons can be provided for thinking that OHP is reliable. Some, like oral history scholar David Henige, have raised concerns that oral histories are prone to change over time. However, C.A. Coady, as well as scholar and hereditary Chief of the Mi'kmaq Grand Council Stephen J. Augustine, note that independent chains of transmission of the oral traditions can be used as checks against each other. In some communities, these scholars also note, members who demonstrated aptitude for recalling oral traditions are assigned the role of ensuring their accuracy. In cases where these sorts of communal checks exist, Coady argues, there is reason to think that oral histories have undergone minimal change.

In *Oral History and the Epistemology of Testimony*, Tim Kenyon develops a point made by Alessandro Portelli in Portelli's account of the oral history of the Italian socialist labor movement. The particular episode in the history of this movement involves the independently confirmable death of Luigi Trastulli in an anti-NATO protest in 1949. Kenyon notes that in his investigation, however, Portelli

> ... discovers that many testifiers blended some events in memory, elided other events altogether, and mistakenly placed themselves at the center of key events. This discovery leads Portelli, not to skepticism about oral history, but to a more complicated understanding of the connections between the truth-value of testimony and the historian's ability to learn from it.[11]

Rather, in Portelli's approach,

> The strict truth of a piece of testimony might fail to be the crucial consideration, not necessarily because truth is a suspect notion ... but because there are many other truths illuminated by an understanding of how even false testimony comes to have its content, in its context, in the mouth of its particularly situated speaker.[12]

According to Portelli,

> Oral sources are credible but with a different credibility. The importance of oral testimony may lie not in its adherence to *fact*, but rather in its departure from it, as imagination, symbolism, and desire emerge. Therefore, there are no "false" oral sources.... The diversity of oral history consists in the fact that "wrong" statements are still psychologically "true," and that this truth may be equally as important as *factually reliable* accounts.[13]

Understanding the content of Indigenous oral histories as a list of propositions probably results in an impoverished reading of the information these narratives contain. Rather, by paying attention to the social, legal, moral, emotional, symbolic, and psychological significance associated with the narratives, including in those points at which the narrative appears to depart from a strict adherence to fact, can result in learning important truths.

It should be noted that this point is not a concession that oral history is non-factual. Rather, the claim is that the meaning and purpose of oral history is not solely identified with its adherence to fact. Understanding an Indigenous oral history by checking off what one believes to be factual from what one believes is not, is not only likely to get you a scolding from the knowledge keeper sharing the story, but, epistemically, you are likely to fundamentally miss the point being conveyed.

I think Stó:lo Nation cultural advisor and historian Albert (Sonny) McHalsie nicely illustrates this in his discussion of some conflicting claims that Stó:lo elders make about the chronology for a story known as the *sxwó:yxwey*. McHalsie believes that this story is referring to a smallpox outbreak that occurred in 1782. However, when he asks the elders about the timeline, he gets different answers. McHalsie explains:

> When I ask the elders today, depending on who you talk to, some elders will say, 'Oh the *sxwó:yxwey* is only a couple hundred years old.' Some elders will say, 'No the *sxwó:yxwey* is thousands of years old.' And so while

you try to disprove or try to prove one of them, you can't really. You can look at the genealogies of some families and say, 'Oh yeah, that must be around 1780.' But then what about the other ones that are saying it's thousands of years old? Well, they're partly correct as well because after the smallpox epidemic there were certain teachings that needed to be retained, and elements of those teachings that were retained were inside the *sxwó:yxwey* story. That's what made it real so that it could be believed and could become part of our culture and our tradition. So those old teachings are encompassed in there. To me, that's why I think that an elder says it's thousands of years old is right because there are teachings within the story that are probably thousands of years old. Within this story that's only two hundred years old.[14]

McHalsie's discussion shows how the tension in the different elders' claims can act to an attentive listener's epistemic advantage. This tension enables the listener to recognize that there are more ancient components within the *sxwó:yxwey* story and to tease out a richer understanding of what the elders are saying when they claim that the story is thousands of years old.

These considerations suggest that there is a plausible case for the truth-conduciveness of oral histories, on a broad conception of truth which includes psychological, symbolic, social, and moral meaningfulness. If so, there is a basis for adopting a legal epistemology that employs a principle like OHP. However, someone doubtful of OHP may be unpersuaded and regard such considerations as inadequate to support OHP's reliability. If considerations along these lines remain unpersuasive to an OHP skeptic, and they still regard OHP as unreliable and, thus, as inappropriate for inclusion in a juridical reasoning process, then perhaps it is more plausible that there is a genuinely deep disagreement.

§4.2 Resolving the Deep Disagreement: The Politics of Recognition

So, what could be done in the face of such deep disagreements? One option is to consult practical reason and ask what legal epistemology promotes the well-being of the overall community of nations that reside on the land currently named Canada. Indeed, according to Lynch, deep disagreements are to be "solved, if at all, by appeal to practical reasons."[15]

One practical reason for adopting OHP may be grounded in the "politics of recognition." Roughly, the idea is that, to promote reconciliation between the Canadian state and the variety of Indigenous nations, political, legal, and institutional recognition of principles like OHP is required as an important component of enhanced recognition of Indigenous legal traditions within the Canadian legal order. However, in *Red Skin, White Masks* Glen Sean Coulthard argues that the politics of recognition often functions to serve the interests of the settler-colonial state. While states adopting liberal tropes of recognition might *appear* more accommodating than they would by practicing an explicit strategy of colonization, the "structural orientation of the settler-colonial state remains the same."[16] Merely surface forms of legal and political recognition for OHP, as well as for Indigenous legal traditions more broadly, are not, ultimately, likely to be a satisfying resolution to this difference of opinion for Indigenous Peoples in general.

§4.3 Resolving the Deep Disagreement: Inter-societal Legal Epistemology

A different proposal would be for the disagreeing legal and epistemological communities to engage in the construction of a mutually agreeable inter-societal legal framework.[17] This option would regard a plurality of legal-epistemic traditions as authoritative at generating legal and epistemic obligations, in setting legal-epistemic norms, and in interpreting law within the lands now called Canada. From this framework, the variety of Indigenous legal traditions and European legal traditions would possess *equivalent authority* in the construction of inter-societal legal and legal-epistemic norms. Such a legal framework would not arise from authority being granted or bestowed by Canada. Rather, such a framework would involve crafting a system of adjudication among distinct legal traditions that can be jointly agreed upon. This inter-societal framework would plausibly require an epistemology with some substantially more significant contribution from legal-epistemic principles like OHP, and other legal epistemic principles found within Indigenous legal traditions.

However, the prospect of actualizing a genuine resolution to the disagreement along these lines is likely to be a long and difficult path. One particularly challenging problem to overcome is the uneven distribution of political, legal, and material power tilting in favor of the settler-colonial state and its capitalist economic system. Inter-societal legal deliberations within such unevenly balanced power structures risk collapsing into the same problem Coulthard has pointed out with the politics of recognition. While there may be surface forms of recognition for principles like OHP at the inter-societal level, there remains no serious challenge to the structural power and epistemologies of the settler-colonial state.

Nevertheless, even though there are challenges with such an approach, the Canadian state has, at least, expressed a desire to place itself on a stronger ethical foundation with respect to its relationship with Indigenous Peoples. For example, whether or not one regards this as genuine, the current Prime Minister Justin Trudeau has stated that, "No relationship is more important to Canada than the relationship with Indigenous Peoples. Our government is working together with Indigenous Peoples to build a nation-to-nation, Inuit-Crown, government-to-government relationship."[18] And, on June 21, 2021, *the United Nations Declaration on the Rights of Indigenous Peoples Act* received royal assent.

If Canada, however, is to actualize an ethical and just relationship with Indigenous Peoples, then its fundamental laws, public policies, and institutions would have to be justified by argumentation that is cogent not only from the juridical traditions of the common law, but also from the perspective of Indigenous legal traditions. A widely regarded principle underlying legitimate political orders is the so-called "liberal principle of legitimacy." This principle holds that "fundamental political principles, laws and institutions, to be legitimate, must be justifiable from the point of view of all reasonable citizens."[19,20] However, to satisfy this principle, Canada's fundamental laws, policies, and institutions, I submit, would have to be justified by argumentation that is cogent not only from settler legal-epistemic perspectives, but also from Indigenous legal-epistemic perspectives. Thus, while significant challenges exist, the extent to which Canada genuinely seeks an ethical foundation for law and justice will determine whether a program of genuinely inter-societal law is possible.

§5 Conclusion

In conclusion, I am uncertain that any of above-mentioned approaches can effectively result in genuine resolution to the conflicts arising across Indigenous and settler legal-epistemic traditions. However, while this discussion might not provide a clear path to the resolution to such tensions, I hope that it does offer a sketch of some of the dialectical space that exists at the intersections of Indigenous and settler-colonial legal and epistemic traditions and develops some options for further reflection and consideration.

Endnotes

1 Maggie Walter and Chris Andersen, *Indigenous Statistics: A Quantitative Research Methodology* (Abingdon, UK: Routledge, 2013), 47–48.

2 For a discussion of various other kinds of deep disagreement and how they differ from this conception of deep disagreement, see Paul Simard Smith and Michael Lynch, "Varieties of Deep Epistemic Disagreement," *TOPOI: An International Journal of Philosophy* 40, no. 5 (2021): 971–82.

3 Michael Lynch, "After the Spade Turns: Disagreement, First Principles and Epistemic Contractarianism," *International Journal for the Study of Skepticism* 6, no. 2–3 (2016): 250.

4 Ibid.
5 Simard Smith and Lynch, "Varieties of Deep Epistemic Disagreement," 976.
6 Ibid., 977.
7 Ibid., 976–77.
8 For extensive discussion of another example, one involving a disagreement over a fundamental epistemic source principle for acquiring knowledge of the distant geological past, see Lynch (2010, 2016). Also see Andrew Aberdein, "Arrogance and Deep Disagreement," in *Polarization, Arrogance and Dogmatism: Philosophical Perspectives* for an example involving a disagreement about how to evaluate the height of mountains.
9 See, for example, Indigenous Foundations, "Aboriginal title," https://indigenousfoundations.arts.ubc.ca/aboriginal_title/. Also see P.G. McHugh, *Aboriginal Title: The Modern Jurisprudence of Tribal Land Rights* for a more extensive discussion of the common law jurisprudence surrounding the legal notion of "Aboriginal title," which we can only touch on in this discussion. One point worth noting, however, is that at the time of the Crown assertion of sovereignty in the Royal Proclamation of 1763, it was acknowledged that Indigenous Peoples possessed "Aboriginal title" by virtue of their pre-existing ownership of the land. This is regarded by Common Law as a "burden on Crown sovereignty" and one that can only be extinguished by the Crown. Thus, establishing ownership and jurisdiction at the time of the Royal Proclamation over a given tract of land is supposed to illicit legal obligations from the Crown to Indigenous Peoples who possess Aboriginal title. If an Indigenous People establish ownership of their traditional territories at the time of the Royal Proclamation, then, presuming their Aboriginal title has never been extinguished by the Crown, that would be grounds for them possessing Aboriginal title and for the Crown owing to them any obligations associated with that. For criticism of the notion of Aboriginal title and its role within the current jurisprudence in the Canadian legal order, see Dale Turner, *This Is Not a Peace Pipe: Towards a Critical Indigenous Philosophy*. For our purposes, we are not evaluating ethical or conceptual problems with the notion of Aboriginal title, of which there are several. Rather, our focus is on the dispute over whether Indigenous oral traditions could provide independently sufficient evidence for ownership of traditional territories at, for example, the time of the Royal Proclamation.
10 Only a cursory summary and discussion of the *Delgamuukw v British Columbia* case is possible here. However, it is worth noting that the case was appealed to the Supreme Court of Canada, which in turn ordered a new trial. However, in their decision on the case, the SCC held that the courts were obligated to admit and consider forms of evidence, such as oral history, distinctive to Indigenous legal traditions. For a more extensive discussion of this case, see Dale Turner, *This Is Not a Peace Pipe*.
11 Tim Kenyon, "Oral History and the Epistemology of Testimony," *Social Epistemology* 1 (2016): 59.
12 Ibid., 61–62.
13 Alessandro Portelli, *The Death of Luigi Trastulli and Other Stories: Form and Meaning in Oral History* (Albany: State University of New York Press, 1991), 51, emphasis added.
14 Albert McHalsie, "We Have to Take Care of Everything That Belongs to Us," in *"Be of Good Mind": Essays on the Coast Salish*, ed. Bruce Granville Miller (Lincoln: University of Nebraska Press, 2007), 117.
15 Lynch, Michael P., "Epistemic Circularity and Epistemic Incommensurability," in Adrian Haddock, Alan Millar, and Duncan Pritchard (eds), *Social Epistemology* (Oxford, 2010), p. 274.
16 Glen Sean Coulthard, *Red Skins, White Masks: Rejecting the Colonial Politics of Recognition* (Minneapolis: University of Minnesota Press, 2014), 25.
17 For further discussion of the inter-societal law approach see Val Napoleon et al. in *Mikomosis and the Wetiko: A Teaching Guide for Youth, Community, and Post-Secondary Educators*.
18 Justin Trudeau, "Statement by the Prime Minister of Canada on National Aboriginal Day," June 21, 2017, https://pm.gc.ca/en/news/statements/2017/06/21/statement-prime-minister-canada-national-aboriginal-day.
19 Karin Jonch-Clausen and Klemens Kappel, "Social Epistemic Liberalism and the Problem of Deep Disagreement," *Ethical Theory and Moral Practice* 18, no. 1 (2015): 371–84.
20 Of course, one need not endorse some form of liberalism to hold that this kind of consensus-based principle of political legitimacy plays an important role in the legitimate exercise of political authority.

References

Aberdein, Andrew. "Arrogance and Deep Disagreement." In *Polarization, Arrogance and Dogmatism: Philosophical Perspectives*, edited by A. Tanesini and M. Lynch, 39–52. London: Routledge, 2020.

Coady, C.A.J. *Testimony: A Philosophical Study*. Oxford: Oxford University Press, 1992.

Coulthard, Glen Sean. *Red Skin, White Masks: Rejecting the Colonial Politics of Recognition*. Minneapolis, MN: University of Minnesota Press, 2014.

Henige, D. *Historical Evidence and Argument*. Madison: University of Wisconsin Press, 2005.

Jonch-Clausen, Karin, and Klemens Kappel. "Social Epistemic Liberalism and the Problem of Deep Disagreement." *Ethical Theory and Moral Practice* 18, no. 1 (2015): 371–84.

Kenyon, Tim. "Oral History and the Epistemology of Testimony." *Social Epistemology* 1 (2016): 45–66.

Lynch, Michael. "Epistemic Circularity and Epistemic Incommensurability." In *Social Epistemology*, edited by A. Haddock, A. Millar, and D. Pritchard. Oxford: Oxford University Press, 2010.

Lynch, Michael. "After the Spade Turns: Disagreement, First Principles and Epistemic Contractarianism." *International Journal for the Study of Skepticism* 6, no. 2–3 (2016): 248–59.

McHalsie, Albert (Naxaxalhts'i, Sonny). "We Have to Take Care of Everything That Belongs to Us." In *"Be of Good Mind": Essays on the Coast Salish*, edited by Bruce Granville Miller, 82–130. Lincoln: University of Nebraska Press, 2007.

McHugh, P.G. *Aboriginal Title: The Modern Jurisprudence of Tribal Land Rights*. Oxford: Oxford University Press, 2011.

Napoleon, Val et al. *Mikomosis and the Wetiko: A Teaching Guide for Youth, Community, and Post-Secondary Educators*. Victoria, BC: Indigenous Law Research Unit, 2014.

Portelli, Alessandro. *The Death of Luigi Trastulli and Other Stories: Form and Meaning in Oral History*. Albany: State University of New York Press, 1991.

Simard Smith, Paul, and Michael Lynch. "Varieties of Deep Epistemic Disagreement." *TOPOI: An International Journal of Philosophy* 40, no. 5 (2021): 971–82.

Trudeau, Justin. "Statement by the Prime Minister of Canada on National Aboriginal Day." June 21, 2017. https://pm.gc.ca/en/news/statements/2017/06/21/statement-prime-minister-canada-national-aboriginal-day.

Turner, Dale. *This Is Not a Peace Pipe: Towards a Critical Indigenous Philosophy*. Toronto: University of Toronto Press, 2006.

Walter, Maggie, and Chris Andersen. *Indigenous Statistics: A Quantitative Research Methodology*. Abingdon, UK: Routledge, 2013.

Suggestions for Critical Reflection

1. Do you think differences of opinion over the evidentiary sufficiency of Indigenous oral traditions are genuine cases of deep disagreement?
2. Of the three approaches considered in this paper for resolving differences of opinion over the evidentiary sufficiency of Indigenous oral traditions, which, if any, do you find the most plausible (truth-conducive features of oral tradition, the politics of recognition, or inter-societal law)? If you think a different approach would be more plausible, explain.
3. Does the inter-societal law approach really evade Glen Sean Coulthard's criticism of the politics of recognition?
4. After witnessing the film *Trick or Treaty?* (see companion website linked below), do you think treaties with the Indigenous nations were instances of deep disagreement?

Additional Resources

For additional resources relating to this reading and its themes, visit **sites.broadviewpress.com/waysofbeing/4-3**

PART V

Ethics

INTRODUCTION

The Good Path: How Should We Live Our Lives?

Ethics, an area of investigation found in value theory, focuses on questions of right and wrong, or morality. In the Western tradition, ethics is further divided into three areas of study: ethical theory, applied ethics, and metaethics. These three areas are also present in the oral traditions of Indigenous communities—although the areas will not be clearly demarcated from each other, or from the other sub-disciplines of metaphysics and epistemology. While the stories of an Indigenous community may include the existence of virtues, like humility or gratitude, they would not be laid out formally in a manner similar to that of the Western canon. Virtuous behavior may appear in a story as part of a character's personality, or it may be part of what is implied by the story. For example, in the Haudenosaunee Creation Story of Skywoman, the virtue of humility is implied through the context of Skywoman being supported by the animals as she falls through the sky. The story, in one context, serves to remind the listener that humans were not the first creation, that they depend on the animals for their existence, and there is an obligation borne of that dependence. In the story, there is no formal presentation of humility and no conceptual analysis as one might find in its Western analogue, but the story, in one context, might serve as an invitation for the listener to consider the right or proper way to act.

The first selection in this chapter offers an epistemological account of what one needs to know to live the right way, to be in harmony with one's surroundings. Joseph Len Miller (Muscogee) introduces the concept of harmony within a metaphysical framework of relationships, which is shared by many Indigenous communities on Turtle Island. This account not only speaks to the consideration of well-being for others (in the broadest possible terms), but also highlights the emphasis on context and self-knowledge. For many Indigenous individuals, living ethically includes reasoning from what they know in order to fulfill their obligations to others, human and nonhuman alike.

Q'um Q'um Xiiem, Jo-Ann Archibald (Stó:lō/ Soowahlie First Nation) addresses memory and Indigenous storytelling in our second reading. A fundamental skill involving the dissemination of knowledge is the storyteller's commitment to memorize stories. This may cause the reader to question the placement of this reading.

Shouldn't it be in the chapter on epistemology instead? While the techniques of passing down stories might be suited to the topic of the previous chapter, this reading includes multiple conceptions of Indigenous values. The reading opens with a story that describes Old Man Coyote as being reluctant to do what he should (care for his relations). Instead, Coyote would rather do what is easy (look for the missing bone needle by the light of the campfire instead of where he lost it). Indigenous stories are more than recorded events: sometimes the story assists individuals in determining how they should live in the world. Lived stories are a part of the reclamation of culture and language revitalization. Stories, especially those known as trickster stories, teach what is important and afford the listener some space to reason.* Like the bone needle, Indigenous stories are tools that should be treated respectfully.

Part V concludes with a keynote address given by Piita Taqtu Irniq, Peter Irniq (Inuit), at the 2006 "Arctic Change and Coastal Communities" Conference, held in Tuktoyaktuk, Northwest Territories. In his address, Irniq encourages a return to Inuit values and culture as a way of dealing with the challenges of colonialism. Life for Inuit has changed considerably since contact with Europeans—and not solely due to the introduction of technology. Today, the Inuit way of life risks being subsumed by a dominant, Western worldview. Irniq suggests that Inuit knowledge, culture, and values provide guidance for what might be described as living a good life. Irniq proposes that being healthy and living a good life will enable Inuit to create solutions to contemporary social, political, and environmental problems.

* Brian Burkhart, *Indigenizing Philosophy through the Land: A Trickster Methodology for Decolonizing Environmental Ethics and Indigenous Futures* (East Lansing: Michigan State University Press, 2019), xxiii.

5.1
"What Do We Need to Know to Live in Harmony with Our Surroundings?"

Joseph Len Miller (Muscogee)

ABOUT THE AUTHOR

Hesci. Joey Miller cvhocefkv tos. Hello. My name is Joey Miller. I'm an assistant professor in the Philosophy department at West Chester University in West Chester, Pennsylvania. Although I am living on Lenapehoking (the ancestral territory of the Lenape), I grew up in Corcoran, Minnesota, on the ancestral lands of the Wahpekute and am of Mvskoke descent (an enrolled member of the Muscogee Nation). I received my BA (2009) in philosophy (applied ethics emphasis) and a BASc (2009) in psychology from the University of Minnesota Duluth. I then earned my MA (2012) in philosophy from Virginia Tech and received my PhD (2021) in philosophy from the University of Washington, Seattle.

KEY TERMS

Harmony, Relationships, Responsibilities, Adaptations, Morality, Knowledge, Roles, Surroundings, Awareness, Well-being, Balance, Environment, Change

Along the highway's gravel pits
Sunflowers stand in dense rows.
Telephone poles crook into the layered sky.
A crow's beak broken by a windmill's blade.
It is then I understand my grandmother:
When they see open land
They only know to take it.

Jennifer Elise Foerster[1]

1. Introduction

Native American ethical systems are often built or rely upon the concept of *harmony*.[2] While precise definitions and explanations will vary among tribes, the main idea, roughly, is that we ought to be working to live *with* our surroundings. Our well-being and the well-being of our surroundings are necessarily tied together. As a result, to survive and thrive our surroundings need to survive and thrive. Thus, Native ethical systems place a great emphasis on one's relationships to one's surroundings.[3]

Harmony is a concept that is used as a standard for relationships. It is an ideal toward which our actions are to aim. Actions that discourage or disrupt harmony are bad or evil, and actions that promote harmony are good. However, if achieving harmony is an aim of morality, or if promoting harmony is something we ought to do (absent any moral requirements to avoid or commit *particular* or *specific* acts—e.g., killing, lying, eating meat, etc.), then it may seem that *any* action that brings about this achievement is permissible.

The main question addressed in this paper is, "For any moral problem, how do I know which of the available options is morally correct?" While I won't be offering an explicit answer to this question, I will offer a Native American account of how to respond to this question. In doing so, I hope to expand upon and tie together some key concepts in Native American moral epistemology.

2. *Harmony as an Ethical Concept*

For the purposes of this paper, and given my particular experiences and understandings, I'll be working with a Mvskoke (Muscogee) conception of *harmony*.[4] While there is no Mvskoke word that directly translates as 'harmony,' my understanding of harmony is based on the phrase *etemeyaske vpokat*, which translates to 'living together peacefully.'[5] Thus, in this paper, when I use the term 'harmony' I'll be referring to the idea of living together peacefully.

Again, harmony is a standard of relationships. In a very basic sense, for there to be harmony some relationship must exist. Given that every person that has ever existed exists in some context (i.e., in some surroundings), everyone has a relationship with their surroundings. Relationships are the roots or foundation of ethics. Relationships confer responsibilities. That's what it means to be in a particular kind of relationship. Being a mother means having the responsibilities of a mother, being a sibling means having the responsibilities of a sibling, etc. Having these responsibilities is what puts us in particular relationships, and failing these responsibilities means you're a bad participant in the relationship (e.g., a bad mother, a bad sibling, etc.). Having the responsibilities of being a friend and failing at these responsibilities means you're a bad friend.[6]

Within Native American ethical systems moral claims such as "you ought not lie" or "you shouldn't cause harm" are justified by the existence of particular relationships. There are no universal moral rules.[7] These are rules to which we may still appeal, but the justification for these rules would be particular and based on context and surroundings. For example, consider the rule "you ought to lend Danny money." It may be a good rule in the context of a friendship, but it may not be a good rule in the context of a parent-child relationship. This means appealing to particular relationships will count as justifying particular claims. If I claim, in a particular context, "you shouldn't steal," and you ask "why?" I could respond by identifying the relevant relationship (e.g., "because that's your mother!"). In other words, I shouldn't steal from my mother *because* she's my mother. Obviously, this justification won't work in any other context that doesn't involve my mother. However, the explanation for why I shouldn't steal from my mother has something to do with what it means to be in this kind of relationship (i.e., what it means to be a mother and what it means to be a child).

To live well one must live in harmony with one's surroundings,[8] and that means fulfilling the responsibilities of one's relationships and treating others with a special kind of love. Living together peacefully requires living with a special kind of love. In Mvskoke this is known as *vnokeckv*. This doesn't refer to a romantic or heteronormative love. This refers to a "love that cares for and tends to the needs of the people ... a compassionate love."[9] Loving of this kind allows us to know what others need and how we can appropriately reciprocate in the context of that relationship. Reciprocation is required to achieve harmony and knowing how to reciprocate requires love. When we take things, or when we're given gifts, these exchanges need to be reciprocated, otherwise an imbalance occurs. These imbalances—taking things or being given things without reciprocation—are instances of disharmony.

Avoiding disharmony and promoting or restoring harmony is a way of maintaining stability or balance. As Cordova states:

> Our survival depends on maintaining a certain degree of stability, which we know more familiarly as "balance." ... Stability, in this sense, requires constant adaptation to changing circumstances.[10]

3. Achieving Harmony: Internal Adaptation and External Adaptation

If the aim of our actions is to achieve harmony, then it appears this can be done in a number of ways.[11] All ways of achieving harmony seem to fall into at least one of two categories: they either involve (1) changing oneself or (2) changing one's surroundings. For example, consider the problem of climate change. The problem can be addressed by either changing one's behavior or preferences (e.g., driving less, shopping locally, adopting a vegan diet, etc.) or by changing one's surroundings (i.e., keeping the same behaviors and habits but helping to promote or develop changes in technology—e.g., renewable energy, sustainable production, more sustainable and efficient farming practices, etc.). Either of these ways of changing can help to address climate change.

This illustrates a distinction between two ways of achieving harmony: *internal* and *external* adaptation, which can be defined as follows:

> **Internal Adaptation**: changing oneself or one's reactions in response to one's surroundings to bring about peace.
>
> **External Adaptation**: changing one's surroundings to bring about peace.

Either one of these kinds of adaptations is capable of achieving harmony. Both can help to promote living together peacefully, but it's not always clear *whether* one option is better than the other. And, if one's better than the other, it's not always clear *which* option is the better or correct one.

Consider the example of climate change. The question is whether one option is better than the other, and, if so, what makes it the better option. Assuming they're both morally permissible, doing both may be best, but imagine you're in a position where both options aren't available. You can do, *at most*, one of the options (i.e., at least, one of the options, but not both). You can either internally adapt by driving less, shopping locally, or adopting a vegan diet, or you can externally adapt by helping to develop or promote the use of new technologies. However, doing both, for whatever reason, isn't feasible. It may be too psychologically demanding, or you may not be in a position, socially or economically, to do both options (e.g., because you can't drive less, shop locally, adopt a vegan diet, while also accumulating the resources and time to be able to contribute to developing, or promoting the use of, new technologies). In this kind of scenario, would one option be better than the other?

There's another distinction that needs to be understood to understand the reason for differentiating between internal and external adaptations. This is the distinction between the *existence* of a problem and our *feeling* of a problem. Moral problems can exist without our recognizing them as such. Similarly, we may think of something as being a moral problem when, in fact, it's not. Just because something *feels* like a moral problem doesn't entail that it *is* one (and vice versa).

This distinction is important because the role of internal and external adaptations is different depending on whether we're focused on problems that merely feel like they're moral problems or on problems that are actually moral problems. While internal and external adaptations can be used in both contexts, they are only helpful in promoting harmony in the context of *actual* moral problems. Imagine a case where you merely feel that there's a moral problem: you've lost your car keys, but you think your roommate stole them. If your roommate had stolen the keys, this would actually be a moral problem. However, since your roommate didn't actually steal them—you just lost them—you merely feel there's a moral problem. In this case, what kind of adaptation would best promote harmony? How should you adapt? You could either adapt internally and change how you feel about your roommate stealing your car keys, or you could adapt externally and confront (hopefully politely) your roommate. Now, if this were a moral problem (i.e., if your roommate had actually stolen your keys) it seems like internally adapting would do very little to promote or bring about harmony. You still wouldn't have your keys and a wrong that had been done (stealing your keys) wouldn't have been addressed. Thus, in the case where your roommate had stolen your keys, internal adaptations don't seem to promote harmony, so you should adapt externally. In the case where you lost your keys (your roommate didn't steal them) either adaptation seems equally permissible since there's no actual moral problem. Adapting internally seems just as good as adapting externally to problems that are merely felt.

Another way of stating this is that for problems of practical rationality, without regard to morality, either way of adapting is permissible. Changing oneself is just as good as changing one's surroundings. When morality is concerned, however, the type of adaptation (internal or external) seems to matter. For the remainder of the paper, I'll be focusing on the existence of moral problems, not the feeling of a moral problem. In the case of actual moral problems where it's not clear which kind of adaptation best promotes harmony, what do we need to know to achieve harmony?

4. What We Need to Know to Achieve Harmony

Before proceeding to address the question that I mentioned at the start of the paper, it's important to distinguish between two related, but essentially different, questions. When deciding between internal adaptation and external adaptation, one question that arises in the context of any problem is:

> Should I adapt internally or externally?

Notice, this is a moral question. In asking this question we're asking what ought to be done. Moral questions are different from epistemological questions. Both are normative (i.e., both are normative in the sense that we're asking what ought to be the case), but moral questions are questions about what we ought to do, whereas epistemological questions are about what we ought to believe or when we can claim to know something. To answer the question above we'd have to offer *conditions of morality*. These are claims or truths *about* morality (as opposed to claims or truths about other topics).

These kinds of questions (i.e., moral questions) are different from the following kind of question:

> How do I know whether I should adapt internally or externally?

This is an epistemological question. To answer this question, we'd have to offer *conditions of knowledge* (i.e., what beliefs or knowledge you'd have to have to know which kind of adaptation to choose). These are claims or truths about knowledge or what it means to know something.

This second question is the main focus of this paper. But although this is the case, I won't be offering a direct or explicit response. Since there are no universal principles prohibiting or encouraging particular actions in Native American ethical systems, I can't offer a particular or individualized answer for how we know what kind of change we should pursue. The kind of change that ought to be pursued depends on one's context and surroundings, and these vary significantly from person to person.

Instead of offering a particular response, I'm going to suggest a *method* of responding to this question. In other words, I aim to offer a series of things that have to be known to answer this question. To answer the main question, an individual must have knowledge of the following:[12]

- oneself
- one's surroundings
- one's role in, or relationship to, one's surroundings

Knowing oneself means understanding what you are and how you operate. As silly as it seems, this means, partly, knowing that you're human and knowing how humans operate (e.g., biologically, socially, psychologically, etc.). It also means knowing how you're likely to respond in a number of situations. Knowing your history, culture, values, behaviors, etc., are all part of knowing yourself.

Knowing one's surroundings means understanding the environment that you're occupying. This includes understanding the land, ecosystems, the people in your community or with whom you interact, the customs, traditions, and history of the places and persons surrounding you.

Knowing one's role in, or relationship to, one's surroundings means understanding the interactions between oneself and the other beings within one's surroundings. It means having a perspective about one's place in the world, as well as understanding the effects of one's actions on the surroundings. This involves more than just people. Knowing your relationships with other people helps to know what responsibilities you have towards them, but knowing your relationship to the land (e.g., the effects of your actions on the land and how you and the land benefit each other) also helps you know what responsibilities you have towards it. Knowledge of one's role in, and relationship to, one's surroundings means knowing the relationships (and responsibilities that define each relationship) and knowing how one interacts with one's surroundings (how one responds to one's surroundings and how those surroundings respond to the individual).[13]

Knowledge of each of these is required before someone can know the answer to the main question. Moral knowledge is dependent upon, or rooted in, knowledge of these three kinds. Determining whether one should adapt internally or externally depends on knowing enough about oneself and one's surroundings to know, for example, which kind of adaptation is easiest, which one best displays good or desirable behavior (e.g., patience, compassion, humility, etc.), which one is most effective, etc. While both kinds of adaptations, internal and external, *can* solve the problem, some solutions are better for one's surroundings. Knowing when this is true, however, requires knowledge of the three previously stated kinds.

Overall, determining the source or cause of disharmony will help one decide whether internal or external adaptation is best. This, however, means knowing whether one's reactions to one's surroundings are appropriate (and this requires knowledge of the three aforementioned kinds). If one's reactions are appropriate (meaning the source of disharmony is outside oneself and this causes you to feel bad), then external adaptation seems to better promote harmony. If one's reactions aren't appropriate (meaning the source of disharmony is one's reaction and there is no other problem beyond one's reaction), then internal adaptation seems to better promote harmony.

One way to live together peacefully is to adapt yourself to your surroundings so that you're not disturbed. This seems particularly useful when one is the source of the problem. If your reaction to something is creating disharmony, then your reaction—yourself—is the thing that should be changed. For example, imagine someone gets incredibly angry at hearing the song "Best Friend" by Toy Box. Assuming the existence of this song itself doesn't create disharmony, and assuming this person's anger promotes disharmony, then the person should change themselves (i.e., adapt internally) and stop responding to the song with anger. They *could* adapt externally and try to make sure the song never plays around them, but since the song itself doesn't create disharmony, this suggests that changing your reaction is a better way of promoting harmony.

Another way to live together peacefully is to adapt one's surroundings to oneself. This seems particularly useful when the source of disharmony is outside of oneself. If your reaction to something is to create disharmony, and your reaction is appropriate, the best way to promote harmony is to adapt externally. That way both sources of disharmony, the cause and your reaction, are being addressed. Addressing the cause will address your reaction. For example, imagine someone getting incredibly angry at the construction of a pipeline that'll disproportionally affect Native American communities in negative ways (e.g., Keystone XL, Dakota Access Pipeline, Line 3, etc.). This anger seems warranted given that instances of racial injustice and environmental destruction are morally wrong. In these cases, the person shouldn't change their reaction—they shouldn't stop being incredibly angry. They should help to change their surroundings and stop instances of, and systems that encourage or allow, the construction of such pipelines.

Internal adaptations can bring about a kind of inner peace. However, inner peace doesn't always help those with whom we have relationships. I may find racial injustice to be a problem, but if my reaction to it is to adapt internally and be at peace with racial injustice (or to ignore its existence), this does nothing to actually help fix the problem of racial injustice. 'Living together peacefully' doesn't just mean finding peace in your surroundings. It means helping to bring peace to your surroundings (i.e., those with whom you have relationships).

To illustrate this, imagine two different people, Karen and Louella. They both hear about the Missing and Murdered Indigenous Women and Girls movement (MMIWG). Karen decides to internally adapt and ignore the problem because it's causing her a lot of stress, anger, worry, etc. This helps her to live peacefully within her surroundings. Louella, on the other hand, decides to externally adapt and works to raise awareness about and help MMIWG. In this case, it's clear that Karen fails to consider those she stands in relation to. Internally adapting in this instance is more problematic than externally adapting. Louella is making the morally better choice by adapting externally and working to fix the problem. This helps not only Louella herself but also everyone else (especially Indigenous women) to live peacefully with each other (i.e., their surroundings).

While knowing how one ought to adapt requires knowing oneself, one's surroundings, and one's relationships with those surroundings, it's also important to understand what it means to live together peacefully. 'Living together peacefully' *could* be understood as 'being at peace with your surroundings,' but it could also mean 'bringing peace to your surroundings.' *Etemayaske vpokat* doesn't refer to merely being at peace with your surroundings, because you shouldn't be at peace with your surroundings if your surroundings are creating disharmony. *Etemayaske vpokat* is achieved by helping to bring peace to your surroundings. It's the promotion of harmony by making sure all our relationships are reciprocal and guided by *vnokeckv* (i.e., love).

5. Concluding Remarks

In this paper, I have focused solely on the knowledge required to know how to live in harmony. Thus, the topic of this paper is a sort of moral meta-epistemology. As previously stated, I can't offer conditions to know how to live in harmony because this varies among individuals. What I hope to have offered is a method for obtaining this knowledge. In other words, I hope to have offered an explanation of what we need to understand in order to know how to live in harmony.

Harmony isn't a standard that's achieved by accident. We can't accidentally bring harmony to our surroundings because we, with our surroundings, are the authors of reality. Harmony requires knowledge, but this knowledge doesn't come easily: it requires awareness, consideration, and familiarity with the people, customs, land, food, animals, and so on that constitute one's surroundings.

Endnotes

1 Jennifer Elise Foerster, *Leaving Tulsa* (Tucson: University of Arizona Press, 2013), 10.

2 Viola F. Cordova, *How It Is*, 123.

3 This idea is explained in much more detail in Brian Burkhart, *Indigenizing Philosophy through the Land*, Viola F. Cordova, *How It Is*, and Daniel Wildcat, *Red Alert!*

4 The importance of harmony to the Mvskoke worldview is explained in Jean Chaudhuri and Joyotpaul Chaudhuri, *A Sacred Path*.

5 This conception of harmony and its role in ethics is expanded upon and explained in Joseph Len Miller, "Etemeyaske Vpokat (Living Together Peacefully)."

6 Further argument for these claims can be found in Joseph Len Miller, "Decolonizing the Demarcation of the Ethical."

7 This is a metaethical position known as *moral particularism*. The main idea is that moral rules or moral judgments are justified in particular situations or circumstances. There are no universal moral rules (i.e., rules that apply regardless of particulars). This contrasts with *moral universalism*: the belief that some moral rules apply universally (regardless of situation or circumstance).

8 Cordova, *How It Is*, 120.

9 Laura Harjo, *Spiral to the Stars*, 20. Harjo also refers to this as 'decolonial love' and explains additional contexts in which this conception of love applies.

10 Cordova, *How It Is*, 120.

11 This is similar to a classical problem with Utilitarianism. Utilitarianism is a moral theory where the morally correct act is the act that produces the largest amount of happiness for the people involved. The problem is that if our only goal is maximizing happiness, then it appears we could justify a number of intuitively bad actions. If my life ending would increase overall happiness, then someone would be justified in killing me. A similar problem applies here: if our goal is achieving harmony, then it appears that could justify a number of intuitively bad actions.

12 This is greatly inspired by V.F. Cordova's explanation of what differentiates "world-pictures" (or philosophical spaces) (83). According to Cordova, confrontations between world-pictures push us to ask three fundamental questions: What is the world?, What is it to be human in that world?, and, What is the role of a human in that world?

13 I will not be explaining how knowledge of these types is obtained because there are many ways of knowing these things. However, social structures and social identities illustrate one way these kinds of knowledge can be embodied and help provide people with knowledge of themselves, their surroundings, and their role in their surroundings. Clan membership is a social identity that provides Mvskoke people with a set of relationships that embody these areas of knowledge. Customs, traditions, histories, etc. are shared among clan members, and there are norms of interaction within and among clans (e.g., only being allowed to engage in romantic relationships with individuals from clans other than one's own). As such, clan membership is one social structure that provides people with knowledge of themselves (e.g., their identity in relation to other people), their surroundings (e.g., customs histories, traditions, etc.), and their role in their surroundings (e.g., norms of interactions).

References

Burkhart, Brian. *Indigenizing Philosophy through the Land: A Trickster Methodology for Decolonizing Environmental Ethics and Indigenous Futures*. East Lansing: Michigan State University Press, 2019.

Chaudhuri, Jean, and Joyotpaul Chaudhuri. *A Sacred Path: The Way of the Muscogee Creeks*. Los Angeles: UCLA American Indian Studies Center, 2001.

Cordova, Viola F. *How It Is: The Native American Philosophy of V.F. Cordova*. Edited by Kathleen Dean Moore, Kurt Peters, Ted Jojola, and Amber Lacy, with a Foreword by Linda Hogan. Tucson: University of Arizona Press, 2007.

Foerster, Jennifer Elise. *Leaving Tulsa*. Tucson: University of Arizona Press, 2013.

Harjo, Laura. *Spiral to the Stars: Mvskoke Tools of Futurity*. Tucson: University of Arizona Press, 2019.

Miller, Joseph Len. "Etemeyaske Vpokat (Living Together Peacefully): How the Muscogee Concept of Harmony Can Provide a Structure to Morality." In *Comparative Metaethics: Neglected Perspectives on the Foundations of Morality*, edited by C. Marshall. New York: Routledge, 2019, 81–101.

Miller, Joseph Len. "Decolonizing the Demarcation of the Ethical." *Philosophical Studies* 177, no. 2 (2020): 337–52.

Wildcat, Daniel. *Red Alert! Saving the Planet with Indigenous Knowledge*. Golden, CO: Fulcrum Publishing, 2009.

Suggestions for Critical Reflection

1. What do we need to know in order to live in harmony with our surroundings?
2. Is there an 'equivalent' to the concept of harmony in the Western philosophical ethical system? Why or why not?

3. How does the concept of well-being figure into other Western ethical theories? How does it differ from its Indigenous counterpart?
4. What do we need to *be* in order to live in harmony with our surroundings?
5. What *role* does harmony play in ethical systems, Indigenous and non-Indigenous?

Additional Resources

For additional resources relating to this reading and its themes, visit sites.broadviewpress.com/waysofbeing/5-1

5.2
"Indigenous Storytelling"*

Jo-Ann Archibald, Q'um Q'um Xiiem (Stó:lō/Soowahlie First Nation)

ABOUT THE AUTHOR

Born in Chilliwack, British Columbia, and a member of the Soowahlie First Nation, Q'um Q'um Xiiem (Jo-Ann Archibald) earned a BEd (1972) at the University of British Columbia (UBC) and continued her specialization in education, earning both an MA and a PhD (1997) at Simon Fraser University. While teaching elementary school, Archibald noted the lack of culturally relevant curricula for First Nations students. She worked with teachers and elders from the Coqualeetza Cultural Education Centre to develop the first curriculum on the history of the Stó:lō people for elementary and secondary students. Archibald was a member of the Board of Directors at the First Nations House of Learning at UBC and its director from 1993 to 2001. She received the Justice Achievement Award in 1995 from the National Association for Court Management for her development of a First Nations justice curriculum. The American Educational Research Association awarded her the Scholars of Color Distinguished Career Contribution Award in 2013. Archibald also provides instruction regarding the teaching of Indigenous stories.

KEY TERMS

Storytelling, Oral traditions, Memory, Synergy, Pedagogy

Storytelling plays a powerful role in the way we create and recall memories. This is particularly true of Indigenous Elders who remember ways of learning the oral traditions from their ancestors, being on and with the land, and helping the younger generation learn from and with Indigenous traditional and lived stories. This concept of memory entails the development of a storied memory, the living of storied lives, the disruption of memory stories, and the awakening and resurgence of storied memories. From time to time, the Indigenous Trickster, Coyote, joins in the storytelling.

I, Jo-ann Archibald, Q'um Q'um Xiiem am from the Stó:lō/Soowahlie First Nation in southwest British Columbia and have ancestry from St'at'imc/X'x'alip First Nation in the Interior of the province. I grew up in Stó:lō territory

* Jo-Ann Archibald (Q'um Q'um Xiiem), "Indigenous Storytelling," in *Memory*, ed. Philippe Tortell et al. (Vancouver: Peter Wall Institute for Advanced Studies, 2018), 233–41.

and know some of its rivers and water systems. The rivers give the territory its name. Q'um Q'um Xiiem is my Indigenous name and means "strong, clear water."

My interest and use of Indigenous stories for teaching and learning purposes developed during my educational career, first as a school teacher and then as a university professor. I have often wondered how traditional storytellers could remember a large number of oral stories without the use of textual or digital tools. As a young school teacher, I could not remember stories without relying on written, literate forms, and I was only comfortable reading stories from books to students. It wasn't until I became a PhD student that I was able to dedicate space and time to my storied interest and to the development of my storied memory. I was drawn to Indigenous Elders and storytellers who told stories from memory. There were a few stories that I became attached to and could remember.

I want to recount one of these stories. As a form of protocol and ethics, I acknowledge the source of the Indigenous stories that I tell. Dr. Eber Hampton of the Chickasaw Nation told a trickster story at a research conference. He eventually gave me permission to use this story and to adapt it to suit my cultural context. I renamed the trickster character Old Man Coyote, because Coyote transcends time and place and has become my trickster of learning. Now it is Old Man Coyote's turn to voice his thoughts.

* * *

Old Man Coyote: Searching for the Bone Needle

Old Man Coyote had just finished a long, hard day of hunting. He decided to set up his camp for the night by starting a fire for his meal. After supper, he sat by the cozy, warm fire and rubbed his tired feet from the long day's walk. He took his favourite moccasins out of his bag and noticed that there was a hole in the toe of one of them. He looked for his special bone needle to mend the moccasin but couldn't feel it in the bag.

Old Man Coyote started to crawl on his hands and knees around the fire to see if he could see or feel the needle. He went around and around the fire. Just then, Owl came flying by and landed next to him. He asked Old Man Coyote what he was looking for. Old Man Coyote told Owl his problem.

Owl said that he would help his friend look for the bone needle. After he made one swoop around the area of the fire, he told Old Man Coyote that he didn't see the needle. Owl said that if it were around the fire, then he would have spotted it. He then asked Old Man Coyote where he had last used the needle. Old Man Coyote said that he had used it quite far away, over in the bushes, to mend his jacket. Then Owl asked Old Man Coyote why he kept going around and around the campfire when the needle clearly was not there. Old Man Coyote replied, "Well, it's easier to look for the needle here because the fire gives off such good light, and I can see better."[1]

***

Searching for the bone needle is like searching for the perfect answer or working towards one's goals. The bone needle could be a storied memory. In the story, Old Man Coyote knew how to use the bone needle, and he had used it previously. However, he did not care for the needle well and subsequently lost it. I identify with Old Man Coyote's comfort around the fire. Sometimes, we get used to doing things a certain way, and the "doing" gets easier with repeated use. However, going out into the dark or returning to places less known takes more effort and courage. This brings me back to the notion of memory and its place in storytelling.

I recall others who travelled on the story memory pathway and provided some direction for me. In the late 1980s, scholarship by Elder Harry Robinson and Wendy Wickwire introduced an important approach for remembering Indigenous stories from the Okanagan region of BC. Robinson recalled his friend, Josephine George, who told her grandson that to remember a story, you must "write it on your heart."[2] Embedding and remembering stories through the emotions—knowing them intimately—establishes a seamless connection to one's memory. Stó:lō Elder Roy Point remembered that grandparents often told stories to children at night and that the grandparents "had memories, miles and miles long with their stories."[3] He also mentioned that children listened to stories for two to three hours at a time. I wondered how the grandparents developed these extensive memories for stories and how children could listen to stories for this length of time. Developing a storied memory means that a storyteller has to keep using memory, repeatedly telling the stories to others. Sometimes, song and art forms are added to the oral telling.

Elder Dr. Ellen White, Kwulasulwut, of Snuneymuxw First Nations, from the Nanaimo area of Vancouver Island, BC, spoke to me about learning traditional Indigenous stories through structured repetition directed by family members. She was trained to be a storyteller from a young age. The role of repetition in developing a storied memory was critical. The traditional stories that she told were detailed and complex and needed to be accurately told and retold. She talked of learning parts of the story, especially the core of the story first.[4] The responsibility for learning traditional stories accurately and intimately is essential for those who become storytellers; it is part of an intergenerational pedagogy of learning.

Now, Old Man Coyote is impatient to get in a word. He knows that the only way to develop his storied memory is through living these stories, so that he can boast about his adventures. Indigenous Elders, however, had another motive and way of developing their storied memories.

Scholars such as Julie Cruikshank at the University of British Columbia, in collaboration with Yukon Indigenous Elders Annie Sidney, Kitty Smith, and Annie Ned, fostered a new appreciation for Indigenous stories through their cooperative research. Angela Sidney's statement "Well, I've tried to live my life right, just like a story" points to a way of appreciating the power and beauty of stories, which are frameworks for presenting life experiences.[5] I am forever grateful to the Indigenous Elders who kept their stories alive in their hearts, minds, bodies, and spirits. They lived the experiential stories that they told. These stories were certainly told from memory, from their experiences, where they could remember emotions, physical actions, and the context of the stories and their tellings.

Elder and Chief Dr. Simon Baker, Khot-La-Cha of Squamish First Nation exemplifies this reinforcement of storied memory. He told me many stories about spending time with his grandmother Mary Capilano, on the land and water, helping her sell baskets to non-Indigenous people. If I asked a question, he would answer with a story. I learned to listen to his many stories and then search in them for what he wanted me to learn. Speaking from and through experience, Khot-La-Cha's activities and events became "alive" once more. I could visualize Simon's actions, identify the emotions of caring or concern, and appreciate the intergenerational closeness of his relationship with his grandmother. Living storied lives has become important for culture and language recovery and revitalization and for appreciating Indigenous people's resiliency and resistance to colonization, which has disrupted this storied memory through legislation, education, and policy.

The storied memories of Indigenous people have been assaulted through decades of colonization, decades during which disease, legislation against cultural and ceremonial practices, family and community separation through boarding or residential schools, abduction of Indigenous children for adoption and fostering purposes, and educational assimilation in public and postsecondary education systems have negatively impacted the intergenerational transmission of culture and memory.[6] However, as Stó:lō Elders remind us, these storied memories were not totally forgotten but were "put to sleep" for a while.[7] New stories of trauma were lived by generations of people who experienced the Indian residential schools that operated across Canada for more than a century. Some of these stories were brought into a broader public consciousness through the Truth and Reconciliation Commission of Canada. Oppression, genocide, and various forms of abuse were remembered and told through residential school survivor stories. But Indigenous Elders and storytellers kept embers of original Indigenous stories alive in their hearts, minds, bodies, and spirits, waiting for the time to spark the return of these storied memories.

Starting in the early 1970s, Indigenous cultural centres were established throughout British Columbia with the purpose of culture and language revitalization. In the Stó:lō area, the Coqualeetza Cultural Education Centre was established in Sardis, BC, at a location named Coqualeetza. Traditionally, its name meant a place where blankets were beaten with a stick to cleanse them.[8] Over the years, this was also the site of the Coqualeetza boarding or residential school, later an "Indian hospital" or tuberculosis sanatorium and then a cultural, political, and social service centre for Stó:lō people. Before the cultural centre was established, a group of Stó:lō people had met on a weekly basis for culture and language revitalization purposes in a member's home. They shared food and documented culture and language from memory because there were few written records that truly reflected Stó:lō perspectives. The Elders' group became a sponsored program of Coqualeetza: a coordinator was hired to organize weekly meetings. Elders were picked up and brought to Coqualeetza. One member also cooked a lunch for everyone.

I was introduced to the Elders through my work as an Indian education coordinator with the Chilliwack School District. I also enrolled in various Coqualeetza cultural learning activities, such as gathering cedar roots, making cedar root baskets, fish-drying camps, and Halq'eméylem language classes. The Elders were involved in a new social studies curriculum program for elementary grades called the Stó:lō Sitel.

I remember a short Stó:lō story "Mischievous Cubs," which the Elders had selected for the Stó:lō Sitel curriculum. One person began telling this story but could not remember it all. Over a few weeks, individuals would contribute a piece of the story or verify another's telling of a section. The Elders said that they needed to think about the story, which really meant that they had to remember or dig into their memory bank. Eventually, the assembled collective narratives became one coherent story. This shared work was a synergistic action—one remembrance "tickle[d]" the memory of someone else.[9]

Sometimes, an unplanned action would reawaken a storied memory. I recall one Elder, Ann Lindley, who said that she had been told lots of stories when she was a child, but she had not thought about the stories for many years, maybe because of colonization or various parental responsibilities. One day, the Elder's coordinator, Wilfred Charlie, called Ann to see if she wanted to go for a car ride with another Elder and himself. Ann agreed but was surprised to learn that Wilfred was taking her to a school, where he wanted Ann to tell the children stories. At that moment, Stó:lō stories were reawakened in her memory, and she subsequently told these stories to the school students.

Indigenous storied memory can be thought of as a bone needle: a useful tool for sewing, mending, and bringing Indigenous stories, storytellers, and listeners together for meaningful engagement. Traditional forms of learning and teaching through stories, intergenerational relationships, and experiences on and with land and nature have contributed to the development of a storied memory. In telling stories, Elders and storytellers portray lives that have been lived like a story, demonstrating their individual, collective, and cultural resilience and resistance to many forms of colonization. Maybe Old Man Coyote needed to keep warm by a good fire, to gather strength, to learn or practise ways of looking after his storied memory. Elder storytellers and friends such as Owl can help Old Man Coyote and each of us search for the bone needle by asking critical questions and showing us how to awaken or spark our oral memories. Today, the term *Indigenous pedagogy* is used to include traditional ways of learning and teaching. These ways are timeless. Indigenous storied memory is a form of Indigenous pedagogy for those who want to look for and then use the bone needle.

Endnotes

1 Jo-ann Archibald, *Indigenous Storywork: Educating the Heart, Mind, Body, and Spirit* (Vancouver: UBC Press, 2008), 35–36.
2 Harry Robinson and Wendy Wickwire, *Write It on Your Heart: The Epic World of an Okanagan Storyteller* (Vancouver: Talon Books, 1990), 28.
3 Archibald, *Indigenous Storywork*, 75.
4 Ibid., 54.
5 Julie Cruikshank, with Annie Sidney, Kitty Smith, and Annie Ned, *Life Lived Like a Story: Life Stories of Three Yukon Elders* (Vancouver: UBC Press, 1990), 1.
6 Royal Commission on Aboriginal Peoples, *Report of the Royal Commission on Aboriginal Peoples*, vol. 1, *Looking Forward, Looking Back* (Ottawa: Canada Communications Group, 1996).
7 Archibald, *Indigenous Storywork*, 80.
8 David M. Schaepe, *Being Ts'elxwéyeqw: First People's Voices and History from the Chilliwack-Fraser Valley, British Columbia* (Madeira Park, BC: Harbour Publishing, 2017).
9 Archibald, *Indigenous Storywork*, 147.

Suggestions for Critical Reflection

1. Why does the author ask permission to use a story? Why is it important to note where a story comes from?
2. Why does the author think Old Man Coyote has not treated the bone needle well?
3. What are the criteria associated with the role of a storyteller?
4. Is there something inherently wrong, or bad, about preferring to do something easy?
5. What is the value of assembling collective narratives?

Additional Resources

For additional resources relating to this reading and its themes, visit sites.broadviewpress.com/waysofbeing/5-2

5.3 "Healthy Community"*

Peter Irniq, Piita Taqtu Irniq (Inuit)

ABOUT THE AUTHOR

Piita Taqtu Irniq is an Inuk cultural teacher who has lived most of his life in the Kivalliq Region of Nunavut. He served as the executive assistant commissioner of the Northwest Territories from 1974 to 1975, and was elected to represent Keewatin Region for four years. He was named director of the Inuit Cultural Institute in 1992 and director of communications for Nunavut Tunngavik Incorporated the following year. Irniq was appointed Deputy Minister of Culture, Language, Elders and Youth with a mandate to be the guardian of traditional Inuit culture and language. From 2000 to 2005, he served as the second commissioner of Nunavut. Irniq has worked to preserve and promote Inuit culture and languages. He attended Sir Joseph Bernier Federal Day and Sir John Franklin residential schools. Irniq has written columns about Inuit life for *Nunavut News/North* and the Ontario Community Newspapers Association awarded him the columnist of the year award in 2007. Recognized internationally for his artistic ability in designing inukshuks, Irniq created an inukshuk for the 2010 Olympics in Vancouver, British Columbia.

KEY TERMS

Harmony, Roles, Humans, Relationships, Cooperation, Connectedness, Support, Trust, Pride, Adaptation, Modernity, Technology, Autonomy, Sovereignty

We were strong in mind and body! We were creative and adaptable!
We were adventurous and fiercely independent!
We lived in very isolated and challenging areas but found ways
to meet and live in harmony with the land!

To have healthy communities in 2006, I believe that we Inuit need to draw on our strengths from the past and find a way to integrate them into our life today. We have to identify our strengths, as well as our weaknesses—what

* Peter Irniq, "Healthy Community," *Arctic* 61, no. 5 (2008): Supplement 1, 1–3, https://journalhosting.ucalgary.ca/index.php/arctic/article/view/63160/47098.

has been shown to us from our experience with change—and find ways to turn this experience into new strengths.

When I was asked to make a keynote speech for this Conference, I thought back to our way of life in Naujaat–Repulse Bay in the 1950s and 1960s, to the community I left in 1964, when Inuit were still living in iglus in the winter and tents in the summer. I was born in an iglu and lived the iglu life for my first 12 years. My parents, and the Inuit we lived with, taught me many things. Today I draw on that knowledge for strength and inspiration in my personal, family, and community life. I believe that all of us have to look to our personal past and that of our culture to find what we need to lead us in the challenges of today and find what can be done to have healthy communities.

I think your culture, Canadian and Western European culture, suffers from a problem. History is not something from which lessons are learned. History is just entertainment, something that makes a good film or book. The way history is treated and taught in schools, from what I have been told, makes history boring. It is just dates, names, and things that happened. I guess the best example is economic history. What did your culture learn from the Depression? How is that knowledge shown today in policies that do not seem to recognize how important social programs and a sense of community are in looking after the needs of all of us? I would like to think that Inuit learn from their history, and because there has been so much change in our recent history, there is a lot to be learned.

Today I am traditional and yet modern; I lived and saw the end of the traditional way of life and the beginning of the modern technological age. In these years of change, I have come to realize the Inuit way of life is disappearing and that my Inuitness is becoming more Europeanized or 'southernized' as we say in the North. Our struggle is to protect values and ways of thinking that are different from those of Southerners but that have a lot to offer to a world suffering from environmental, social, and political pain.

My fellow Inuit and I went from the iglu to microwaves in less than 40 years; this is where I want to start. Inuit, as the last traditional hunting society in the Northern Hemisphere, were a very adaptable people and we felt good about it. We all know that there is no going back to the old way of doing things.

In the "other" days, Inuit *tapiriingniq* (teamwork) was most important to our survival. Families, related in some way, would live together to help each other in all manner of activities; be it harvesting, traveling or companionship. From the time I was a little boy, my father always used to direct my brother-in-law and me to go out and collect the caribou meat that he caught a few days before; we stayed together as an extended family so that we could work in *tapiriit* (teams). He used to say that together we were stronger.

Relatives' and friends' relationships were very important for the survival of the family. We had many age-old practices that dictated how we should share food and how different members of the group would interact together to ensure that we would live together harmoniously. We had elders and shamans who held the respect of the members of the group and passed down the directives and practices for the group. I am not saying that everything from the past was perfect or even right but it was our way. Most importantly, we knew how to work together and to respect differences.

From what I can remember, cooperation of both the husband and wife was always extremely important. Both of my parents knew their roles and followed them carefully. My father's responsibility was to be the boss of hunting and fishing. He was responsible for his dog team, and the tools that we needed to survive. As a knowledgeable hunter he was always seeing to our family's safety, and he knew where the animals were, most of the time. He knew the dangers of the land and knew how to forecast weather. He was also a very spiritual person; he truly believed in his culture. Because he was a good hunter he always shared food and helped his community. He taught me many things, expecting me to learn by observation and by practice. He taught me that violence against women was not acceptable. He knew how to communicate his wisdom and knowledge to other people. He was a role model for both men and women.

On the other hand, my mother, as many mothers were, was the boss of the iglu and tent. Besides being the seamstress and cook, she had the authority to bring up all her children. To me, my mother was everything in life! She was a "family doctor" and "family counselor." When I got sick as a young boy, she knew just how to talk to me and get me thinking that I was not sick. Like my father, she was very humorous and knew how to make us laugh. She was generous and very considerate of others. She used to say, "be particularly kind to those who have just lost one of their parents. Be respectful." I had a strong attachment to my mother.

My family, as I was growing up, included my parents, my sister (16 years older than me), her husband, and my little brother. We learned about how partnerships work in the family. My brother-in-law and I were taught about the ways of hunting and to be completely connected to the land that we walked on. No matter how old we got, our parents were our bosses for life, and you know, at that time it worked well.

Sharing and patience and survival went together in the past. It was not hard for members of the family or groups of families to learn how important these qualities were because those who did not practice or develop these qualities could be at risk for surviving.

A practice that existed in the past was *Nalunaijainiq*. When two people had conflicts, they used to talk, find solutions, and move forward to become friends again. To resolve issues between people was essential in the past because of how much we depended upon each other for survival. Today we seem to have abdicated this conflict-solving ability to the by-law officers, the RCMP, and the courts. We are frustrated that the formal, legal system does not help us to overcome the problem and become friends again. It creates divisions and problems in our communities. In the past Inuit knew that they had to forgive and move on after conflict had occurred. In the past it was easy for Inuit to forgive.

Today we must identify the strengths in our 'Inuitness' and find ways to integrate the strengths into our present-day lives. We must be proud of who we are and where we came from; we must be strong enough to accept the challenges of today as we accepted the challenges of the past. Today we are called upon to move away from our families and communities for education or employment, but remember, we were always adventurous and independent. We can take our families in our hearts and use their strengths to build our new lives. If our families did not give us strength and guidance then we were always adaptable and ingenious—we found ways to learn these skills.

Today we do not always have the strength of our families and relatives around us, so we must find helpers and support from friends, co-workers, church associates or maybe more distant relatives. We must build healthy support groups around us to replace our extended families of the past. We need the support for companionship, language, country food, connections; we need help with bringing up children in today's world, with the challenges of employment, housing, and doing our taxes. We needed our family in the past and we need them today. Today we may need more helpers because the world we live in is much more complicated, and none of us can be good at everything.

Today we have many challenges to face and maybe the worst of these challenges is that the directives and practices are less well known to ordinary people. We need medical practitioners, counselors, and mechanics; we need food, clothing, and furniture stores; we need educators of all descriptions just to make it through an average day. We must put some trust in all of these people to provide us with the services that we require, but we will know little about them and yet have to trust them for the part of our lives that they help us with. They cannot know us the way our families did in the past, so their advice has to be tempered with who we are and where we come from. No longer are the rules simple and known by all. Today we do our best and hope that all will work out.

We all need housing. Today some of us own our houses, some of us rent from employers or privately and some of us rent from various housing associations. Most Inuit live in social housing. Some of us live as guests in others' houses for a few days or weeks, or we are forced to live in tents, shacks or cabins because we do not qualify for housing of our own. In the end Nunavut does not have enough housing for all who need it, and this situation increases the stress that we live under. Using the Inuit way of looking at these challenges, we have to make the best of what we have and find the strength to improve our situation as much as possible.

Perhaps the opportunity is today, while our Nunavut is still very young, to give more responsibilities to men, women, and young people alike. Just like her ancestors, my mother was the keeper of the *qulliq* light; Miriam Aglukkaq lit the *qulliq* earlier today to symbolize the authority and responsibility of women.

Family connectedness is an Inuit trait. Perhaps the time has come to have men and women work together for the betterment of our communities and for the survival of our families. We must be imaginative, innovative, and courageous to make this happen. We must have more determination, honesty, and trust to make sure that we give men and women more responsibilities and thereby encourage them to provide leadership. Perhaps this is where we should re-introduce to the political system the idea of a two-member constituency in Nunavut, the idea that you need one woman and one man in each constituency to provide the balanced leadership required to direct the legislature. Together, men and women, we are stronger!

Finally, we need to protect and make use of our way of understanding ourselves in relation to nature. We have accomplished some of this. The new Wildlife Act says that wildlife is to be treated with respect. We are a part of nature. We have a relationship, the same one we have always had, with land and sea animals and all other living things. Nature is not a resource to be exploited so we can become bigger and more important. Nature—the land—is our home. With nature we have a relationship just like the relationships between people that I have described.

We must be proud to be Inuit! We must encourage our children to know about our culture and share this pride. Healthy communities can come only from healthy individuals, and we all have to work to that end. This interrelationship has always been true of Inuit culture, and must continue for the sake of our children and grandchildren.

Suggestions for Critical Reflection

1. What do you think is the goal of Irniq's address? Why?
2. Did you think the address achieves that goal? Why or why not?
3. What are the persuasive elements of this address?
4. How do the roles of the father and mother in Inuit culture differ from those in Canadian and Western European culture?
5. Why do roles have value? Is this value inherent?

Additional Resources

For additional resources relating to this reading and its themes, visit sites.broadviewpress.com/waysofbeing/5-3

CLOSING

This text began as an idea long before I knew that I would be an academic. As a student, the philosophical thought of my people and other Indigenous communities was not on the syllabus. Although this project is finished, it is by no means complete. There are so many topics, issues, and groups that are not present within these pages. Centring the voices and philosophies of the people living on Turtle Island is a continuous journey. I give you a map that is not fully drawn. I provide a direction, but not a well-established path. Walk carefully as you travel. I wish you well in your travels, keeping in mind that *Cokv Kerretv Heret Os*.

PERMISSIONS ACKNOWLEDGEMENTS

Alvarez, Joel. "Native American Epistemology through Dreams." 2023. Original work commissioned for this anthology.

Archibald, Jo-Ann (Q'um Q'um Xiiem). "Indigenous Storytelling" (pp. 233–42), from *Memory*, ed. Philippe Tortell, Mark Turin, and Margot Young, published by the Peter Wall Institute for Advanced Studies. Copyright © 2018 Jo-Ann Archibald. Reprinted by permission of the author. https://doi.org/10.2307/j.ctvbtzpfm.30.

Boyer, Kurtis. "What Are We? Exploring Indigenous Models of Mind." 2023. Original work commissioned for this anthology.

Cordova, Viola F. From Section V: "Coda: Living in a Sacred Universe" (pp. 229–32), *How It Is: The Native American Philosophy of V.F. Cordova*, ed. Kathleen Dean Moore, Kurt Peters, Ted Jojola, and Amber Lacy; foreword by Linda Hogan, Tucson, AZ: The University of Arizona Press, 2007. Copyright © 2007 The Arizona Board of Regents. Used by permission of The University of Arizona Press, conveyed through Copyright Clearance Center, Inc.

Deloria Jr., Vine. Chapter 5: "The Problem of Creation" (pp. 78–84, 95), from *God Is Red: A Native View of Religion*. First published by The Putnam Publishing Group, NY; third edition published in 2003 by Fulcrum Publishing, Golden, CO. Copyright © 1973, 1992, 2003 Vine Deloria Jr. Used with permission of Fulcrum Publishing, conveyed through Copyright Clearance Center, Inc. Chapter 3: "Power and Place Equal Personality" (pp. 21–28), from *Power and Place: Indian Education in America*, by Vine Deloria Jr. and Daniel R. Wildcat. Golden, CO: Fulcrum Resources, 2001. Copyright © 2001 Vine Deloria, Jr., and Daniel Wildcat. Used with permission of Fulcrum Publishing, conveyed through Copyright Clearance Center, Inc.

Fixico, Donald L. Excerpt from Chapter 3: "American Indian Circular Philosophy" (pp. 41–52), *The American Indian Mind in a Linear World*. First published by The Haworth Press; reprinted 2009 by Routledge. Copyright © 2003 by Taylor & Francis Books, Inc. Reproduced by permission of Taylor and

Francis Group, LLC, a division of Informa plc, conveyed through Copyright Clearance Center, Inc.

Irniq, Peter. "Healthy Community," from *Arctic* 61, no. 5 (2008): Supplement 1, 1–3. https://doi.org/10.14430/arctic96. Copyright © 2008 The Arctic Institute of North America. Reprinted by permission of the Arctic Institute of North America.

Kimmerer, Robin Wall. "Skywoman Falling" (pp. 3–10), from *Braiding Sweetgrass: Indigenous Wisdom, Scientific Knowledge and the Teachings of Plants*. Copyright © 2013, 2015 by Robin Wall Kimmerer. Reprinted with the permission of The Permissions Company, LLC on behalf of Milkweed Editions, www.milkweed.org.

LaDuke, Winona. Excerpts from Chapter 6: "In the Time of the Sacred Places" (pp. 71–75, 78–79, 81–82, 83–84), *The Wiley Blackwell Companion to Religion and Ecology*, ed. John Hart, Wiley Blackwell, 2017. Copyright © 2017 John Wiley & Sons, Ltd. Used by permission of John Wiley & Sons, Ltd., conveyed through Copyright Clearance Center, Inc.

Landa, Diego de. "Letter to the King, from Montejo Xiu and others, April 12, 1567" (pp. 115–17), from *Yucatan Before and After the Conquest*, translated by William Gates, 1937. New York: Dover Publications, 1978. Copyright © 1937 by The Maya Society.

Miller, Joseph Len. "What Do We Need to Know to Live in Harmony with Our Surroundings?" 2023. Original work commissioned for this anthology.

SHAKÓYE:WA:THAʔ, or Red Jacket. "Speech to the Iroquois Six Nations" (1805; pp. 283–87), from *Lives of Celebrated American Indians*, by Daniel Drake. Boston: Bradbury, Soden & Co., 1843.

Santana, Alejandro. "Did the Aztecs Do Philosophy?" *APA Newsletters: Newsletter on Hispanic/Latino Issues in Philosophy* 8, no. 1 (Fall 2008): 2–9. Copyright © 2008 by The American Philosophical Association. Reprinted by permission of the author.

Simpson, Leanne Betasamosake. Chapter 6: "Endlessly Creating Our Indigenous Selves" (pp. 83–94), from *As We Have Always Done: Indigenous Freedom through Radical Resistance*, published by the University of Minnesota Press, 2017. Copyright © 2017 by the Regents of the University of Minnesota. Used by permission of the publisher.

Smith, Paul Simard. "The Epistemology of Deep Disagreement and Indigenous Oral Histories." 2023. Original work commissioned for this anthology.

Tibbles, Thomas Henry. Excerpt from Chapter VII: "Standing Bear's Religion—What Army Officers Think of Him" (pp. 72–75), *The Ponca Chiefs: An Indian's Attempt to Appeal from the Tomahawk to the Courts*. Boston: Lockwood, Brooks and Company, 1879.

Weaver, Hilary N. "Indigenous Identity: What Is It, and Who Really Has It?" *American Indian Quarterly* 25, no. 2 (Spring 2001): 240–55. http://www.jstor.org/stable/1185952. Copyright © 2001 University of Nebraska Press. Used by permission of the University of Nebraska Press, conveyed through Copyright Clearance Center, Inc.

Whyte, Kyle Powys. "On the Role of Traditional Ecological Knowledge as a Collaborative Concept: A Philosophical Study," *Ecological Processes* 2, no. 7 (2013). https://doi.org/10.1186/2192-1709-2-7. Copyright © 2013 The Author; licensee Springer. Used under CC BY 2.0, https://creativecommons.org/licenses/by/2.0/.

ABOUT THE EDITOR

Andrea Sullivan-Clarke (Muskogee Nation of Oklahoma) is a Native American philosopher whose research focuses on the philosophy of science, particularly the social dimension of knowledge creation. She is a first-generation college student who holds a PhD (2015) and MA (2009) from the University of Washington and a BA (1999) from Oklahoma State University, all in philosophy. A member of the wind clan of the Muskogee Nation of Oklahoma, Sullivan-Clarke has published in topics relevant to Indian Country, such as allyship, land acknowledgment statements, and Settler-Colonial Ignorance.

ABOUT THE ARTIST

Portia Po Chapman (BFAH, B.Ed) is a Kingston, Ontario-based freelance Indigenous illustrator, visual artist, and drum maker. Along the south shores of Chuncall Lake, she developed her characteristic style and Creation-focused imagery in the woods where she communed with the land. It was while sitting beneath grapevines that hung from cedars and hawthorn trees that she first drew her inspiration. The sunlight cascading through the dense vines presented bright, crisp figures outlined by the vines' dark silhouettes. The illustrations presented in this book echo the essence of laying beneath those vines as whispers of ancestors are felt and heard. Whether in black and white or full, robust blocks of colour, Po's beautiful artwork shares a truth of Turtle Island: "We are still here!"

From the Publisher

A name never says it all, but the word "Broadview" expresses a good deal of the philosophy behind our company. We are open to a broad range of academic approaches and political viewpoints. We pay attention to the broad impact book publishing and book printing has in the wider world; for some years now we have used 100% recycled paper for most titles. Our publishing program is internationally oriented and broad-ranging. Our individual titles often appeal to a broad readership too; many are of interest as much to general readers as to academics and students.

Founded in 1985, Broadview remains a fully independent company owned by its shareholders—not an imprint or subsidiary of a larger multinational.

To order our books or obtain up-to-date information, please visit broadviewpress.com.

broadview press

www.broadviewpress.com

This book is made of paper from well-managed FSC® - certified forests, recycled materials, and other controlled sources.